DISCOVERING CREATIVITY

DISCOVERING CREATIVITY

Proceedings of the 1992 International Creativity & Innovation Networking Conference

Stanley S. Gryskiewicz, Editor

Center for Creative Leadership
Greensboro, North Carolina

The Center for Creative Leadership is an international, nonprofit educational institution founded in 1970 to foster creative leadership and effective management for the good of society overall. As a part of this mission, it publishes books and reports that aim to contribute to a general process of inquiry and understanding in which ideas related to leadership are raised, exchanged, and evaluated. The ideas presented in its publications are those of the author or authors.

The Center thanks you for supporting its work through the purchase of this volume. If you have comments, suggestions, or questions about any Center publication, please contact Bill Drath, Publication Director, at the address given below.

Center for Creative Leadership
Post Office Box 26300
Greensboro, North Carolina 27438-6300

Copyright ©1993 Center for Creative Leadership

All rights reserved. No part of this publication may be reproduced, stored in a retrieval system, or transmitted, in any form or by any means, electronic, mechanical, photocopying, recording, or otherwise, without the prior written permission of the publisher. Printed in the United States of America.

CCL No. 319

Library of Congress Cataloging-in-Publication Data

International Networking Conference on Creativity and Innovation (6th : 1992 : Center for Creative Leadership)
    Discovering creativity : proceedings of the 1992 International Creativity and Innovation Networking Conference / Stanley S. Gryskiewicz, editor.

    p. cm.
    Includes bibliographical references.
    ISBN 0-912879-73-4 (alk. paper)
    1. Organizational change—Congresses. 2. Creative ability—Congresses. 3. Leadership—Congresses. I. Gryskiewicz, Stanley S. II. Title
HD58.8.I585 1992
658.4'092—dc20

CONTENTS

ACKNOWLEDGEMENTS ix

INTRODUCTION
Stanley S. Gryskiewicz xi

CONTINUOUS IMPROVEMENT

Hard Organizational Development—A Business Approach to Quality:
The Osteonics Story
Frank D. Anthony 1

The Positive Impact of Humor in the Workplace or TQM (Total Quality
Mirth) in Organizations
Lindsay Collier 7

Introducing the Integrated Programme for the Creative Training of Leaders
César E. Diaz-Carrera 11

The Vision of Quality *Versus* the Quality Vision: Leading Cultural
Changes for Innovation
Linda H. Green 15

Flying High: Exploring Whole Systems and Quality
W. Christopher Musselwhite 19

COMM=Unity—A Process for Understanding Connecting
Charles D. Rose 23

Seven Levels of Change Model: A Process for Linking Creativity,
Innovation, and Continuous Improvement
Rolf C. Smith, Jr. 27

DIVERSITY

Creative Community Development—Where It Really Begins
Aleksandra Chwedorowicz 35

Managing Diversity in Communication and Problem Solving With
Effective Levels of Abstraction
Mary C. Murdock 41

Entrepreneurs: Who Are They and How Do We Find Them? A KAI Study
Robert B. Rosenfeld, Michael Winger-Bearskin, David A. DeMarco, and Charles L. Braun 45

Learnings From Selection or How to Develop Intuition Into Shared Insight
Marc Tassoul 53

NEXT GENERATION

The Fire This Time: Coping with Sudden Imposed Change
B. Kim Barnes 63

Creating Breakthrough in Organizations: Beyond the "Whack-a-Mole" Theory
Lindsay Collier 67

Process Explorations with Cyberquest
John W. Dickey and George DiDomizio 71

A Hypermedia System for Discovery and Innovation Support
John W. Dickey, Dingshin Yu, Bruce Wright, and Thomas T. Wojcik 75

Leadership and Creative Leadership: Some Personal Reflections
Per Grøholt 79

Teaching Creativity by Distance Learning Methods
Leslie J. Jones 83

Change as a Creative Catalyst: A Model for a Regenerative Mindset
Joseph M. Miguez 87

Learning to Create Shared Vision
W. Christopher Musselwhite and Cheryl P. De Ciantis 91

PARTICIPANT THEMES

"What I Tell You Two Times is True"
John Cimino 97

The Touchstone: Discovering the Transformative Story Within
Cheryl P. De Ciantis 101

The Art and Discipline of Debriefing
Hedria P. Lunken 105

Leadership Development Theory and a Model for Intervention in the
Development of Leaders
Charles J. Palus and Wilfred H. Drath 109

Risk-taking and Innovation Performance
Charles W. Prather 119

RESEARCH

Work Environment Differences Between High Creativity and Low Creativity
Projects
*Teresa M. Amabile, Regina Conti, Heather Coon, Mary Ann Collins,
Jeffrey Lazenby, and Michael Herron* 123

Discovering the Unseen Leader
Robert C. Burkhart and David M. Horth 127

Introducing a Creativity Improvement Program for the Federal Express
I.S. Organization
J. Daniel Couger, Pat Flynn, and Doris Hellyer 139

Creativity in Project Work: A Longitudinal Study of a Product
Development Project
Göran Ekvall 143

MBTI and KAI Bias on Creativity Courses
Jane Henry 147

An Inquiry Into Cross-cultural Creativity Training: Results From a
Five-week Study Tour in Bergen and Bratislava
Scott G. Isaksen and K. Brian Dorval 151

The Dynamic Nature of Creative Problem Solving
Scott G. Isaksen, K. Brian Dorval, Ruth B. Noller, and Roger L. Firestien 155

Profiling Creativity: Nature and Implications of a New Research Program
Scott G. Isaksen and Gerard J. Puccio 163

New Insights Into Different Styles of Creativity
Leslie J. Jones 167

Managing Creative People at Work
Will McWhinney 171

A World of Ideas: An Innovative Research Approach for Business
Kelly B. Morgan 177

Bridging Theory and Practice: Disciplinary Implications for the Field of Creativity
Mary C. Murdock, Scott G. Isaksen, Suzanne K. Vosburg, and Dave A. Lugo 181

Critical Thinking: An Essential Ingredient for Effective Leadership
Luke Novelli and Sylvester Taylor 187

Creating Together: Who or What Generates the Creative Energy in a Collective Effort?
Kurt Possne 197

The Relationship Between the Kirton Adaption-Innovation Inventory and the MBTI Creativity Index
Sylvester Taylor 201

Creativity East and West: Intuition vs. Logic?
Jacquelyn Wonder 207

SUCCESS STORIES

Creativity Research at the Delft University of Technology
Jan Buijs and Kees Nauta 209

On Becoming a Facilitator: Discovering Oneself
Jan Buijs and Kees Nauta 213

Innovation in the U.S. Military
Dale W. Clauson 217

Creating an Innovation Course in a Large Corporation
Tony L. Jimenez 221

Promoting Targeted Innovation in Japan Through R&D Division Liaison Between Different Industries
Shigeru Kurebayashi 225

Developing Creativity in Japanese Companies
Yuji Nakazono 237

Innovative and Creative Change
David Tanner 247

ACKNOWLEDGEMENTS

Edited books which capture the cutting-edge thinking of conference presenters just do not spontaneously occur. First, you must have quality written papers that accurately mirror the presentations. They must represent the ideas of an international cadre of presenters who have dispersed to the four corners of the globe. The process must happen quickly, to preserve the timeliness of the ideas. The ideas must withstand the filters of language translation and editing.

In order to do this, you must have support. I want to take this opportunity to acknowledge the following people who provided the support:

Heather George—our project manager—in between her undergraduate degree in international relations and the start of an MBA degree;

David Hills and Carol Andresen—my research and administrative assistants—who provided some extra editing help;

Ellen Hamman and Joanne Ferguson—publication staff who further proofread and edited prior to Joanne's design layout.

I would also like to acknowledge the fact that our success relates in large part to the community we formed to turn the project around—and to the creative climate at the Center for Creative Leadership which supported our collective effort.

Conferences just don't happen on their own either. I want here to recognize the Center people who shared and implemented this dream with me over the years:

Carolyn Stoll—my former assistant and co-first mate for the '92 ICINC voyage of discovery;

David Horth—shared the leadership with Carolyn, contributing to process and content in numerous significant ways;

Carrie Ganim—managed conference mailings and registration—as well as communication with presenters.

Also to be credited are the planning/networking groups, Prism and Periscope:

Prism
Jacynthe Bedard-Menard ('94 ICINC – Quebec)
Vicki Connell (Torrance Center for Creative Studies)
Stan Gryskiewicz (Center for Creative Leadership)

David Horth (Center for Creative Leadership)
Scott Isaksen (Center for Studies in Creativity)
William Shephard (Creative Education Foundation)
Carolyn Stoll ('92 ICINC)
Mary Wallgren (Procter & Gamble Company)
Jerry Norton (Eastman Kodak Company, Retired)
Rolf Smith (Office of Strategic Innovation)
David Tanner (DeBono International Forum)

<u>Periscope</u>
Patrick Colemont (Belgium)
Per Grøholt (Norway)
Marjorie Parker (Norway)
Tudor Rickards (United Kingdom)
Hans Smeekes (The Netherlands)

Thank you—all!

INTRODUCTION
Higher Order Horizons Through International Community Building

In our amazing world, there is a microscopic organism that almost totally defies classification. Here is a true story of the myxomycetes (MIX-o-my-seat-tees). It begins its life as a tiny, airborne bubble—almost as ephemeral as an idea—almost invisible even under a microscope. It floats on the breeze, eventually to come to rest on a leaf or on the earth. There it turns into an amoeba-like creature that moves about, exploring the world in which it finds itself.

At some point, it receives an invitation to convene with peers. Whether this is a genetic, a chemical, or a psychic message, we do not know. But we can observe these individuals coming together to form a temporary community. This community begins to communicate and cooperate and becomes more than an aggregate of individuals. It becomes a functional organism (now visible to the naked eye if we know where to look). This organism moves about and explores, sharing what it learns as a group with each other.

Then, responding to some unknown mandate, this congregation takes on some of the properties of a plant. It rests from exploration. Some individuals cooperate to form root filaments, others a platform, others a stem-like structure, and still others—raised aloft on the stem—begin to manufacture tiny, gossamer bubbles—almost like ideas—which are released to float on the wind. All individuals have shared in the creation of these bubbles; some individuals accept the task of articulating them, of publishing them, of typing out the formulation, of manufacturing the ideas in tangible form.

Some of these bubbles land and become dormant for a time, resting until the season is right to start new, wider-spread colonies and communities to repeat the cycle of renewal and change.

These colonies become overlapping circles, blanketing the world with the almost intangible film of the ideas of

> individuals,
>   community,
>   growth,
>   change,
>   renewal,
>   creativity.

Perhaps like this marvelous little creature, we sense that we, too, at times may be virtually invisible as individuals—or at least easily overlooked in the great commotion of the larger world.

The number of conferences that focus on creativity has quadrupled in the last five years. In 1985, there were two. In 1990 there were seven international conferences in which creativity and innovation were the major themes. These conferences have moved beyond the study of creative problem solving towards the management of innovation and cooperation within and between organizations. These annual events stimulate discussion and communicate new understanding.

One clear result is a growing perception of the importance of international networking—out beyond the boundaries of a person's day-to-day existence. And once people have become aware of the benefits, they know what's possible and will seek the experience again.

Often, these conferences and networks only need some group—or some<u>one</u>—to act in an administrative capacity to nurture the formulation stage. Once critical mass is formed, the network will continue to meet, renew, and create interest—as long as the topics are perceived as current and the people who represent these topics are knowledgeable and fluent in discussion.

More recently, networks have formed as study groups using electronic networking software—along with face-to-face meetings—to allow almost continuous dialogue between members. Such real-time discussion, feedback, and learning is—in the true sense—an innovation.

However, network members need to be willing to share information and respond to questions in a straightforward, candid manner. If they are seen only as takers, and not contributors, they will sabotage the effectiveness of the networking process. Network effectiveness is based on trust: If trust is in any way reduced among the members, the network is doomed to fail—or to degenerate into a meeting where pleasantries are merely exchanged.

The papers within this book represent the ideas of those attending the 6th International Creativity & Innovation Networking Conference (ICINC) hosted by the Center for Creative Leadership in Greensboro, North Carolina, in the fall of 1992.

It is my experience that conference participants are pulled in two opposing directions. One direction is a pull to pursue their own agenda: a particular insight, a friend, an answer, a confirmation, a research question . . .

But there is another pull, a pull to form community with those attending—a strong community that will continue to bring both scholars and practitioners together in the future.

I have chosen to label this dialectic tension, this motivational disequilibrium. Over the years I have personally experienced this tension in work groups I have been part of and in conferences such as the one described here. It seems to appear when inquisitive, intrinsically motivated individuals who are pushing the boundaries come together to commune—in order to accomplish a task they cannot do alone. I want to label this dialectic <u>autonomy versus community</u>.

Discovering Creativity — *Introduction*

We welcomed and nurtured this tension and all the good things that caused it; but we could not ignore the dilemma either. Conscious choices in both directions were encouraged to insure the success of the conference.

Participants did not give up personal freedom in a move towards community—nor did chaos result from the proclamations of individual positions. Rather, we learned that by becoming part of a community we are provided with a platform to accomplish things beyond our own imagination.

Perhaps a more meaningful way of organizing this conference conceptually is to ponder a quote of Václav Havel's in his book, *Disturbing The Peace* (1991, Random):

> ... there is a basic tension out of which the present global crisis has grown. ... I'm persuaded that this conflict ... is directly related to the spiritual condition of modern civilization. This condition is characterized by loss: the loss of metaphysical certainties, of an experience of the transcendental, of any superpersonal moral authority, and of any kind of higher horizon. It is strange but ultimately quite logical: as soon as man began considering himself the source of the highest meaning in the world and the measure of everything, the world began to lose its human dimension, and man began to lose control of it. (pp. 10-11)

The individual-centered framework of autonomy overlooks our need for the transcendent. Research focusing on the self-absorbed citizens of the 1970s—by Yankelovich and others—suggests that prolonged pursuit of the true meaning of one's self leads to loss of transcendent meaning of the community and spiritual frameworks.

Conference participants can create this transcendent experience together if they remember to focus on the ideas of their colleagues as well as their own ideas. The conference was designed and implemented for the sharing of new insights and learnings and to bring value to the group experience. And in this exchange we created trust—and in turn we created community. And through the creation of community we have a chance to create this higher-order horizon we are seeking.

In addition, as a community—a cooperating congress of individuals—we have learned that we can acquire greater visibility, stronger voice, and greater opportunity for influence. Ultimately, in this community some of us are explorers, some conveners, some listeners and organizers, some spinners of lines of communication, some scribes or typists of the written record of our individual and our collective words. Collectively we contribute according to our gifts and preferences, both to fellow individuals and to the fluid communities of the mind. We serve and are served. We support and are supported. We extend beyond a particular room or this conference. And in a very tangible way we extend our community and impact through this publication. Except by choice or great disaster, we need never be alone with our ideas or without impact.

Ideas impel—not compel. But it is possible for the impelling flow of ideas to solidify into a confining web or even into the foundation for tyranny. Yet we know internally that one of the antidotes to this paralyzation of festering ideas is free communication between trusting people. Like myxomycetes, we came together from all corners of the world and created this community in September of 1992 in Greensboro, North Carolina. We spun both tangible and intangible links of our own choosing—to make overlapping circles, wrapping the world in a nurturing, creative, and renewing blanket of ideas—into this community called ICINC.

Now we are capturing this event through the publication of our individual and collective contributions.

Stanley S. Gryskiewicz

Note: For the purposes of this publication, Session 7 and a paper by a non-presenter have been added to the "Participant Themes" section.

- apply the principles involved in managing change
- commit resources
    - education and training
    - time for planning, decision making, and problem solving
- recognize the importance of communication—even when there are unanswered questions
- use the steering/management team as process champions and mentors

Phases: A Business Approach to Quality—Osteonics

1) communicating vision, values, mission statement

2) ensuring readiness of steering committee
   - education
   - training
   - organization development

3) communication of vision, values, mission to operations

4) refining of vision to include self-directed work teams

5) selection of leaders/facilitators

6) communication to operations

7) training of leaders/facilitators

8) selection of cell members

9) communication of selection process to operations

10) training of cells

Elements of a Business Approach to Quality

Communication

- vision
- values
- mission statement
- business goals
- status of business
- customer needs

Education

- world-class quality
- what other companies do
- managing change
- economics of business

Training

- process skills
- problem solving
- decision making
- effective meetings
- process flow
- cost-time analysis
- facilitation skills
- team dynamics
- listening
- feedback
- managing change
- customer service
- conflict resolution
- technical skills
    - new processes
    - cross-training

Systems

- policies and procedures
- staffing
- performance appraisal
- compensation

Frank D. Anthony, Anthony and Associates, 53 Water Street, Lebanon, NJ 08833, Tel: (908) 832-9315. Education: B.S. degree from SUNY; MBA in management from Fairleigh Dickinson University.

Discovering Creativity   CONTINUOUS IMPROVEMENT

THE POSITIVE IMPACT OF HUMOR IN THE WORKPLACE OR TQM (TOTAL QUALITY MIRTH) IN ORGANIZATIONS

Lindsay Collier

Many people have come to the conclusion that work is supposed to be a painful activity—five days of pain for which we are rewarded a two-day weekend. Fun work is somewhat of an oxymoron that ranks with "professional wrestling" and "Senate ethics." What if work could become an enjoyable, fun experience for people? Think of the difference it could make! Effective use of humor in the workplace is one powerful way of making work an enjoyable experience, but humor is quite often considered inappropriate in the workplace. Part of the reason is in our assumption that "humorous" and "serious" cannot take place at the same time. In many organizations, the use of humor is considered as time away from the seriousness of work. Yet, humor is one of the most powerful resources available to us to help us be more effective in carrying out our work. Here are a few reasons why.

1. Humor can help us achieve higher states of health and lower states of stress. If you don't believe this, read Norman Cousins' book, *Anatomy of an Illness* (1979). Laughter is one of the most powerful medicines available to us. It can have tremendous impact on our physical and mental well-being. In Norman Cousins' case, he suggests, it cured a terminal illness. In business, it can cure us from terminal professionalism.

2. Humor helps bring out the creativity in us. Anyone who has worked with and observed the creative process knows there is a direct connection between fun and laughter and creativity. When people are having fun at their work, creativity naturally follows. When is the last time you had a great idea while you were in a state of depression? There are many depressed people in organizations these days. Could that be one reason for the lack of creativity? Our sense of humor is the most powerful resource we have to move us from a depressed state to one of excitement and optimism.

3. Humor helps to build relationships and helps us communicate more effectively. When you are sharing a laugh with someone, you create a bond with them. It is difficult not to like someone you are laughing with. Sharing a humorous moment is a great way of building rapport. It is also a great way to create open thinking patterns between people.

4. Humor can improve the learning process. People have a tendency to remember things that strike them as funny. Integrating that fact into the training activity makes a lot of sense.

5. Finally, humor helps people cope with change.

To sum it up: Humor can have a very powerful and positive effect on the business of work and can be entwined very effectively in our everyday work life in a way that enhances both our feelings about work and the quality of our output.

A Little About the Forms of Humor

One of the greatest myths about humor is that it is always in the form of jokes. A joke is only one form of humor, but this particular form has its limitations. One limitation is that jokes must be remembered and the other is that they tend to victimize some people. Using humor effectively doesn't involve victimization. Other, perhaps better, forms of humor include cartoons, analogies, quotations, funny signs and slogans, stupid questions, and aikido (sometimes called Joke Jitsu). Examples of these are all around us. Next time you are in a bookstore, browse through the humor section. For the price of one business book, you can usually buy about three good humor books (David Barry, Woody Allen, Gary Larson, Jay Leno, etc.) which could have twice the impact on your potential.

Humor may be used in positive or negative ways in the workplace. Positive humor tends to be spontaneous and stem from a caring about people and a desire to bring them together. It is connected with the situation at hand and reinforces it positively. Negative use of humor tends to be rather contrived and may subtly tear people apart, cover up feelings, or mask incompetence. Negative humor can have the exact reverse of the effects previously discussed.

How to Use Humor to Achieve "Funtastic" Results in Your Work

Find a "Smile Mindset" and use it often. Associated with humor is an interesting "chicken or egg" type of question: "Do you laugh because you feel good?" or "Do you feel good because you laugh?" The fact is, when you laugh, your body doesn't really know there is a reason—it just feels good anyway. So, if you carry some laughter or smile-producing memories around with you, they can be used anytime as anchors to make you feel good. Or you may just choose to laugh about absolutely nothing. When you are driving to work in the morning, smile or laugh. You don't need a reason—the effect is the same and it will help make your day better. While you're at it, smile at people in other cars—make their day better too.

Take yourself lightly and your work seriously. You are the most fun you can have and the safest source of humor you can find. Remember that your serious work can be enhanced with humor.

Discovering Creativity   *CONTINUOUS IMPROVEMENT*

Take humor breaks often. A good example might be the start of a meeting that has a serious topic. This may sound like the worst time for a humor break but it might actually be the best. When there is a lot of stress involved in a topic you are working on, it is useful to reduce that stress to allow for some creative thinking and a humor break may be the best way. In fact, anytime you are experiencing a mental block in your work may be time for a break.

Do something strange from time to time. Athletes know that muscles need to be stretched before and after exercise. Think of the mind as having muscles that need stretching. If we are going to maintain our creative capability, we need to stretch into the unknown every now and then. How do you do that? You may want to call Dial-A-Prayer and argue with it or drive through a McDonald's drive-up window backwards or go reminisce with someone you don't know. It's up to you—just make sure it is a stretch and that it's also safe.

Make your memos funny. People will remember your writing if you are able to insert some subtle, funny statements that connect to what you are saying.

Smile at everyone. A recent study showed that robbers tend not to rob people who are smiling. Not being robbed is only a start at what is possible to achieve when you spend time smiling.

How might you access your own humor?

In late 1991, we designed and built a "Humor Room" at the Eastman Kodak Company. It was a wonderful idea and we had some very creative people working on the design. We worked mostly on our own time because we knew there was little support from management; they were deathly afraid someone may think Kodak people were enjoying their work. The room was designed to be a totally different environment where pictures of George Eastman were replaced by those of W.C. Fields and other similar characters. The total cost was about equal to sending one executive to Pecos River for outdoor training. Contained in the room is a full library of creative and humorous materials, creativity software, various stress-relieving gadgets and idea stimulators, and a viewing area for humorous videos. As a side benefit, because of its environment, the room proved to be a wonderful place for groups to have ideation sessions.

Reference

Cousins, N. (1979). *Anatomy of an illness as perceived by the patient: Reflections on healing and regeneration.* New York: Norton.

Lindsay Collier, Creative Edge Associates, Post office Box 352, West Henrietta, NY 14586. Tel: (716) 334-4779.

INTRODUCING THE INTEGRATED PROGRAMME FOR THE CREATIVE TRAINING OF LEADERS

César E. Diaz-Carrera

Our inborn capacity for Creativity becomes withered through the socialization process instilled in us from an early age. Homogeneous schooling, social habits, and labor inertia contribute substantially to this deteriorating trend.

The Integrated Programme for the Creative Training of Leaders assumes, as a starting point, the inevitability of Change and Crisis. Change is the only thing that is permanent (Heraclitus) and in this light even we, human beings, are nothing but a continuous process of Change. On the other hand, Crisis is a crucial questioning which leads to a fundamental restatement of the issue. This approach is already a positive interpretation of the meaning of Crisis perceived as a "breakthrough" rather than the more popular and catastrophic interpretation of Crisis as a "breakdown."

IPCTL is a truly unique program for the creative training of leaders which takes into account the essential distinction—overlooked by other programs of leadership training—between personal and applied creativity. Other specific features of this program, structured around four three-day modules, include :

- Its meta-disciplinary character. The form of the **IPCTL** is not just at the intellectual/conceptual plane. Metasystems thinking is combined with intensive work at the energetic, emotional, ethical, and ontological level.

- A highly formative value of the course asks each participant to commit himself or herself wholly, as the total integrated person that he or she is, to the course experience.

- As a corollary of the above the **IPCTL** has a *deeply transformative character* beyond the useful information it contains.

In short, the **IPCTL** has been designed to help the world leader to more successfully face the contemporary challenges in a planet ridden by unprecedented change and global crisis. To achieve this aim the leaders taking this program will:

- Explore and gain access to their inner power as creative human beings.

- Raise their awareness both to their own personal hidden potential and to the key issues in the world today.

- Enlarge and, at the same time, learn to effectively focus their vision.

- Learn how to encapsulate that vision within a mobilizing mission.

- Generate principles of action and charismatic authority through *commitment* and *integrity*.

- Improve the decision-making, communication, and problem-solving skills needed by future-oriented creative leaders.

CONSCIOUSNESS
& Commitment
M.A.E.

Where do I come from?
Meaning to own life

CHARISMATIC
AUTHORITY
Integrity

DECISION
C. & C.C.
How can I:
– Perform
– Communicate
– Serve?

ADEQUATE
⟶
RELEVANT

IPCTL ⟶ *ACTION*
L.C.
IDENTITY
I am my commitment
into ACTION

Direction to Action
FOCUSED ENERGY
E.P.P.
Experience/Effectiveness/Usefulness ⟶ GOALS
What can I do?

SUSTAINED
EFFECTIVENESS

Figure 1
Integrated Programme for the Creative Training of Leaders (IPCTL)

Discovering Creativity   CONTINUOUS IMPROVEMENT

2. CHANGE

Openness to the Paradox/Ambivalence

Opportunity Communication

1. VISION

3. VALUES

Commitment Become Yourself

LEADERSHIP

Thought/Action Decision

6. CHARACTER

4. POWER

Efficiency Influence

Effectiveness Results

5. AUTHORITY

Figure 2
The IDEC Model of Creative Leadership

~~~

César E. Diaz-Carrera, IDEC, Institute for the Development of Creativity, CIFE, Center for Research and European Training, IDEC Rodriguez San Pedro 24, 28015 Madrid, Spain. Tel: 34 1 593 25 92. Education: Ph.D. in modern philology from the University of Madrid; Doctoral studies in political science and sociology, European University Institute, Florence; Master of Arts in comparative literature and political science, University of Washington.

CONTINUOUS IMPROVEMENT   *Discovering Creativity*

THE VISION OF QUALITY *VERSUS* THE QUALITY VISION: LEADING CULTURAL CHANGES FOR INNOVATION

Linda H. Green

In a dramatic era of change, the twenty-first century is emerging as a technological renaissance. Technology, however, is a double-edged sword, with extinction and obsolescence resulting in economic disparity on one edge, and opportunity through innovation and reformation on the other. Leaders must exploit the edge of opportunity, through the utilization of technology as an integral part of continuous improvement.

Strategic planning must address opportunities paved by new technology and the opening doors of change. Disadvantages associated with rapid change, illustrated by the obsolescence of machinery and the lack of technically trained people, must be understood in order to take advantage of the numerous challenges and competitive advantages offered by technology.

An increasingly diverse and competitive global market requires manufacturers to implement flexible systems, where parts produced can be modified or customized quickly and efficiently, with no sacrifice to quality. The global market also challenges economies of scale, which resulted from mass automation in factories, to compete against niche marketing, total quality management, and flexible manufacturing.

Such new actions require a cultural change to solidify leadership and insure the empowerment of people. Without attention given to these cultural changes, the true capability of the technologies deployed can seldom be realized. Leadership must nurture change from within while simultaneously encouraging, not stifling, creativity.

Businesses' focus on short-term profits, at the expense of long-term survival, often results in a failure to incorporate quality function deployment. Meanwhile, competitors drastically reduce turnaround time by implementing real-time engineering and fail-safe systems. Computer-automated design and computer-assisted manufacturing further streamline the task, making instantaneous design and equipment retrofitting a reality.

Innovation for continuous improvement has become an imperative in day-to-day operations of any organization. It requires trusting the people on the front line to provide constant evaluation, while empowering them with the authority to utilize flexibility in decision making for corrective actions. Automated process controls resulting from technological renovations cannot and should not replace measures of responsibility and accountability of the human beings involved in the process. Authority lines may be shifted or realigned as necessary, but should not be depleted.

While it may not be necessary to reinvent the wheel, all workers can polish the spokes by constantly recognizing performance of others and clearly understanding their contribution to the finished product. This awareness must be coupled with the authority and the ability to make a change where operationally beneficial. Any redesign requires a basic understanding of the wheel's ties to the mission. Input by those ultimately involved will enhance the potential of the redesigned wheel's successful implementation.

The mission of the organization is at the very heart of the issue. For anyone to contribute significantly, they must be clearly aware of the mission or purpose for which the organization was formed. Every action thereafter can be attributed to strategies which can be linked to the overall mission. *Innovation which is fostered in a team environment will be more readily accepted, modified as needed, and implemented.* Constant feedback and ownership of decisions at all levels will insure success and continued improvement which will ultimately result in fulfilling the vision of the organization.

Development of leadership at all levels requires management to readdress perceptions of blue-collar mentality. Cultural acceptance of technological innovations must be understood and appreciated by the entire organization to reap the total benefits of modifications.

Plant managers and CEOs far too often fail to recognize the importance of a strategic plan which addresses:

1. A mission or purpose formed, accepted, and understood by all;
2. The employee, customer, or supplier's role in the strategic plan;
3. The importance of communicating the mission in concise terms which can be understood and appreciated by all stakeholders;
4. The necessity of working as a team to form and accomplish the strategic plan, as opposed to dictating the decisions of the upper managers.

In touring a small transformer operation, a head engineer reflected upon the humbling experience of becoming a "shop floor engineer." He graduated from a state university with honors, and was quite anxious to prove the merits of his education. While he desired to work in a research and development capacity, his first assignment was in a manufacturing facility, which utilized real-time R&D on the shop floor. He felt demoralized when in the first month he was required to work on the production floor to enhance his understanding of the operations.

He walked into the manufacturing facility (where the average education of production workers was estimated to be equivalent to a ninth grader), feeling proud of his accomplishments and certain that he could improve the performance of the facility. He now knowingly admits that within the course of one week, he learned he had no understanding of the knowledge, perseverance, and team efforts required to perform the work on the shop floor. The operational creativity he observed was astounding!

Discovering Creativity CONTINUOUS IMPROVEMENT

In this one week he learned that *intelligence and education are not necessarily synonymous*. Many of the illiterate production workers were exceptionally intelligent and creative by necessity. So who should lead and who should follow for innovation and creativity to flourish?

The underlying message is that each is a leader within their own environment. It is the power of the network of sharing and understanding that makes their efforts complementary. It is the utilization of technologies and science coupled with the ingenuity and persistence of the production-line worker and the day-to-day successes based only on continuous improvement, that encourage advancement. This type of cultural revolution is not limited to organizations, but equally important for governments to deploy.

The Virginia Center for Innovative Technology, and other state and federal technology transfer centers, encourage networking and partnerships between the three constituencies of education, government, and industry. Such efforts force strategic planning to focus on future technological needs and encourage participation by all potential constituents. This team effort requires cultural changes for these organizations in order to maximize the overall benefits of innovation and creativity.

George Bernard Shaw has been credited with saying, "Some men see things as they are and say 'Why?' I dream things that never were, and say 'Why not?'" Every organization will benefit from the vision of the dreamer and the realism and fortitude of the follower.

~~~

Linda H. Green, Virginia Center for Innovative Technology, Danville Community College, 1008 South Main Street, Danville, VA 24541. Tel: (804) 797-3553. Education: Undergraduate degree from Averett College in accounting and management science with a minor in computer science.

FLYING HIGH: EXPLORING WHOLE SYSTEMS AND QUALITY

W. Christopher Musselwhite

Ten minutes into the presentation the trainer is acutely aware of Bob flagrantly reading the morning paper. Not only is Bob, a participant in a week-long leadership-development program, reading a fully opened newspaper, he is doing so while seated at the front of the classroom. Although annoyed, the presenter is not surprised by this behavior. Bob was identified as the program's problem child the first day and for three days he has lived up to the early assessment. The current program component is entitled "systems" and Bob's attitude toward "systems" is reflective of his attitude toward the entire program: "I am above this; I already know all of this."

Fast forward three hours and find Bob in the hallway outside the classroom; he is jumping, laughing, shouting, and encouraging his classmates as he enthusiastically flies paper airplanes. Bob is "playing" (he's actually beyond play) the role of quality inspector in the simulation *Paper Planes, Inc.* Bob's evaluation later in the day provides the following reflection:

> I started the session believing this was just another simplistic exercise that couldn't teach me anything new. Boy, was I wrong. This simulation really captures the essence of the toughest issues organizational leaders face: An understanding of how seeing anything less than the big picture creates divisiveness, lowers commitment, and lessens quality.

The gestalt of this simulated experience is an eye-opener for many of the participants whose companies have explored such popular business remedies as total quality, just-in-time, customer focus, continuous improvement, work redesign, self-managed teams, commitment, and time-based innovation. Many of them have latched onto one or more of these cures in efforts to remain or become competitive. The result has often been short-term improvement that does not seem sustainable and the occurrence of new unanticipated auxiliary problems. The problem symptoms, in fact, seem to shift somewhere else.

The term "gestalt" is used to describe the experience of *Paper Planes, Inc.*, because in its clinical sense, gestalt means the experience of seeing and understanding something in its "wholeness." It is this quality of seeing a problem in its entirety or within its "whole system" that poses the greatest challenge to organizations and their leaders and consequently offers the greatest opportunity for understanding and improvement.

The Simulation

Paper Planes, Inc., presents participants with a traditionally designed work task of building paper planes. The work is divided functionally such that each person performs only a small piece of the overall job and consequently does not understand the overall process. These paper planes are needed by an international consortium for use in preliminary wind tunnel design tests for a proposed plane that will travel halfway around the globe in two hours by flying to the upper limits of the stratosphere. Once each plane is completed it is inspected and tested by the quality inspectors before delivery to the customer. When questioned for causes for the poor quality, typical responses are to blame others, point fingers, and complain about the customer.

The participants are given the opportunity to redesign the production process any way they choose. This redesign is an unstructured group activity. When the redesign is completed the participants are given another opportunity to again make planes.

This second run of the simulation produces phenomenally different results. Points of comparison between the two runs of the simulation include cost of materials and labor, selling price to avoid a loss, quality index, and time to market.

Lessons Learned

Bob reported his greatest learning to be "the importance of everyone understanding the big picture." Other learnings from the simulation debriefs include:

Having a goal or vision: An understanding of the desired product or end result is essential. People are too often asked to work on a part of a task and do not understand how what they do contributes to the desired end result.

Collaborative teamwork: A lack of awareness of the interdependency of jobs results in finger-pointing and blaming behavior. Collaborative teamwork is critical if this type of awareness is to develop. Collaborative teamwork can replace blaming behavior only if the team's task is viewed in its wholeness.

Communication is essential: No matter how traditional or innovative the work design, communication is essential. The act of constructive communication can do more than anything else to improve quality and productivity. However, if the work flow and organizational structure impede efforts to communicate rather than enhance them, then good communication will remain elusive.

Structure gives rise to behavior: The structure or design of work actually creates the negative, ineffective behaviors in individuals. When the work is redesigned by the participants and communication can take place, the same people doing the same task with the same materials and time constraints demonstrate much more constructive and effective behavior. The responsibility for poor performance is usually a function of the system rather than individual incompetence. Yet, it is individuals who are sent to human resources or training programs for fixing.

Quality and whole systems: Quality is ultimately the effect of all the interactions within the entire system. The way the jobs within the system are designed and interfaced are directly reflected in the quality.

Learning as continuous improvement: The concept of continuous improvement is directly related to the degree to which the organization or system encourages risk and learning. If behavior that leads to mistakes is not encouraged then learning cannot take place and continuous improvement will never become part of the organization's culture.

Adaptive or innovative change: During the simulation redesign and debrief it becomes apparent that different individuals have different preferences for dealing with changes in the system. Michael Kirton (1976) describes this continuum of preference as adaptive and innovative. On one end of the continuum adaptors prefer to make small incremental and frequent changes, constantly improving the system. This preference is reflective of a continuous improvement process. On the other end of this continuum innovators contrastingly prefer more radical, wholesale change of the system. Innovators are more likely to challenge the existing paradigm; to think outside of the box. Participants typically experience their preferred style during the simulation. This difference in style is the greatest point of contention in the redesign process. Both preferences for approaching system change are useful and both can have inherent problems, such as continuing to improve a dinosaur or throwing the baby out with the bath water. It is in fact the interaction and compromise of the two styles within a team context that can result in the most effective system change.

Team participation requires process: Given the success of the redesign, the redesign of the production process remains difficult. Conflict will emerge. Adaptors and innovators will bump heads. A "willingness" to participate collaboratively in team decision making does not guarantee the desired outcome. People thrown into a collaborative situation, especially those without experience operating in this mode, need assistance to guarantee success. The participants in *Paper Planes, Inc.,* experience the struggle of team participation and discuss how the redesign could have been even more effective with adequate facilitation. Managers who are skeptical of team participation often throw their people into an unplanned, unstructured decision-making process and, as they flounder, the manager responds with "I told you so."

As with the business remedies mentioned earlier, each of these learning points is related. These learnings when examined in isolation look and sound great. Any good consultant could make a sound argument for any one of these as a viable solution to organizational problems. The dilemma is that taken in isolation each of these lessons will only result in the problem popping up somewhere else in the system. It is when these learning points are embraced in their wholeness that synergy is discovered. It is difficult to communicate with a whole-system perspective. It is certainly easier to talk about Just In Time or total quality or self-managed teams. But with experiential learning and simulations such as *Paper Planes, Inc.,* the dialogue becomes easier and the concepts become clearer.

Reference

Kirton, M. J. (1976). Adaptors and innovators: A description and measure. *Journal of Applied Psychology, 61,* 622-629.

~~~

W. Christopher Musselwhite, Blue Ridge Resource Group, 415 Woodlawn Avenue, Greensboro, NC 27401. Tel: (910) 272-9530. Education: Master's degree in management systems engineering; Ed.D. in adult education–training and development from North Carolina State University.

COMM=Unity—A PROCESS FOR UNDERSTANDING CONNECTING

Charles D. Rose

Sue Rosen and Charlie Rose sang a gentle song with repeated lyrics. Upon invitation the participants joined in singing, "Welcome everyone, welcome everyone, welcome everyone to Our Heart. Sharing all we have, sharing all we have—give and receive."

Following the song, there was an introduction that postulated leading as an art and creating as connecting and integrating. Some other concepts were:

As people are conscious beings, a conscious awareness of connections grows into an intentional choice to follow the force that moves from separation toward unity through the continual, conscious practice of the process of change. And, since the process of change is also the manifestation of the force that creates Diversity within the Unity, this connecting/integrating/creating dance has no end. We are all conductors at every moment, conductors of all energy. These conductors help make connections.

All the arts share some common characteristics:

- They make use of metaphor, symbol, sound, movement, rhythm, and contrast.
- They are spun from the self.
- Even if they use words, they go beyond the verbal.
- They are spontaneous in generation.
- They are expressive of a deeper level of human awareness.
- They catalyze a deeper sense of awareness in the receiver.
- They are intentional.
- They are expansive.
- They are inspirational.
- They celebrate.
- They are connecting.
- They are integrating.

When these characteristics are manifested in ourselves, they promote conductivity. We try to let ourselves live all of our life as an art by living for each moment to be an expression of our intentional openness to the spontaneity of discovering what is in that moment. That is living life as an art, for expressions are as varied and unique as the beings on this planet.

By allowing ourselves to be involved in the Perpetual Process of Peaceful, Perceptive Playfulness we come together in celebrating the Union in COMM=Unity.

After the introduction, Sue guided the participants through an exercise called COMM=Unity of the Self. This experiential exercise is designed to assist and encourage integrative thinking, introspection, inspiration, and creative self-empowerment. Participants were instructed to randomly select, sight unseen, a card with a "value" word printed on the back. (They do not look at this word.) Then, a basket of objects was brought to each person, and the person blindly selected one object out of the basket. These instructions followed:

> Look at your card now. Each of these things you've selected, the value and the object, have messages for you. Listen to these messages. Your task now is to take these messages together and write a statement or two that expresses how integrating the messages you've received either already expresses a way you live your life as an art or would like to in the future.

After some time for reflection and writing, each person was then asked to physically "sculpt" themselves into a pose that conveyed the essence of those statements they wrote. This was all done nonverbally.

A greeting ritual ensued in which, moving around the room in their sculpted pose, each person greeted another and noticed how their poses were effected and perhaps altered through the interactions. This was done in silence. Facilitators observed people moving from a state of tension/separation to one of relaxation/connection (with self and others). They used what was given to create meaning.

COMM=Unity—Discovering Personal and Collective Metaphor

Upon invitation, participants walked randomly around the room, in imagined isolation and silence, to find the perfect spot for them at that moment. This was to be their "sacred space" where they would feel safe and strong. They then selected from piles of playthings (toys, costumes, unusual artifacts) whatever seemed appropriate to their sacred space. They were reminded that they could be silly as well as serious in these "sacred spaces." After decorating the "interiors" of their space, they experimented with nonvocal sounds (observing rhythms being created throughout the group) and then with vocal, nonverbal sound (observing the melodies being added). They compared the experience to entering a room and understanding something about what was happening without understanding a word spoken.

Then in shared silence, they each created their own active, personal metaphor following the form of this example: "I am the Dolphin sending out a gentle, loving invitation to play." Speaking from their personal spaces, they verbally shared these personal metaphors with the rest of the group. In silence, then, using gestures of offering and invitation, they entered and experienced each other's "sacred spaces." Returning to their own spaces they each created, in shared silence, an active, collective metaphor for the entire group. They then shared these diverse individual collective metaphors and wrote them down on flip charts. Next, they voted—one person, one vote, and no voting for your own idea—for the metaphors which best expressed the group at that moment. At this point, the few collective metaphors with the most votes are generally handed to three "word carvers," selected randomly. These "word carvers" were given less than ten minutes to select one of these elected metaphors or to construct a composite, active collective metaphor that draws on the spirit of those previously offered. This group chose (and most groups choose) the latter. The entire group agreed before this effort began that they would accept this end-product as the metaphor most expressive of that group, that COMM=Unity at that moment.

The active collective metaphor created together through this process by the group attending was, "We are an expansive tree at the center of the forest, by a stream, gathering sunbeams."

Charles D. Rose, COMM=Unity, Route 1, Box 97, Thurmond, NC 28683. Education: Wake Forest University.

SEVEN LEVELS OF CHANGE MODEL: A PROCESS FOR LINKING CREATIVITY, INNOVATION, AND CONTINUOUS IMPROVEMENT

Rolf C. Smith, Jr.

This paper presents a new perspective and framework for managers who are trying to accelerate the rate of change. Companies do change and are changing, but the speed with which they accept new ideas and *different* ways of doing things is frustrating at best—leading to cynicism and resignation in once highly motivated, forward-thinking employees.

Creativity, innovation, and continuous improvement are about ideas. Correspondingly, ideas are about change: When someone has an idea, new thought processes are started and thinking changes; when an idea is implemented—when someone does something with it—things change. Some changes are extremely easy to make while others seem virtually impossible. Leaving for the office five minutes earlier in the morning to beat the "rush hour" traffic and drive more efficiently is an easy change to make. On the other hand, the concepts and principles which Total Quality Management (TQM) requires drive organizations and people to change on a much larger scale.

The framework which this paper offers is divided into seven distinct levels—from easy to impossible—across a spectrum of continual change *(continuous innovation)* over increasing levels of difficulty. Each level is progressively more complex, more different, more challenging to undertake than the preceding level. Understanding this spectrum of innovative change can help leaders fully institutionalize *comprehensive process innovation* (i.e., innovation that is continuously ongoing rather than occurring as unrelated events in the face of crisis). The levels of change model can be superimposed on the vision of any organization and then imbedded within its goals, culture, and day-to-day operating environment. When an organization moves from learning about TQM to doing, actually implementing the Quality process, the model quickly becomes an integral part of it.

Change and Individual Styles of Creative Thinking

The manner in which people interact with their environment in solving problems has a strong impact on the levels of change at which they are comfortable working. Individual creative style runs across a spectrum of (1) *highly adaptive* (focused largely on maintaining and improving the existing situation and working on well-defined problems) to (2) *highly innovative* (focused on doing things differently driven by ill-defined and unstructured problems or messes; Kirton, 1976, 1992). People with adaptive tendencies do particularly well with organizational change and proposing creative ideas which are readily accepted and smoothly implemented. People with innovative tendencies often orient more towards individual change or changes which are strategic in nature and which radically change the status quo.

How the Seven Levels Model Makes Innovative Change More Acceptable

At the lower levels of change, smaller, more immediately useful, and easily implementable ideas can be pursued by people who view themselves as more practical and conventional. Changes at these levels tend to be adaptive in nature, focusing on continuity with existing systems through incremental advances. Because they can be implemented relatively quickly, such changes are frequently "bottom line" oriented. They are typically perceived as "sound" *improvements* with relatively low risk/high stability factors. All of this combines to facilitate relatively easy acceptance of such changes by the organization.

People who view themselves as more progressive, nonconforming, and conceptual in their thinking tend to conceive and advocate ideas at the higher levels of change where longer-term, more far-reaching and potentially higher payoffs may evolve. The more such ideas move from the tactical toward the strategic, the more *different*—"original" and pioneering—the changes tend to be. Similarly, the higher the levels of change an organization participates in, the more it departs from conventional wisdom and tradition—with correspondingly higher perceived risks. Such higher level changes are not readily accepted by the organization and, in fact, are often resisted.

According to Kirton, people have a natural tendency to approach tasks and problems in one of two ways: The thrust of the one is basically *improvement* while that of the other is *difference*. Lower levels of change imply *evolutionary* improvements (incremental), while higher levels aim at very different, *revolutionary* (fundamental) advances.

Change is directly connected with action—with *DOING*. Change occurs when someone does something with an idea.

Consider someone arriving for their first day of work on a new job: They immediately experience both knowledge and culture shock on a massive scale. They are confronted with a mass of new ideas and must respond by *DOING* something with them, and they begin to change rapidly in virtually every dimension. The Seven Levels of Change model offers some interesting insights for approaching such challenges.

1. **DO THINGS RIGHT**
   - Follow procedures
   - Become more effective
   - Understand standards
   - Clean up your mess

2. **DO THE RIGHT THINGS**
   - Set priorities
   - Do what's important first
   - Use 80:20 thinking
   - Become more efficient

3. **DO AWAY WITH THINGS**
   - Stop doing what doesn't count
   - Eliminate waste
   - Ask "Why?"
   - Become more productive

4. **DO THINGS BETTER**
   - Think about what you're doing
   - Think of ways to improve things
   - Listen to suggestions
   - Help, coach, and mentor others

5. **DO THINGS OTHER PEOPLE ARE DOING**
   - Take time out to think
   - Read, observe, notice, study
   - Find best practices everywhere
   - Copy!

6. **DO THINGS THAT HAVEN'T BEEN DONE**
   - Consider crazy ideas
   - Try things *you* think will work
   - Try new technologies
   - Ask "Why not?"

7. **DO THINGS THAT *CAN'T* BE DONE**
   - What's impossible for you today?
   - Imagineer a perfect process
   - Where will it take real magic?
   - "Wouldn't it be amazing if . . . ?"

Figure 1
**A Strategy for Creativity, Innovation, and Continuous Improvement:
Seven Levels of Change at Work**

Level 1: *Efficiency*—**Doing** Things Right

The easiest way to begin is by learning to do things right—the basics of the new job. This is usually done with the help of a supervisor who understands the operation and can explain standard procedures to the newcomer. For the newcomer the immediate focus is on changing enough to quickly become relatively <u>efficient</u> in the job. Changes at Level 1 are based largely on adjusting to new standards and procedures, and involve low risk and low effort. The theme at Level 1 is *Efficiency*.

Level 2: *Effectiveness*—**Doing** the Right Things

Moving into change at Level 2 requires developing an overall picture and then focusing. This involves a thorough understanding and analysis of all the aspects of an operation, process, or service activity in order to identify and then focus on those things which have the most important impact and make the largest contribution. The Pareto Principle states that generally 20% of all the things being *done* actually yield 80% of the total payoff. To maximize effectiveness energy must be shifted to and focused on doing that 20% (the right things) very well indeed and *then* applying Level 1 thinking to Level 2 priorities to *do the right things right*. The theme at Level 2 is *Effectiveness*.

Continuous improvement is often defined as doing things right and doing the right things simultaneously. When someone has made enough Level 1 and Level 2 changes to be comfortable in a new job or situation they have become competent. Thus transitioning through Level 1 and Level 2 (efficiency and effectiveness) is largely change at a personal level and leads to the overarching theme of *Competency*.

Level 3: *Cutting*—**Doing** Away With Things

This level of change involves extinction—*cutting out* the 80% of things that only yield 20% of the value in an activity and then *redirecting* and *refocusing* those freed-up resources to leverage higher levels of change. In the simplest case, change at Level 3 focuses on eliminating waste. If this can be done systemically while keeping all organizational interrelationships, processes, and subsystems in perspective, major results company-wide can be achieved. Quality gurus such as William Conway point out that almost any organization can realize 25% savings by simply eliminating waste in equipment, products, processes, people's time, and so forth. Changes at this level also include taking the initiative to do things without the need for approval, and involve low risk and low effort. Level 3 change has the potential to directly affect the bottom line and to be highly visible, both internally and externally. The theme at Level 3 is *Cutting*.

Level 4: *Improving*—**Doing** Things Better

Change at this level involves careful analysis of the priority "core" activities (the high payoff 20% left after Level 3 change) and figuring out ways to improve or fine-tune them. For example, this could include ways to speed things up, shorten delivery time, increase functionality, or reduce downtime. Work process redesign initiatives are large-scale efforts to bring about Level 4 changes in combination with Level 3. Level 4 change involves making something *more* effective, *more* efficient, *more* productive, or *more* valuable—frequently with customer ideas and input. The theme at Level 4 is *Better*.

Level 5: *Copying*—Doing Things Other People are Doing

Moving to change at Level 5 is the first clear transition from incremental thinking to fundamental change across the spectrum of continuous innovation. Copying, *learning from*, and "reverse engineering" can all dramatically boost innovation quickly and at significantly lower costs than starting from scratch. *Benchmarking* how other organizations are doing things (regardless of what industry they're in), and then further enhancing their discoveries and achievements (using Level 4 thinking), is the hallmark of the successful adapting innovator. This concept, legitimized today by the Quality movement, puts copying in a whole new light. Unfortunately, American leaders are still largely uncomfortable with this level of change. To some degree it is because they are so inwardly focused that they often are not aware of what others are doing that might be worth copying. Further, *Not Invented Here (NIH)* thinking in many organizations resists imitation strongly and the wheel is often reinvented. The Japanese, on the other hand, are long-time world leaders in adapting and creatively improving the products and processes of others—making the "best of the best" even better by synergistically combining thinking at Level 4 and Level 5. The theme at Level 5 is *Copying*.

Level 6: *Different*—Doing Things No One Else is Doing

"When you come to a fork in the road, take it!" urged Yogi Berra. Change at Level 6 involves taking a fork—either doing something <u>very</u> *different* or doing something <u>very</u> *differently*. This level introduces a degree of novelty and uniqueness which moves a group or organization firmly "out-of-the-box" with what they are doing. Such trailblazing and potentially greater risk-taking can bring about genuinely *new* things, often by synthesizing seemingly unconnected concepts, technologies, or components—or by totally shifting perspective with *lateral thinking* around the possible uses of a product. In process-oriented operations, Level 6 at the extreme combines Levels 3, 4 and 5—cutting, enhancing, copying, and adapting—into *reengineering*—completely revolutionizing processes and procedures to the degree that they become so different that they are no longer recognizable. The theme at Level 6 is *Different*.

CONTINUOUS IMPROVEMENT   *Discovering Creativity*

Level 7: *Impossible*—**Doing** Things That Can't Be Done

"What is today *impossible*, but if possible would fundamentally change the way you do business?" Joel Barker's famous question reframes thinking for Level 7. Technology, market constraints, resource limitations, or company culture are too often seen as posing insurmountable barriers. Thus, discoveries at this level frequently build on *paradigm shifts* and truly audacious visions. They lead to tantalizing thrusts into the unknown which are seen as bold, significant and long-term. Change at this level reflects the *highest* degree of imaginative thinking and is almost invariably perceived by others as revolutionary—*shocking*—in its departure from convention. Yet such thinking and such change is vital. Einstein pointed out that: "The significant problems we face today cannot be solved at the same level of thinking we were at when we created them." Very few Level 7 changes are actually implemented as first conceived. Instead they are almost immediately barraged with Level 4 ideas aimed at improving their perceived weaknesses. Those that survive frequently produce enormous innovative spikes which result in heightened plateaus of new thinking, performance, operations, and technology. Such changes can profoundly affect an industry or create an exciting new one. Lockheed Corporation's famous Skunk Works, for example, has continuously produced quantum leap innovations in military aircraft and space technologies—such as the F-117 stealth fighter made famous during Desert Storm. Its ultra radical design is a perfect example of the impossible—change so different that it cannot be compared to anything else known at the time. The theme at Level 7 is clearly *Breakthrough*.

So What? Putting Things in Perspective

An organization needs to leverage the strength of its people's diversity—their varying styles of creativity, motivation, risk-taking quotients, thinking, and vision. To be able to form cohesive teams, people must be able to operate across the level(s) of change in an area *they most prefer*. Each individual has an area of focus on the spectrum of change where they are comfortable working and where they are most likely to welcome continuous change. It is in that area of change that they will transition into proactive *changemasters* and form into cohesive teams. However, as teams become accomplished and comfortable at lower levels of change, they will naturally bootstrap themselves up to the more challenging changes at the higher levels—and the process of *continuous innovation*.

Using the Seven Levels of Change Model

How can this model, these seven levels, best be used?

Whatever the program, initiative, or "flavor of the month" in the company, one thing is sure—it will call for a wide range of changes. The trick is getting people to begin making the changes, to actually <u>DOING</u> something. By using the seven levels to "categorize" the changes desired or needed it is possible to focus and energize people around ideas and changes which they can <u>and will</u> undertake and implement successfully—*because they are operating at their own level of change.*

First, think about the way you think. Reflect on the levels of change at which you typically operate—the kinds of ideas you usually have; that will give you insight into your comfort zone relative to change. Then reflect on a specific change you have successfully made or been involved with at each of the seven levels; that will give you insight into how you deal with change at each level. Such reflections are the first steps to take in understanding how to get other people to consider new ideas. However, others may not perceive a change to be at the same level at which <u>you</u> perceive it to be.

Second, every change requires time, resources, and personal energy. The higher the level of change, the more time, resources, and personal energy the change will require in implementation. Further, it is not a straight-line relationship; it is geometric and literally explodes in terms of challenge and difficulty as the change level increases.

Third, once a change has been made at <u>any</u> level, everything goes back to zero—and the levels of change model can immediately be applied to the change just made. It can be done more efficiently, more effectively; it can be done better or differently; aspects of it can be cut out and eliminated; and it can be copied.

Finally, to change the way you do things, you must change the way you think. You must move your thinking—your way of seeing and understanding things—to match the level of the change you wish to make. If the change involves other people, you must similarly bring them first to that level of thinking before you will be able to successfully move toward implementing the change.

References

Kirton, M. J. (1976). Adaptors and innovators: A description and measure. *Journal of Applied Psychology, 61,* 622-629.

Kirton, M. J. (1992). Adaptors and innovators: Problem-solvers in organizations. In S. S. Gryskiewicz and D. A. Hills (Eds.), *Readings in innovation* (pp. 45-67). Greensboro, NC: Center for Creative Leadership.

Rolf C. Smith, Jr., The School for Innovators, 10682 Beinhorn Road, Houston, TX 77024. Tel: (713) 984-9611. Education: B.A. in mathematics from the University of San Diego; M.S. in computer science from Texas A&M University; Ph.D./ABD in artificial intelligence from Texas A&M University.

CREATIVE COMMUNITY DEVELOPMENT—WHERE IT REALLY BEGINS

Aleksandra Chwedorowicz

Change which probably looks and tastes differently in different parts of the world seems to have become an inseparable dimension of our lives everywhere. Particularly in Eastern Europe, in all kinds of communities, both leaders of different caliber and ordinary people face the challenge of finding their way in completely new and constantly changing situations which are determined by new factors and complicated by combinations of factors. Situations become more and more interrelated and focusing on one problem at a time does not take the problem solver far. What we face are issues rather than problems, difficult to deal with even when vast interdisciplinary knowledge is available. Situations are never the same, and solutions which worked elsewhere, prescriptions and entire systems which proved effective in other cultures are of little help, unless a very flexible approach is adopted. In the new political, economic, and social order in Poland, again and again we discover, often too late, that hope must not be placed in the expertise of the experts, that political leaders alienated from their original communities get lost in the jungle of generalized problems and ideas, that alliances built only for strategic reasons can be no basis to a creative, successful step into the future. All these lessons seem to point to a need for a paradigm shift in how we face the new, in our approach to change.

Poland's difficulties are surely not a separate case. Larger and smaller communities every now and again do face multidimensional changes which render their experience and knowledge of little use and their assumptions, attitudes, and behaviors inadequate.

A very important question in such situations is asked just as it is asked in Poland is "Who will be capable of facing the situation?" This is a question about leaders as well as about communities that would be strong and creative enough to find the way to bring about the new.

The claim of this paper is that in the time of multidimensional change that we are facing, those most capable of finding the way will be very closely spiritually bound groups or teams—cores of communities rather than single individuals—and that the primary mode of their search for ways and solutions will be intuitive rather than rational and analytic.

Spiritual group leadership, though only just budding in Poland, seems to have a good chance for powerful development and deserves wider attention. Examination of the phenomenon with its underlying assumptions may add to what we know about creative leadership and community development.

Numerous definitions of leadership emphasize different aspects of a leader's role, from goal setting to explaining and articulating new values and perspectives. In all of them the integrative role of leader is taken for granted. Different styles of leadership receive a lot of attention ranging from authoritarian to participative. What probably deserves more attention is that the majority of our contemporary leaders, whatever styles they prefer, can be described as answering or aiming to answer the question of direction, of "where to go" and "what to do" more than anything else. The integrative role these leaders perform, while providing their followers with answers, can be graphically presented as orienting a group of subjects who have moved in random directions towards the same point.

Managers as leaders set goals for their employees and divide large, perspective objectives into small individual goals. Social or political leaders state their groups' missions and create images of "where they are going" or "what they want" so that people who follow them look or move in the same direction. What happens is illustrated as follows:

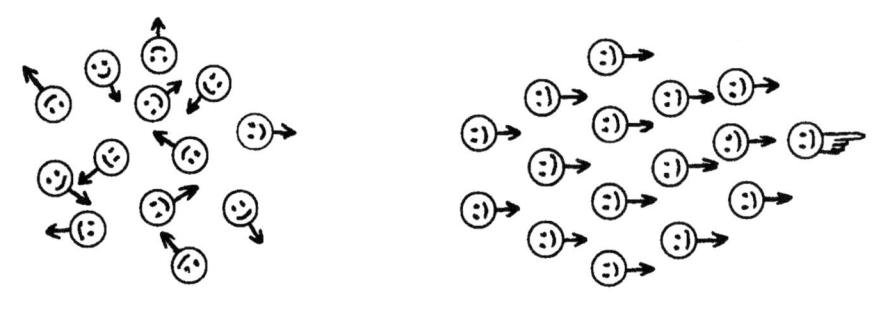

The "where" or "what" vision people want to reach or make in some future time or space provides direction. It also creates tension between what there is (reality) and the dream, and thus releases the energy necessary to span the gap between the two.

What happens, however, when the goal (the dream) placed beyond the immediate reach of the followers gets blurred or disappears? The seeming temporary unity of the group disintegrates. The subjects lose the direction and once again become single and directionless. The recent experience of the people in Poland who were laid off from work by the tens of thousands is probably the best illustration of the phenomenon.

Integration by "where" or "what" type of leadership is superficial and unstable. Relationships developed while pursuing a common goal need not be deep or lasting. As the above figure shows, moving all in one direction need not necessarily mean getting closer to one another. The empty space between the followers of "where" or "what" leaders is wasted space where a lot could happen but doesn't. The picture also illustrates the distance developed between the leader and the individual followers. Once he or she has started performing the role, the leader is no longer one of the followers and is no longer aware of

Discovering Creativity

what it is like to be one of them. Can they ever be really together? Whatever connections are between them, they are the long "via-the-goal" connections.

Observations made above, though obvious, are very important. As it seems, this is where the problem of contemporary disintegration of communities is most deeply rooted. Whether in the factory, in the office, or at school, or every so often even in the family, we live in non-communities or, at best, weak communities which do not produce much sense of community, which fail to provide an environment the individual needs to live a creative life, to develop, and to be in good health. It is the role of community to provide nurture in infancy, security in which to mature, a framework of identity and belonging, a network of caring individuals, experience of being needed, a framework of shared assumptions and values. In a "where" or "what" type of community, individuals contribute to and rely on their communities in a very narrow and shallow way and only so long as they accept the "where" or "what" as their goal. Can there be any substantial contemporary alternatives to "where" or "what" type of community integration?

A useful list of psychological theories for individual development follows. Whether renowned ones like Maslow's or Piaget's or only locally important ones like Kazimierz Dabrowski's or Tom Boydell's, they all very clearly point to a basic direction in individual development. As an individual makes progress in development, the proportion of his or her openness, contact, penetration, understanding, exchange, participation, and insight into the external world increases. The more advanced you are in development, the less concentrated on yourself, the less concerned with your security and survival you are, the more freedom you have in experiencing and exploring your environment and the more perceptive you are of what is going on and of other people. Calling the process of maturing "individual expansion" it is possible to present it graphically as the development of spheres of potential capabilities of richer dialogue with the environment and deeper penetration.

I propose Boydell's theory of development of being and present it graphically in the following way (Boydell, 1990):

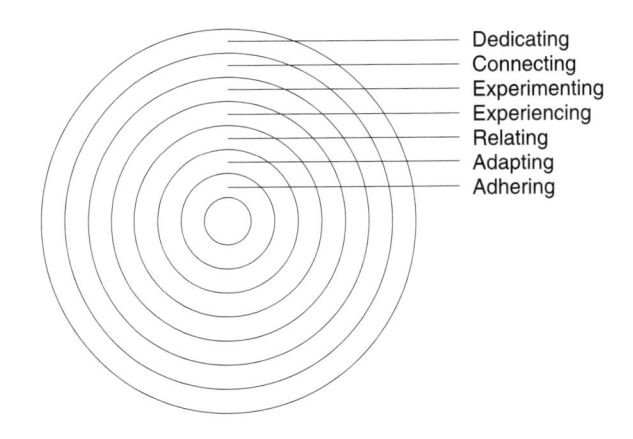

Dedicating
Connecting
Experimenting
Experiencing
Relating
Adapting
Adhering

DIVERSITY *Discovering Creativity*

Assuming that individuals do "expand" it is possible to think about integration and strong community building in terms of development of its members. Attention can be shifted then from where to go or what to do to the question of how to be, how to do. Instead of being pulled in one direction, the members can be pulled together gradually developing more and more advanced modes of being. The process is illustrated by the gradual filling of the open space between community members, so that more and more people fall within the reach of other people's awareness, understanding, and willingness to help, and in turn, become more capable of understanding and offering help to others as shown below:

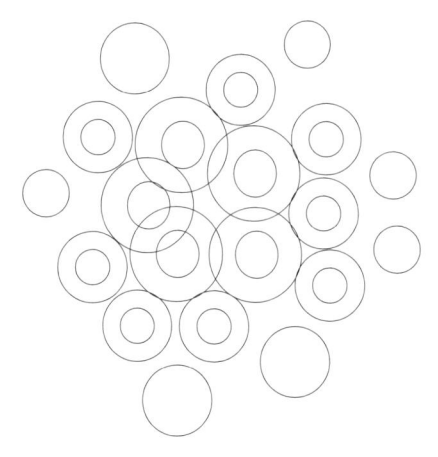

This is how a dense network of one-to-one relationships and communications is created. This network provides the basis to the process of the gradual "tuning in" of each individual to the others, especially to those closer to the core group who show more mature modes of being. It is also the basis for the phenomenon of mutual resonating and amplifying which goes on from the core of the community outwards, resulting in surges of energy and motivation throughout the entire group.

The Polish model of spiritual group leadership for community integration and development begins the integrative process with the development of a core group or team of people whose repertoires of modes of being are possibly the richest today of those having reached the highest levels or stages of personal development. What is spontaneously created when a group of a few such people come together is the common space of intensive multidimensional exchange, where each member contributes and expects to find more than just the sum of individual contributions. The space in-between them is the area where they share and discuss, but also where they "listen together"—tune in to voices coming from the environment and search for patterns that might emerge from the apparent chaos. Amplifying one another's insights and impressions, as a group they become more sensitive to information. Resonating to one another's modes of being, they develop what might be called "the same spirit."

With this surge of energy, they transcend their individual limitations, develop a broader perspective and a better understanding of patterns which emerge from apparent chaos. A "listening" attitude allows them, each time a decision is needed, to develop a general holistic picture of the situation and intuitively to grasp what is most important. What emerges is not just communicated to the rest of the community; it is shared and collectively elaborated.

The way core groups develop into communities resembles an organic process. New people are attracted and gradually become closer and closer members of a growing group. Once they have established closer relationships they undergo some change themselves and, in turn, they attract new people. What might be called a community border is a constant movement—new people coming and old members leaving, relationships and participation becoming stronger or weaker.

It is difficult to say how long-lasting development can be expected of communities created around spiritual group leadership, how many of them will flourish, how many new ones will be started. While some groups seem to aim just at integration of members of disintegrated communities, others try to match mutual love with innovation in economy and perhaps have a chance of success. Whatever they manage to do, the phenomenon creatively budding at the time of change in Poland deserves attention.

Reference

Boydell, T. (1990). Modes of being and learning (Transform Working Paper No. 8).

Aleksandra Chwedorowicz, Local Government Training Center, Lodz City Council, 104 Piotrkowska Street, Lodz, Poland. Tel: 042 33 75 71. Education: Has studied literature and psychology.

MANAGING DIVERSITY IN COMMUNICATION AND PROBLEM SOLVING WITH EFFECTIVE LEVELS OF ABSTRACTION

Mary C. Murdock

There are many aspects of group process that influence productive outcomes. Few are as challenging to manage as sociolinguistic differences. How we think and how we use abstract or concrete language to express similarities and differences is a major concern in creativity training. To effectively manage sociolinguistic differences, creativity professionals must consider balancing novelty and usefulness in both content (task) and process (group dynamics).

Primary and Secondary Diversity: Making the Novel Useful in Group Dynamics

Loden and Rosener (1991) identify six primary and eight secondary dimensions of diversity that are helpful organizers for managing differences in group process. They note that primary dimensions of diversity such as gender, age, race, physical ability, sexual orientation, and ethnicity are more likely to be innate and to have ongoing impact in our lives. They describe secondary dimensions of diversity like educational background, income, marital status, military experience, parental experience, religious beliefs, work experience, and geographical location as those that arise from specific experience and that can be more easily changed. Primary and secondary dimensions of diversity are inherent in every group and are present to a greater or lesser degree in all interactions.

Managing these dimensions of diversity in creativity training presents a compressed conflict that might be described as a "mixed blessing." On the one hand, having diversity in a group or team is important for increased likelihood of novelty and change on a task. On the other hand, that same novelty will not always be welcomed by the group, nor will it be automatically useful or applicable for action on a task. The same is true of primary and secondary diversity in group dynamics. Group members of different genders or ethnic backgrounds speak different "languages," value different ways of taking action, and communicate the meaning of their actions in different ways. To maintain a balance of novelty and usefulness in group dynamics, primary and secondary dimensions of diversity must be managed along with novelty and usefulness in task.

Because there is novelty in creativity training in primary or secondary diversity within a group working on a task as well as in the task itself, sociolinguistic awareness in creativity training is important. Holden (1988) commented on the importance of communication performance in organizations to creativity professionals. His comments illustrate the novelty involved in group dynamics: "Everything about other people's functions, including their occupational language, is 'foreign'" (p. 22). In later comments he suggest five sociolinguistic factors that illustrate what creativity professionals should consider to make novelty of cross-cultural group dynamics useful: (a) the degree to which written forms of a foreign language present barriers; (b) the difference in emphasis on the role of written and oral communication; (c) the influence of setting on interpersonal language behavior; (d) the difference in social purposes of language in a society; and (e) different attitudes toward the level of language proficiency that is expected or respected in others (p. 22).

The differences in thinking and the languages that are needed to communicate them that Holden noted in organizations are also applicable in problem-solving groups. How we structure our problem-solving approaches semantically not only influences the effectiveness of group outcomes (Isaksen, Dorval, & Treffinger, 1993; Isaksen & Treffinger, 1985) but also the ease with which we understand and manage primary diversity dimensions such as gender (Tannen, 1991). Managing diversity at the organizational or group level, however, begins with the thinking skills of individuals. One thinking skill that is necessary in managing primary and secondary diversity is abstraction.

Characteristics and Functions of Abstraction as a Thinking Skill

Understanding and using abstraction effectively depends on an awareness of its characteristics and function. Some characteristics of abstraction are that it is:
- related to cognitive, rational and semantic perspectives (cognitive = thinking; rational = has logical order and form; semantic = having to do with words);
- concerned with things and their qualities;
- operationalized on a continuum that moves from a high level or large degree (macro) to low level or low degree (micro) of specificity in words and meaning; and
- situational and dynamic.

These characteristics can be sorted into two kinds of functions: (a) naming and (b) doing. Naming or defining and identifying qualities is an important aspect of abstracting (Upton, 1961). Mark Twain noted that the difference between a word is the difference between lightning and lightning bug. The naming distinction between the bug and the lightning will not be a semantic quibble if one has had the "doing" experience of being hit by either. A productive way to use abstraction that combines both naming and doing is to consider it as a "locator" to identify an appropriate level of commonality in ideas and concepts that will communicate sufficient shared meaning for effective action. Focusing on identifying the movement of abstraction on a continuum and on locating the position of this movement can help people adjust to changing levels of abstraction during the flow of a discussion or conversation. Once the movement is identified, they can give or receive clarification.

Using Abstraction Ladders to Develop Commonality in Oral Communication

Because the application of abstraction in thought and language is dynamic and varies with situation, effective use depends on awareness of the movement of a conversation along a ladder of abstraction. There are a variety of "ladder" techniques that help to define and locate levels of abstraction in problem solving and written communication (Isaksen, Dorval, & Treffinger, 1993; Isaksen & Treffinger, 1985; Seaburg, 1991). There are, however, fewer applications of these techniques for learning to listen for and use abstraction in discussion, especially in regard to dimensions of primary and secondary diversity.

Oral communication operates on the same continuum of specificity of abstraction that written communication does. However, the flow of every conversation will have as many "ladders" of abstraction as there are general topics and each will have a top and a bottom level of specificity. In addition, discussions are more likely to have a mixture of very specific examples and very broad concepts that result in a variety of dynamic switches from high to low and low to high. The challenge is to identify the ranges of abstraction in the discussion, locate the highest and lowest points, analyze the distance between each, and to adjust thinking and speaking accordingly. One technique to determine where a discussion is going and what the commonalities or differences in language and concepts are within, is to identify key words in a conversation and reorganize them on paper along an abstraction continuum. As you are listening, try to identify concepts and locate them on a high-low abstraction continuum. Notes taken in ladder structures can then be shared for definition and clarification.

The management of diversity in groups is not a task for the faint of heart; it requires knowledge, skill, and courage. Achieving commonality and valuing diversity not only on task, but on primary and secondary dimensions in group dynamics, however, can be learned and improved. Recognizing movement along an abstraction continuum involving primary and secondary diversity is like packing for an unknown destination; you know you'll need a suitcase, but you don't know exactly what you'll need when you arrive. Given the challenge, pack descriptive techniques and use abstraction to locate a productive destination.

References

Holden, N. (1988). Modeling firms as communicators with and interpreters of foreign business environments. In P. Colemont, P. Grøholt, T. Rickards, & H. Smeekes (Eds.). *Creativity and innovation: Towards a European network* (pp. 19-24). Dordrecht, The Netherlands: Kluwer Academic Publishers.

Isaksen, S. G., Dorval, K. B., & Treffinger, D. J. (1993). *Creative approaches to problem solving*. Buffalo, NY: Creative Problem Solving Group—Buffalo.

Isaksen, S. G., & Treffinger, D. J. (1985). *Creative problem solving: The basic course*. Buffalo, NY: Bearly Limited.

Loden, M., & Rosener, J. B. (1991). *Workforce America! Managing employees' diversity as a vital resource*. Homewood, IL: Business One Irwin.

Seaburg, M. B. (1991, February). Critical thinking via the ladder of abstraction. *English Journal*, 44-49.

Tannen, D. (1991). *You just don't understand: Men and women in conversation*. New York: William Morrow Co.

Upton, A. (1961). *Design for thinking: A first book of semantics*. Palo Alto, CA: Pacific Books.

~~~

Mary C. Murdock, Center for Studies in Creativity, State University College at Buffalo, 218 Chase Hall, Buffalo, NY 14222. Tel: (716) 878-6223. Education: Bachelor of Arts in English from the University of North Carolina at Greensboro; Master's of Education in gifted education; Doctorate in educational psychology from the University of Georgia.

ENTREPRENEURS: WHO ARE THEY AND HOW DO WE FIND THEM? A KAI STUDY

Robert B. Rosenfeld, Michael Winger-Bearskin, David A. DeMarco, and Charles L. Braun

Entrepreneurs constitute a significant economic and cultural influence on societal change and innovation. To maintain a competitive edge, the corporate community needs to identify, understand, and characterize the attributes of successful entrepreneurs. Creating an entrepreneurial environment—the current trend in corporate America—necessitates fostering innovative behaviors, which include the support and promotion of novel thought, the advocacy of idea originators, and the removal of outworn bureaucratic barriers. In order to create this environment, organizations must either build or reinforce three pillars: (1) the implementation of systems and processes that foster innovation, (2) the development of leadership that drives innovation, and (3) the capability to demand and support the diversity necessary to generate innovation. Our study was motivated by an essential but often overlooked component—what we call "capability in diversity." This concept aims to make the most of diversity in all its forms, including cognitive styles. Using the Kirton Adaption-Innovation Inventory (KAI) and its subscale scores (Kirton, 1976), we examined the creative styles of a group of successful entrepreneurs. Compared to a group of technology managers and Kirton's original sample population, we found that the entrepreneurs exhibit a distinct creative style profile. By examining this profile and subsequently encouraging successful entrepreneurial behaviors, organizations may understand how better to nurture innovation.

Adaption-innovation (A-I) theory offers a new understanding of creativity by adding the dimension of creative style to capacity, and proposes a continuum of styles, ranging from "adaption" (paradigm building) to "innovation" (paradigm pioneering) (Isaksen, 1987; Kirton, 1987). Kirton's recognition that individuals who work with reliability, precision, and efficiency in organizations manifest "adaptive creativity," while those who challenge existing thought and proliferate novel ideas manifest "innovative creativity," has promoted an appreciation of diversity in creative styles (Kirton, 1989; Rosenfeld, Dubras, Winger-Bearskin, & Braun, 1990).

The KAI score consists of three subscales: originality (the degree of preference for proliferating ideas); efficiency (the level of interest in methodical effectiveness); and rule/group conformity (the extent of accommodation to a group's norms or rules). Whereas most researchers have looked primarily at the interdependence of the subscales within the overall KAI score, we believe that the independent workings of each subscale must also be examined when interpreting KAI results (Rosenfeld, Winger-Bearskin, Marcic, & Braun, 1992). Two people with the same overall KAI score, for instance, could have different subscale scores, which in turn reflect different problem-solving styles. Looking more closely at subscale score alignments can only enhance the usefulness of A-I theory and its measure, the KAI.

By dividing the subscale continuum into four zones (adaptive, mid-range adaptive, mid-range innovative, and innovative), we devised an uncomplicated way of looking at the subscales (Rosenfeld & Winger-Bearskin, 1989, 1990). Zone boundaries were established by the factor trait norms that Kirton used to calculate standard deviations from observed means on each subscale. One standard deviation on either side of the theoretical mean maps out two zones, mid-adaptive and mid-innovative. Scores extending beyond these zones constitute the adaptive and innovative zones (see Table 1).

Using zones to express the relative positions on the subscales seems conceptually easier than using raw scores for the subscales, each of which has a different minimum, maximum, and mean. In addition, designating specific zones facilitates discussing ranges of subscale scores and accessing unique combinations, particularly within specific populations.

Table 1
KAI Zones

	Adaptive	Mid-Adaptive	Mid-Innovative	Innovative
KAI	32-77	78-96	97-114	115-160
Originality	13-31	32-39	40-46	47-65
Efficiency	7-16	17-21	22-25	26-35
Rule conformity	12-28	29-36	37-43	44-60

Note. KAI = Kirton Adaption-Innovation Inventory

In our study, 44 entrepreneurs from a wide range of businesses took the KAI, generating not only total KAI and subscale scores, but also zone placements. Successful entrepreneurs were defined as individuals (a) who had founded, not simply taken over, a business; (b) whose business had a positive cash flow after two years; and (c) for whom the business was the primary means of financial support. We then compared their KAI results with those of 189 managers from one division (which tends to have an entrepreneurial culture) of a large company, and with Kirton's original sample population. We were thus able to test the following hypothesis: entrepreneurs' overall KAI scores, subscale zone scores, and subscale zone alignments should differ significantly from those of the managers and Kirton's sample population.

Results

Except for efficiency, differences between the populations were statistically significant at the .01 level. Kirton's original sample and the entrepreneurs were significantly different at the .01 level. Z-tests rejected the null hypothesis of equality of all means (KAI, originality, rule conformity, and efficiency) between manager and entrepreneur samples, as well as between Kirton's sample and entrepreneurs. Differences were significant at the .01 level. The differences in both mean and variance suggest that these are different population distributions. If this is true for entrepreneurs, then other populations may also exhibit less predictable subscale correlations with the total KAI score (see Table 2, Table 3, and Table 4).

Table 2
Means of the Three Populations

	Kirton's Sample	Managers	Entrepreneurs
n	562	189	44
KAI			
M	94.99	102.33	125.16
SD	17.9	16.39	12.2
Originality			
M	40.78	44.33	55.14
SD	8.89	8.06	6.04
Efficiency			
M	18.82	19.43	22.36
SD	5.59	5.07	5.7
Rule conformity			
M	35.39	38.62	47.68
SD	8.56	7.03	5.18

Table 3
Population Differences in Means and Distribution
Managers vs. Entrepreneurs

Variable	Z Value	F Value
KAI	10.6	1.8*
Originality	9.9**	1.78*
Efficiency	3.15**	0.79
Rule conformity	9.7**	0.84*

* Significant at .01 level of confidence.
** Significant at .001 level.

Table 4
Population Differences in Means and Distribution
Kirton's Sample vs. Entrepreneurs

Variable	Z value	F value
KAI	7.6**	2.15*
Originality	14.6**	2.17*
Efficiency	3.97**	0.96
Rule conformity	14.3**	2.73*

* Significant at .01 level of confidence.
** Significant at .001 level.

The correlations between the subscales in the manager sample and the correlations between the subscales in the entrepreneur sample show very different patterns: (a) the correlation between rule conformity and efficiency is weak (.333) in the entrepreneur data, but this correlation is stronger (.490) in the manager data; (b) the correlation between rule conformity and originality in the entrepreneur data is .303, and not significant, while the correlation between these two terms in the manager data is .604 and significant at the .001 level (see Table 5 and Table 6).

Table 5
Pearson Correlation Coefficients
Entrepreneur Sample

	KAI	O	R
Originality	.674**		
Efficiency	.663**	.058	
Rule conformity	.756**	.303	.333

n=44   1-tailed signif:
* .01
** .001

Table 6
Pearson Correlation Coefficients
Manager Sample

	KAI	O	R
Originality	.834**		
Efficiency	.669**	.278**	
Rule conformity	.869**	.604**	.490**

n=189   1-tailed signif.:
* .01
**.001

This last point indicates that those managers who tend to be innovative in originality will also tend to have a corresponding innovative rule conformity score. By contrast, entrepreneurs with innovative originality may have relatively less innovative rule conformity, although their overall scores will remain in the innovative range.

Overall, the entrepreneurs in this study possessed both innovative originality and innovative rule conformity scores, with efficiency ranging across the continuum, with a mean approximately centered on the scale. This wide range of efficiency subscale scores for entrepreneurs differed from both managers and Kirton's original population with reference to alignment. Further examination of individual entrepreneurs' efficiency scores reflected the type of efficiency expected for the types of businesses that each owned, thus sustaining our argument that continued investigation of subscale alignment may yield more fruitful understanding of A-I theory.

Although this study does not reflect an individual's actual capacity, it does uncover another dimension of the successful entrepreneur's attributes.

Additional studies may further our perceptions of other populations as well. In conjunction with the zone placements, subscale scores may prove valuable in career counseling for potential start-up entrepreneurs. Although further research is needed, this study may enable the financial, investment, and venture capital communities, who perhaps undervalue cognitive diversity, to better understand the behaviors of start-up entrepreneurs and thus increase the success rate of new ventures. Looking beyond the business community, more appreciation of diverse styles will create an environment in which individuals can manifest their own unique strengths.

Innovation within organizations depends on understanding and supporting the entrepreneurial spirit. Individuals who manifest entrepreneurial behaviors need appropriate systems and processes to help release their creative potential, leaders who can advance innovation through the corporate labyrinth, and the capability to make the most of diversity by identifying and promoting a variety of cognitive styles.

References

Isaksen, S. G. (1987). *A new dimension for creativity research: Examining style and level of creativity.* Paper presented at the KAI Conference, Hertfordshire, England.

Kirton, M. J. (1976). Adaptors and innovators: A description and measure. *Journal of Applied Psychology, 61,* 622-629.

Kirton, M. J. (1987). *Manual of the Kirton Adaption-Innovation Inventory* (2nd ed.). Hatfield, England: Occupational Research Centre.

Kirton, M. J. (1989). A theory of cognitive style. In M. J. Kirton (Ed.), *Adaptors and innovators: Styles of creativity and problem solving* (pp. 1-36). London: Routledge.

Rosenfeld, R. B., Dubras, M., Winger-Bearskin, M., & Braun, C. L. (1990). Adaptors and innovators: Partners and opposites—a revolutionary theory with practical implications for agents of change. In M. McDonald (Ed.), *Forging revolutionary partnership: Organizational Development Network 1990 Conference proceedings* (pp. 277-283). Portland, Oregon: Organizational Development Network.

Rosenfeld, R. B., & Winger-Bearskin, M. (1989, December). *KAI subscale scores.* Paper presented at the 1st European Conference on Creativity and Innovation, The Netherlands.

Rosenfeld, R. B., & Winger-Bearskin, M. (1990). *Problem-solving profiles.* Rochester, NY: Idea Connection Systems.

Rosenfeld, R. B., Winger-Bearskin, M., Marcic, D., & Braun, C. L. (1992). *Delineating entrepreneur styles: Application of adaption-innovation subscales.* Manuscript submitted for publication.

Robert B. Rosenfeld, Idea Connection Systems, Inc., 311 Park Avenue, Rochester, NY 14607. Tel: (716) 442-4110.

Michael Winger-Bearskin, Idea Connection Systems, Inc., 311 Park Avenue, Rochester, NY 14607. Tel: (716) 442-4110.

David A. DeMarco, Idea Connection Systems, Inc., 311 Park Avenue, Rochester, NY 14607. Tel: (716) 442-4110. Education: Ph.D. in organometallic chemistry from Purdue University.

Charles L. Braun, Idea Connection Systems, Inc., 311 Park Avenue, Rochester, NY 14607. Tel: (716) 442-4110. Education: Master's from State University of New York, Buffalo.

LEARNINGS FROM SELECTION OR HOW TO DEVELOP INTUITION INTO SHARED INSIGHT

Marc Tassoul

Summary

In this paper, the question of how to exteriorise implicit "intuitive" information is addressed through a process I have termed "Selective Confrontation." The process is meant to be used during creative problem-solving sessions. After having generated ideas, team members are asked to select a number of ideas intuitively. On the basis of this selection, arguments are collected to make the selection process visible and explicit. These arguments are then developed into criteria and sometimes into new problem statements.

Introduction

Creative Problem Solving (CPS) is, like many things, a coin with two sides; in this case one side is for creating and one side for evaluating and selecting. The first aspect, that of creating, receives quite a lot of attention in the field of Creativity and Innovation, but the selection process is often underrepresented. It might be that for creative people, this part of the process is not as popular, since many creative ideas have to be abandoned during this phase. Whereas generating ideas can be very informal and non-committal, converging is much more an act of responsibility and involvement, where consequences and implications are taken into account and hidden agendas make their appearance.

In my experience with creative problem solving, mostly within product innovation projects, I find that lots of ideas already exist in the organization before doing a project. Actually, this is a natural state of affairs; lots of valuable things lie within easy reach, but we don't see them as valuable. It is through events like CPS sessions, with newly formulated goals and conditions and, when possible, with new teams, that the "obvious" is not taken for granted and old ideas can be reevaluated against new problems.

So, what techniques might there be to extricate or exteriorise this latent information? Some techniques consist of mapping information through association, both individually and in a group, both in language and in pictures (e.g., brain mapping). Other techniques use analogies: to imagine real (biology) or hypothetical ("if I were superman") situations where comparable problems have been solved. An excellent technique for analyzing problems is to ask session participants to "draw their problem" without using textual language. All these techniques help to build insight and provide for tools to share this "information."

The idea for Selective Confrontation comes forth from setting up sessions with different teams for the divergent and the convergent steps (see de Groot & Buijs, 1991, for an account of a comparable session). The idea-generating sessions are mainly powered by Industrial Design Engineering students foreign to the problem, whereas the selection steps are executed with experts in the field. The first phase is directed at obtaining a wide scope of ideas, an inventory of possible solutions, and then rounded off by a first selection and clustering. The second phase concentrates on gathering expert information on the field of application (e.g., trends, markets, end-users, etc.), one of the objectives being a more complete and explicit view of the problem field to assist the client in selecting the best options. It is during these sessions that a process was tried and gradually developed in which criteria were generated on the basis of intuitive selection of ideas and concepts.

Evaluation and Selection

The first convention of creative problem solving is to postpone judgment in the creative divergent phases of the process. With associative techniques, it is immediately followed by "quantity breeds quality" which brings participants to focus on the actual production of ideas, forgetting about (self-)judgment. And like many processes in nature, the large number of ideas first produced has to be brought back to a viable amount of concepts before some of these come to maturity.

The primary function of selecting is, of course, to find the "best" proposition from a collection of ideas. But there are a number of points to take into account:

- The ideas resulting from a creativity session are often "vague" and abstract; they have to be developed further before one can simulate their effect and understand the degree to which they accomplish the desired effect;

- there is a trade-off between risk and costs: if you develop lots of ideas, the risk of choosing is low, but costs will be high; conversely, if one makes a choice at an early stage, costs will be low but risk will be higher (e.g., jumping to conclusions);

- furthermore, costs in the first phases of a project are often low compared to those of later stages of a development project, whereas these first phases are often determinants for the overall costs of the project.

It is easy to see the dilemmas with which we are confronted. They all have to do with simulating the functioning of a proposed solution in order to find out its effects and deciding upon further action. The more concrete and explicit the concept is, the easier it will be to evaluate its potential and the less risky it becomes to make a choice.

The purpose of this paper is not to give a full overview of selection techniques but some elements are important. A part of the selection process can be explained as a rational activity, especially when concepts have reached a certain level of elaboration. But even with a fully developed product:

- What criteria do we take into account?
- How important are these criteria and what weight factors should be used?
- Is the list of criteria complete or have we overlooked certain aspects?
- What if the result doesn't feel right?

It is obvious that not all the information needed will be available at the beginning of a project. Depending on the concepts chosen in certain phases, more specific information will have to be gathered and criteria will have to be further specified parallel to the development of concepts into marketable products.

Selection Techniques

In the literature on decision making, one finds that rational models of decision-making processes often lead to an oversimplification of the process. One model for decision making, "successive limited comparisons," restricts the amount of criteria. This choice involves selecting alternatives and evaluation criteria simultaneously. Since this process can only result in a partial solution, it is repeated as conditions and aspirations change and as accuracy of predictions improves. Decision making can thus be perceived as a cyclical, incremental learning process. Complex decisions are evidently more than a simple choice between alternatives: They start to look like problems! (Hicks, 1991, referring to Lindblom, 1959).

In Figure 1, an overview is given of a number of techniques for evaluation and selection used during problem solving and new product development. The list is not exhaustive, it is solely meant as an illustration of some techniques being more explicit than others. These techniques can be used effectively during the different stages of a project when a concept is developed starting from an abstract (implicit) idea into a marketable (explicit) product. To this effect, a development project should be seen as a learning process. Information has to be collected and synthesized into the final product and in each development phase, appropriate selection techniques can be chosen depending on how far the concept has been developed.

from **implicit**

- intuitive
  - gut feeling
  - simplicity and elegance
- inventory
  - clustering and naming clusters
  - PMI: Plus, Minus, and points of Interest
- argumentative
  - paired comparison
  - itemized response
- confrontative
  - court of justice (judge, advocates, and jury)
  - devil's advocate
- criteria and weighed criteria
  - checklists
  - product life cycle
- efficiency
  - strength, weight, consumption, etc.
  - ROI - Return on Investment

to **explicit**

Figure 1: Selection Techniques[1]

[1]The distinction between clusters of techniques (e.g., confrontative and argumentative) is questionable—what it mainly illustrates is the implicit–explicit axis; some of the techniques (e.g., itemized response) are mainly used to locate points on which the concept can be improved.

The Process of Selective Confrontation

The technique will now be dealt with in more detail, and the various steps and some interventions you can use to improve the information-gathering process will be demonstrated.

An example of a process which includes selective confrontation is given in Figure 2. The mess-finding, problem-definition, and idea-implementation phases have been left out for clarity.

From a collection of ideas generated in a previous session, and presented to experts (let's say 20 to 30 ideas), participants are asked to select five ideas with the greatest potential and two ideas with the least chance of being further developed. These results are added resulting in a selection of "good" ideas and "bad" ideas. One should try to have some four to eight ideas in total. The subset of concepts resulting from this intuitive selection is then used to "extricate" pro and con arguments of the selected concepts. Up to this point, the process is similar to the "itemized response" and PMI techniques. But next to localizing possible improvements, it focuses on generating criteria. Through role-playing, these comments are first developed into arguments and later on into goals and conditions from which explicit criteria can be refined.

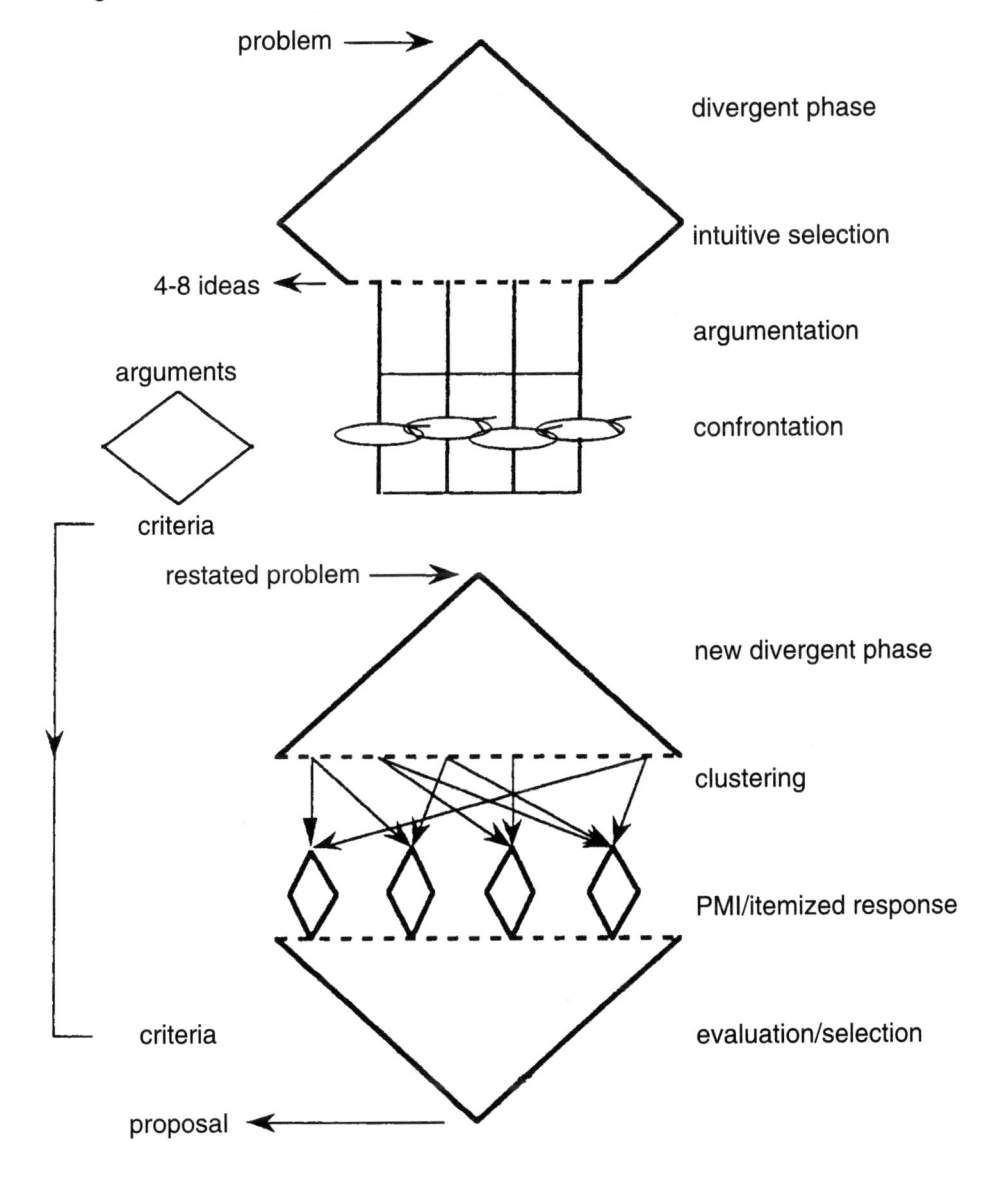

Figure 2
A Process Example of Selective Confrontation

At this stage, three variations on a role-playing scenario have to be followed. Let's assume Anne (one of the team members) is the president of the company and Bill one of the employees.

Bill likes the idea, but his boss, Anne, is not convinced but is inclined to listen to the arguments her collaborator is pointing out; Bill should try to sell the concept to Anne by arguing his case, and Anne will try to oppose this initiative in a confrontative manner. The facilitator (and team members) can assist the process by further investigating the arguments.

An example of such a dialogue might be:

- B. I like the idea because I think it is elegant.
- A. What do you mean by elegant?
- B. Well, it looks simple and has a nice form.
- A. To proceed with your first point, why should it look simple?
- B. Well, the simpler it is, the easier it will be to develop and to produce, and to end-users, its functioning should be obvious.
- A. Fair enough. What about the second point, the nice form?
- B. Well, it should appeal to our customers.
- A. Do we know who our customers are?
- B. Yes and no, we have some ideas but we will have to determine more precisely for whom the product is meant.
- A. etc.

In a very short time, a comprehensive list of arguments can be collected. Each answer can be developed into needs and wants that can be used in a more explicit list of criteria. At the same time, further actions can be identified in the "learning" process.

The first dialogue was done on a "good" idea for which positive arguments had to be used. A similar role play should be done on "bad" ideas. By finding out why these ideas are judged negatively, another set of criteria will be generated:

- A. Why should we not develop product "bad"?
- B. I don't think it is a good idea because we don't have the capacity to produce it.
- A. Why is that?
- B. We haven't got the tools nor the technology, it might take too much time to develop the product, we have to get the idea on the market before our competitors, and having to develop a new technology might be too much of a risk.
- A. etc.

Discovering Creativity   DIVERSITY

It is obvious that all these arguments have to be worked on, but one can see that with just these two dialogues, quite a lot of arguments have been collected in a large number of fields: development, time-to-market, sales, target group, end-user, user instructions, aesthetics, production, and competition.

Yet a third stage should be included. It consists of going against a first intuition. An idea judged positively at first sight has to be criticized with all the possible arguments the experts can come up with; the same goes with "bad" ideas that have to be "sold." This third stage is essential as it will force participants to break through mindsets, presumptions, and thinking patterns. Participants cannot rely on routine; they will have to create new arguments to defend an (at first sight) artificial opinion. It is important to note that after this third stage, a new set of selected ideas often emerges, including some of the "bad" ideas!

These role-playing scenarios have to be dealt with playfully, they have to be mingled and used on all the ideas previously selected. It should become a challenge to generate arguments. These arguments do not necessarily have to be correct; by looking behind these arguments, relevant points will come to the surface. Of course, some feedback should be given by the problem owner on the facets that might need further elaboration, but then, this is part of the "normal" interaction between facilitator and problem owner. To obtain a complete and balanced set of criteria, much care should be taken to select "relevant" experts (including consumers and end-users).

The arguments collected through selective confrontation will need further elaboration. Part of developing these arguments should be done with experts attending the session. The steps would consist of clustering the arguments, filtering out redundancy and less relevant arguments, taking care that each cluster is completed, and finally translating these arguments into a balanced set of criteria.

Conclusion and Comments

The process of Selective Confrontation as presented in Figure 2 was used as an illustration of the (learning) mechanism. It depends on the problem and the personal preference of the process facilitator to determine how useful such a mechanism is at a certain stage of a development process.

Intuition is an important facet in this technique. People are asked to give some holistic opinions on the basis of past experience, spontaneous liking or disliking, and many other subconscious mechanisms. In the process of making explicit intuition, presumptions and mindsets come to the surface and new sets of ideas are often the result. Moral: "Trust your intuition—it's a powerful tool, but you have to check it!"

A few words of precaution are important in this context:

- Intuition is fragile. Trust and respect are essential to have people experience and express their intuition;

- don't expect nor try to make intuition explicit in all its facets (e.g., "It just feels right");

- intuition is "right," the arguments that follow are constructs (logical, social, political, etc.) that will influence (and often also "pollute") this insight; therefore, some time should be spent on "fixating" or recording these intuitive insights before proceeding;

- and finally, include enough time for incubation—like creativity, intuition needs time to ripen.

A final conclusion is that Selective Confrontation will help you develop valuable information on attributes and criteria for product concepts, and values and beliefs from the participants. It is a powerful tool to accelerate the process of developing abstract concepts into explicit proposals. It should result in a feeling of ownership and commitment and could thereby improve the odds of project success.

References

de Groot, R., & Buijs, J. A. (1991). Students and industry experts used as a creative tandem in new business development. In Rickards, et al. (Eds.), *Learning from practice, report of the Second European Conference on Creativity & Innovation.* Delft, The Netherlands: Innovation Consulting Group TNO.

Hicks, M. J. (1991). *Problem solving in business and management: Hard, soft and creative approaches.* London: Chapman & Hall.

Additional Sources

Agor, W. H. (1986). *The logic of intuitive decision making, a research-based approach for top management.* New York: Quorum Books.

Argyris, C. (1990). *Overcoming organizational defenses, facilitating organizational learning.* Boston: Allyn and Bacon.

Buijs, J. A. (1987). *Innovatie en interventie.* Kluwer, Deventer.

Buijs, J. A. (1992). Fantasies as strategic stepping stones: From SWOT analysis to SWOT synthesis. In Rickards, et al. (Eds.), *Quality breakthroughs, report of the Third European Conference on Creativity & Innovation.* Delft, The Netherlands: Innovation Consulting Group TNO.

Firestien, R. L., & McCowan, R. J. (1992). Effects of creative problem solving training on quality of ideas generated in small groups: A working paper. In L. Novelli (Ed.), *Collected research papers, International Creativity & Innovation Networking Conference.* Greensboro, NC: Center for Creative Leadership.

Goldberg, P. (1990). *De kracht van intuitie.* Uitgeverij Kosmos–Utrecht/Antwerpen (original title: *The intuitive edge*, Los Angeles: Jeremy P. Archer Inc.).

Isaksen, S. G., & Treffinger, D. J. (1985). *Creative problem solving, the basic course.* Buffalo, NY: Bearly Limited.

McWhinney, W. (1992). *Paths of change, strategic choices for organizations and society.* Newbury Park, CA: Sage Publications.

Miller, W. C. (1987). *The creative edge: Fostering innovation where you work.* Reading, MA: Addison-Wesley.

Roozenburg, N. F. M., & Eekels, J. (1991). *Produktontwerpen, struktuur en methoden (Product design, structure and methods).* uitgeverij Lemma - Utrecht.

Snelders, D. (1992). *Understanding the role of product design in consumer choice by means of laddering.* Working paper, Faculty of Industrial Design Engineering, Delft.

Vanosmael, P., & De Bruyn, R. (1990). *Handboek voor creatief denken.* Kapellen, Belgium: DNB/Pelckmans.

Westcott, M. R. (1976). *Toward a contemporary psychology of intuition: A historical, theoretical, and empirical inquiry.* New York: Holt, Rinehart and Winston.

~~~

Marc Tassoul, Delft University of Technology, Faculty of Industrial Design Engineering, Post Office Box 5018, 2600 GA Delft, The Netherlands. Education: B.Sc. in aeronautical engineering; M.Sc. in industrial design engineering.

THE FIRE THIS TIME: COPING WITH SUDDEN IMPOSED CHANGE

B. Kim Barnes

Just before I was to begin designing a program on managing change, my home was among 3,000 destroyed in the Oakland firestorm. The irony was not lost on me at the time, but there were other things to think about. The learning would come later.

In the aftermath of the fire and the ensuing months, I paid attention to my own responses and those of family and friends. I began to see how this experience could be a powerful metaphor to help me gain understanding about coping with sudden, imposed change. The kind of change, in fact, that is taking place around the world as fundamental restructuring occurs in the economic and political landscape. The kind of change about which I had been asked to develop a program.

Looking back, I am, for the most part, comfortable with the actions my family and I took to restore our lives to something that is not the same but absolutely acceptable and even interestingly different. I recognize that our loss was mitigated by a good insurance policy; this doesn't exist for most people caught up in a large-scale organizational or political change. The particular action steps that were so useful to us may need to be modified to accommodate differences in personality, cultural values, and life experience.

Assume the worst.
When we were evacuated from the fire area, our house had not yet begun to burn. Of course, I hoped our home would be spared, but realized that it would be better to be surprised by learning it had survived than to expect it to be there and find it gone.

Let go of any illusions of control.
Visualization of a positive future which you can help bring about is productive; imagining you can control the forces of nature, of the economy, of global politics is not. Imagining how you or others could have prevented the disaster is not productive. First grieve and then get on with life after the firestorm. The time for learning how to prevent repetition of the loss will come later in the process when you can make a realistic assessment of what you can and cannot control.

Take time to grieve, but not more than you need.
Two days later, after the fire was out, we were allowed to walk in. It was a shock to see our neighborhood looking like Beirut after the bombings. Our home was gone; in its place a strangely beautiful ruin. We cried and hugged.

Then we began to dig. There was more grieving to do, of course, but it was never after that day the central focus of our lives.

Celebrate the best of what was lost.
The first thing I found intact was a plate my grandmother had painted. The glaze a little rearranged but otherwise perfect, it seemed a loving message from the past. That night the sunset was especially glorious, echoing the fire of two days earlier. The full moon shone through what had once been our bedroom window. We brought fruit and flowers (for life) and candles (for hope) and had a small, quiet ceremony in which we appreciated all the house had meant to us, then let it go and promised to keep that which was best in our hearts until we could rebuild.

Visualize a positive future.
Confidence in yourself and those around you to achieve in the face of adversity is stimulated by your vision. Our vision shortly after the fire was not specific but rather a sense that we would find a good way to live our lives until we could rebuild. Having the knowledge that we would be whole again, although changed, helped us through the most difficult time.

Revisit your values and appreciate what you still have.
We were all alive and well; things are just things. We were temporarily homeless, but did not face it as a permanent condition. Seldom in our fast-moving lives is there an opportunity to learn what is deeply important. I was surprised to learn how easily my attachment to things—even wonderful things—was overcome.

Empower yourself to take action.
The immediate cause of the fire may or may not have been someone's carelessness. The more important cause was that people like me choose to live in a part of the world that is prone to wildfires and earthquakes and choose to use unsuitable building and landscaping material. The latter we can do something about; the former is a choice that involves risk that we need to accept or make a different choice.

Energy spent on blaming is not being spent on resolving the problem. It prevents us from moving on.

Guide and use your support system.
I soon found myself uncomfortable with expressions of sympathy. It was easier to accept help; friends who showed up in work clothes to help us dig or who offered to shop for necessities were deeply appreciated. We learned to ask directly for the kind of help we needed and came to realize how important this was to those who wanted to help and didn't know how.

Be forgiving toward yourself and others.

For weeks I was aware of being unusually impatient. An airline that lost luggage was the object of my wrath for 48 hours. I wryly noted that I seemed to be overreacting about something relatively trivial when I had accepted the loss of so much with more equanimity. Even while this was going on I found it amusing and tried to communicate that to the poor baggage control officers who had to take my calls.

Knowing that the overheated reactions are temporary helps to keep them from escalating, especially if you can let the recipients know that you are blowing off some steam.

Make a conscious effort to learn from the experience.

Noticing your own reactions in a tough situation is like the eye trying to see itself; too much self-consciousness is distracting. Still, this kind of experience offers tremendous opportunities to learn and thus create meaning and value from an experience that is otherwise cruel and senseless.

Don't be afraid to take time off from the serious business of rebuilding your life.

Sometimes we allow situations to define us. A "fire victim" should be suffering, not having a good meal in a restaurant or taking a vacation. I found that the moments I spent enjoying my grandchildren, having a relaxing evening out or reading a good book enabled me to conduct my more complex life with renewed energy and grace.

How does this relate to coping with other kinds of changes; the kinds of changes that inevitably occur in the life of organizations and their employees such as the loss of a job, a contract or customer, a change in leadership, ownership, mission? The loss of productivity and morale that can occur during and after rapid, large-scale change in an organization is well known.

A sudden change that causes serious loss is like a firestorm to those in its path. You can't stop it, but you can survive it; you can even grow and change in unexpected and interesting ways because of it. The best insurance for coping with sudden organizational change is a good support system and a sophisticated set of skills. Individuals and groups that have put these in place before the change have the best chance of surviving and even thriving under otherwise adverse circumstances. Fire consumes; it also refines.

(Excerpted from *The Mastery of Change: Thriving in Uncertain Times*, ©1992 by Barnes & Conti Associates, Inc.)

~~~

B. Kim Barnes, Barnes and Conti Associates, Inc., 940 Dwight Way, Suite 15, Berkeley, CA 94710, Tel: (510) 644-0911.

CREATING BREAKTHROUGH IN ORGANIZATIONS: BEYOND THE "WHACK-A-MOLE" THEORY

Lindsay Collier

With all the different programs that organizations are engaging in these days, one would think that there are some great things being achieved. Total Quality Management, for example, must be the "savior" of American business—that which will take us to the twenty-first century. TQM has its plusses, but it certainly is not something that is going to help us create a great future for business. Many TQM programs have, indeed, proven to be very disappointing uses of resources. Creating excellence is the price of staying in the game these days. Creating the new future of business comes from innovating and anticipating the future, and that's where the concept of breakthrough comes into the picture.

One of the key blockages to the creation of breakthrough is the typical obsession we tend to have about the past. We have always grown by building on past accomplishments and solving problems of the past. Real breakthrough, however, will come only when we are able to stand in the future we want to create and have that future provide the pull. Robert Fritz (1989) discusses the difference between reactive/responsive and creative orientation in his book, *The Path of Least Resistance*. I like to think of this as being analogous to a game I used to play at carnivals when I was a teenager called the Whack-A-Mole game. For those of you who have not had the pleasure of playing this, permit me to explain it to you. You stand in front of a countertop with holes in it and your weapon is a large mallet. As the game proceeds, wooden moles will emerge from random holes, one at a time, and you smash them down with your mallet as quickly as you can. The object is to smash as many moles in the time allowed.

Now, isn't this similar to what is done in businesses? The moles are problems and the object is to smash as many problems as you can in the time allowed. The problem is, since we are so obsessed with problem solving, we totally forget about ever creating anything. The creative orientation suggests that you define what you want to create and are driven by the tension between that and the current reality. There is a tremendous difference between creating what you want and trying not to get what you don't want!

The Nature of Breakthrough

Breakthrough involves the creation of a new pattern or paradigm, rather than the improvement within an existing one. It extends the boundaries of possibility in processes and results and creates new potential. It is also discontinuous, not building on the past, but rather, letting go of it.

Why is it So Elusive to Us?

We have a strong tendency to be trapped in our "boxes." There is rarely much incentive to come outside these boxes because it may be dangerous out there. The majority of people are accustomed to being safe and rather like it that way. As a matter of fact, there is a certain acceptance about non-achievement in work. Not achieving particularly great results, along with a good excuse is often very acceptable. We sometimes have our excuses lined up early for the failure we are programming ourselves for. Large organizations are designed to protect what they have rather than to create something new. The more successful the products of an organization, the stronger are these forces of protection and the weaker is the ability to be innovative and to create something new. Nearly all breakthrough products come from new companies and not the giant companies associated with the product. There are some wonderful breakthrough product ideas just waiting in the spider webs of these large companies, and most will never see the light of day.

Another major block in our ability to create breakthrough thinking lies in our inability to be good listeners which results in a tendency to engage in poorly focused conversation. It was once said that "No great idea ever entered the mind through the mouth." Making assertive statements about what we *are going to* achieve in the future, however, has a powerful effect on helping us realize these achievements.

What potential was set into motion when Kennedy said we will have a man on the moon by a certain time? But we rarely make these statements today—it's more comfortable to be passive and non-assertive.

If we are going to achieve breakthrough, we must learn how to carry out appropriate conversations. Conversations aimed at possibilities will help us create the visions we need for success. Conversations of opportunity will create the bridge between possibilities and action. And, when it is time for action, the conversations need to be focused on what needs to be done and how to overcome the breakdown on the way to its accomplishment.

A Process for Achieving Breakthrough in Organizations

At the risk of oversimplifying this, let me suggest an approach that may get you on the way towards achieving breakthrough in your organization.

1. Get people turned on to and excited about possibilities. Breakthrough will never come from people who have no excitement or passion about what they are doing. This involves doing what is necessary to produce a creative orientation (and stop mole-whacking)—the excitement and energy will follow.

2. Begin a shift in mindsets. This involves some serious shifts in thinking and what I call a "paradigm workshop." There are some very powerful techniques to help people in this process. The need here is to start thinking of possibilities where only impossibilities previously existed. This is not easy—but it sure is fun.

3. Create strong visions of the future and really drive them home with everyone in the organization. These need to be positive visions (creating health vs. preventing illness) and need to be attainable even though requiring a stretch by those achieving the vision.

4. Expand creative thinking capabilities and nurture conversations for possibilities and opportunity. Training people in creativity is rather useless if there is not a strong environment for breakthrough. Gone are the days when idea generation, just for the sake of saying you've been creative, is appropriate.

5. Focus on action and create conversations for action. A strong, real commitment is an absolute necessity here.

6. Remember the well-known words, "Just Do It." You can never steal second base if you keep your foot on first. Movement in any direction is often better than no movement at all.

Reference

Fritz, R. (1989). *The path of least resistance: Learning to become the creative force in your own life.* New York: Fawcett.

Lindsay Collier, Creative Edge Associates, Post Office Box 352, West Henrietta, NY 14586. Tel: (716) 334-4779.

PROCESS EXPLORATIONS WITH CYBERQUEST

John W. Dickey and George DiDomizio

CyberQuest (CQ) is a hypermedia hardware/software system developed to help individuals or groups generate ideas and ways to implement them. To date CQ has been employed in over 450 cases, which have covered a wide span from the highly technical, to management, to product development and marketing, to social service provision.

Process Experiments

Some of the most interesting exercises with CyberQuest have come through a wide variety of process "experiments." The first experiment involved use of Merck's voicemail system (DVX). George (the second author) put John (the first author) onto the system so that they could exchange messages and ideas. George proposed an aim, or purpose—the first step in the CQ system. John then used CQ in Blacksburg, Virginia, to generate some relevant concepts. These were read into the DVX so that George, and others, could respond with ideas. These responses were communicated by DVX (or by fax) and subsequently typed into CQ by John. After a certain time period, all ideas were printed and sent to the respondents.

The next process experiment included teleconferencing. George set up a meeting for John with three advertising agencies in New York. John took the portable CQ system there and started with a 15-minute demonstration. This was followed by a 40-minute trial session on a "dream" of interest to Merck. George facilitated the session by phone from his home in Pennsylvania. At least that was where he said he was. (Many of us believed he was using the cellular phone in his car, on the way to Atlantic City, a famous gambling resort.)

Several other sessions were conducted in a similar way. In one, George was in his office in Pennsylvania with a group of three other people, and John was in Blacksburg with the system. The aim and key words were selected earlier. John read concepts over the phone to the group (the original plan was to send them by fax, but John's fax machine was not working). George would write these down on easel pads, and facilitate the group in idea generation. John then would type these into CQ. The session lasted for about two hours. John sent the resulting report off the next day by overnight mail (although it could have been sent as a computer file by phone/modem).

In another session George was visiting an associated firm in the Washington, D.C., area and John again was in Blacksburg. The same procedure was followed. The unique aspect of this effort, however, was that nobody at the other end (except George) had seen CQ in operation. George simply asked them to "play the game" for a while until they got the hang of it, which surprisingly they did with ease. It turned out to be one of our most interactive sessions.

Next we tried video-conferencing. This was done in connection with a meeting of an industry group known as the "Techno-Innovation Consortium." About 10 of us met in West Point, Pa., in one of Merck's videoconferencing centers. George went to Rahway, N.J., to another of the company's video conference centers. The session was productive, although a little "slower" than others, perhaps because most of the participants did not know each other.

The next adventure was a videoconference as part of the European Conference on Computer-aided Language Learning (EUROCALL) in Helsinki. Four of us were with CQ at Merck's Video Concepts Center at West Point, Pa. We were connected to two other conferees from Tele (Finland's AT&T) on-stage in an auditorium at the Helsinki University of Technology. About 150 people in the audience were able to view the videoconference interaction via a large screen at the front of the room.

The session was for demonstration purposes and lasted for 20 minutes. The selected aim for the CQ session was to improve nonverbal language learning (e.g., in understanding "body language"). John showed various CQ computer screens and the conferees on both sides of the Atlantic responded with their related ideas, screening advice, and packaging suggestions. (Actually, to be safe, the whole process was scripted ahead of time—but still using CQ in that endeavor.)

Still another experiment was made as part of an introductory computer programming class at Virginia Tech. The class was divided into teams and each given the assignment to develop code for a selected section of a new computer program. The aim of the session with CyberQuest was to identify valuable (and perhaps innovative) aspects for the program.

John produced an hour-long videotape of relevant screens from CQ. Most, for example, showed concepts that related to the aim through the key words. Pauses were inserted to allow the viewers time to write down their ideas (with some examples given to start the thought process). The videotape then was aired two nights over the cable network to both the dormitories and local access TV to the town of Blacksburg (for those students living off-campus).

The students were asked to type their ideas into a word-processing program and submit them on disk at the next class session (although they could have sent them via electronic mail or electronic file transfer just as easily). The ideas subsequently were discussed in class and given a verbal screening. They then were copied from disk, checked for redundancy, and put into a CQ case file using an electronic cut-and-paste procedure. The result was a list of 87 ideas that were handed out to the student teams at the next class meeting.

An unexpected outcome was that some of the students videotaped the show themselves, then completed the exercise later. This had two advantages.

Discovering Creativity   NEXT GENERATION

First, those not having easy access to the cable system or those who could not see it at the designated times could still participate. Second, various parts of the videotape could be replayed (with stop action) to review concepts and allow sufficient time for the generation and recording of additional ideas.

Of course some students—being creative nonstudents—did not watch the show at all. They simply asked others what it was about and then wrote up their ideas accordingly.

Lower-tech Experiences

Somewhat "softer" process explorations with CQ have involved such trials as:

(1) Running two CQ sessions simultaneously on one machine.

(2) Addressing an aim in one session, then taking the implementation of one of the resultant ideas as an aim for a second session.

(3) Using the Nominal Group Technique as part of the Idea Generation step in CQ.

(4) Running a session at different times and places and with varying degrees of interruptions.

(5) Using CQ as part of a luncheon talk, with ideas written down via the Crawford "blue slip" method.

Summing Up

All of these experiments demonstrate that there are many ways to use CyberQuest. As for topics that are apt subjects for CQ itself, the variety of these experiments is limited only by the imagination of those involved. Each trial presents unique opportunities both for success and failure. It has been astounding that relatively few did not work well. A lesson here might be that most new ideas are not as hazardous as they might at first appear. We can also conclude that most take a lot more work than expected or that most observers are likely to appreciate from the apparent casualness of the activities.

~~~

John W. Dickey, Virginia Tech and IdeaPlex, Inc., University Center for Innovation Research & Support, 104 Draper Road, Blacksburg, VA 24061-0520. Tel: (703) 231-7307. Education: B.S. degree in civil engineering from Lehigh University; M.S. and Ph.D. degrees in civil engineering from Northwestern University.

George DiDomizio, Boulder City Productions, 700 Hill Road, Green Lane, PA 18054. Tel: (215) 234-4510. Education: Bachelor of Business Administration degree from Ursinus College.

A HYPERMEDIA SYSTEM FOR DISCOVERY AND INNOVATION SUPPORT

John W. Dickey, Dingshin Yu, Bruce Wright, and Thomas T. Wojcik

The CyberQuest System

CyberQuest (CQ) is a hypermedia system for the support of problem solving, design, and broadscale innovation. It has been used now in over 450 "real world" cases in 12 countries. It employs computer data bases (e.g., on CD-ROM) as well as video, audio, and even aroma discs to assist individuals and groups in coming up with ideas AND ways to implement them.

CQ guides the user through six basic steps:
1. Problem description and analysis
2. Word selection
3. Idea generation
4. Idea screening
5. Idea packaging
6. Reporting

In step one CQ asks for a short (50 character) description of the aim to be accomplished via any ideas generated with the system. The user then selects four key words, from a list of about 200 provided by CQ, that best connect to the main words written in the aim.

Once the key words have been chosen, they are employed in step three to match against concepts in various data bases. These concepts come from over 45 sources and cover a variety of disciplinary areas. They, too, have four key words describing them, again taken from CQ's list. If a match is located between the words describing the aim and those connected with a concept, the assumption is made that there is some similarity. The matching concept is then displayed on the screen and the user asked to draw an analogy to obtain an idea to help accomplish the aim.

In step four the ideas are screened. This involves assigning a "status" to each, depending on whether the idea has been tried before, and its implementability. Each idea thereafter is rated for its importance in meeting the aim and the effort required to implement it.

Packaging and evaluation, step five, require the user to look for combinations (i.e., "packages") of ideas that are more productive, beneficial, and cost-effective than any one idea by itself. The subsequent packages thereafter are evaluated according to selected "themes" or criteria, and decisions made between them.

In the final step, reports are created displaying the ideas, sources, screening results, and final packages. Another feature of CQ is that the generated ideas can be put back into the system's data bases and employed by a succeeding user who may be facing a similar problem or opportunity.

Throughout the CQ process, the user also has several options. These include (1) entering notes related to any idea, (2) identifying goals that supplement the aim, (3) employing selected analytic tools (e.g., a spreadsheet), and (4) accessing a variety of information sources. All these give the user a high degree of capability and flexibility in creating ideas and finding ways to implement them.

Experience With CyberQuest at Hoechst Celanese Corporation

Hoechst Celanese Corporation's (HCC) division in Charlotte, N.C., has initiated a highly energetic program to encourage innovation by its employees, especially in new product ideas. Toward this end they have acquired CyberQuest and run over 20 cases so far. Some of these are listed in Table 1. As can be seen, these cover a wide range of activities—from naming and "selling" the innovation process itself, to improving management (both in the company and the community), to creating and marketing new products.

**Table 1
Examples of HCC Cases**

Naming a Forthcoming HCC Book on Innovation (3 sessions)
Naming the Innovation Process Being Pursued at HCC (2 sessions)
Selling Management on the Value of the Innovation Process and CQ
Allocating New Office Space
Designing an Innovation Laboratory
Providing Medical Services to Another Site
Quality Management in Local Government
Speciality Air Filtration Product Concepts and Marketing
Process for Cellulose Acelytation Polymerization

The number of participants involved has ranged from two to twelve. They have spent anywhere from two hours to one-and-a-half days in the effort. Several hundred ideas have come from these sessions. The majority have been screened and a small number put into packages. In the "Air Filtration Product" case, for example, a group of three worked for three hours on idea generation, followed several days later by a screening session with the leader and the Innovation Office. More processing is anticipated to develop packaging and to employ some of the analytic tools in CQ to help assess them. The medical expansion case was a unique one in that the session was held in a medical examination room (CQ is portable and can be rolled around to nearby sites).

Implementation

Since CyberQuest has been in operation only 12 months at the time of this writing, only a few results can be reported. Looking at Table 1, we find that the innovation book as well as the process have been named. Upper management remains convinced of the value of the process, although, with expenditures mounting, they are asking more about benefits and payoffs. Many of the ideas on space allocation are being built into future plans and should become apparent in the next few months as building efforts move forward. The Innovation Lab has been constructed, incorporating a great many of the ideas generated by CQ.

Implementation of the planned medical service extension is now underway. The local government that participated with HCC in the CQ session on Quality Management is readying itself to undertake that effort, although funding is extremely tight at the moment. Progress also is being made on the ideas from the product development cases. These, however, are more recent and take much longer to implement.

On a more general note, it can be said that many people in the organization approach CQ (and the Innovation Program itself) with a skeptical or cynical attitude. A majority of these can be convinced after some exposure to the system. Others, of course, will not be swayed. They may feel completely satisfied with their current activities or be loathe to make any changes, even of known value. There also is some unhappiness with the fact that the Innovation Program is getting priority in funding while most others are being forced to be very careful in their expenditures. These responses are not uncommon. They also occurred when the Quality Management Program was initiated at HCC ten years ago. The point is that CQ, and innovation in general, have to be re-justified and resold on a continual basis.

John W. Dickey, Virginia Tech and IdeaPlex, Inc., University Center for Innovation Research & Support, 104 Draper Road, Blacksburg, VA 24061-0520. Tel: (703) 231-7307. Education: B.S. degree in civil engineering from Lehigh University; M.S. and Ph.D. degrees in civil engineering from Northwestern University.

Dingshin Yu, Environmental Design and Planning, Virginia Tech, 104 Draper Road, Blacksburg, VA 24061. Tel: (703) 231-7571. Education: Bachelor of Architecture from Qinghua University Beijing, People's Republic of China. Master's degrees in science in architecture, and urban and regional planning from Virginia Polytechnic Institute and State University.

Bruce Wright, Hoechst Celanese Corporation, Post Office Box 32414, Charlotte, NC 28232-2414. Education: B.S. in chemical engineering from the University of Idaho; Ph.D. in chemical engineering from Rensselaer Polytechnic Institute.

Thomas T. Wojcik, Hoechst Celanese Corporation, Post Office Box 32414, Charlotte, NC 28232-2414. Tel: (704) 554-3414. Education: Graduate of Frostburg University.

LEADERSHIP AND CREATIVE LEADERSHIP: SOME PERSONAL REFLECTIONS

Per Grøholt

Leadership is creating purposeful (goal-oriented) interaction to achieve results. At the core of the definition is the creation of interaction. It is a relational concept. Leadership creates connections that work, both goals and results. It is not necessarily to interact but to create interactions. This is the what of leadership, not the how. All who do the what practice leadership.

In my opinion, this is the most parsimonious way to explain the substance of leadership. Perhaps I am wrong.

When presenting this definition to executives they at first hearing accept it—then they go through a process of disagreement, and end up wondering what leadership really is. The full discovery process may take years.

The difficulty is to intuit the difference between content and process and then, even harder to grasp, the difference between processes and creating processes. I am talking about a higher order of understanding. A second order of learning.

Be aware that I am not talking about decision making, problem solving, planning and control, goal setting and results, motivation, cooperation, etc. Leadership creates interactions that result in the above.

In other words, leadership is the simultaneous integration of tasks and people. It is not tasks and it is not people. But without people there is no leadership. It is the integration of hard and soft, of inner and outer reality, of spirit and matter (heaven and earth).

At a more practical level I have developed some leadership principles which I use as a tool for dialog with executive groups in order to start this discovery process.

The first twelve principles on leadership and responsibility follow. I also include the last three principles on change and development. (The other twelve are on line and staff relation, goal setting, loyalty, and communication.)

Leadership Principles—A Basis for an In-company Dialog

All employees are co-workers in a company.

A leader is a co-worker with line responsibility for other co-workers.

Leadership

1) The role of leadership is to create goal-oriented (purposeful) interactions to achieve results.
2) All co-workers have a responsibility to create goal-oriented interactions—to act as leaders.
3) The leader is responsible for seeing that leadership is practiced according to the principles outlined here.

Task Responsibility

4) The leader must clarify the tasks of the co-workers. They also must insure that the co-workers understand and accept them.
5) Co-workers have the responsibility for everything, including consequences, that happens within their clearly defined tasks.
6) By delegation, the co-workers get full responsibility for decision making and accomplishment of the task. The leader is responsible for delegating correctly.

Area Responsibility

7) A leader has total responsibility for everything that happens in their area.
8) The cause and time something happens never serves to lessen the leader's total responsibility.
9) Total responsibility cannot be delegated.

Responsibility for the Whole

10) In addition to their own responsibilities, the co-workers are responsible for the whole of the company.
11) Responsibility for the whole is shown when your actions, within and outside of your task and area, agree with company goals and values.
12) To be active is to take on responsibility for the whole.

Change and Development

- All co-workers are responsible for working continuously with change.
- The leader must prepare for change and development by giving co-workers freedom, responsibility, and challenges.

- The leader should assure that an element of learning and development exists in every co-worker's task.

Leadership Principles—Some Remarks

"Goal oriented" refers to the future purpose and efficiency of requirements. Results relate to individuals, company, and society. Profit is just one aspect of the results.

All co-workers have leadership responsibility. That follows from the definition. Leadership is a mutual process. The leader is not outside the team, but inside—where all have leadership responsibility.

The word leader refers to formal leaders who also are co-workers. We need strong leaders to create strong co-workers.

Only formal leaders have total responsibility—that is area accountability outward and upward. To be a formal leader of an area, however, is not leadership—it is a responsibility called accountability.

Other principles refer to the holistic principle. All co-workers are responsible for the entire organization.

The above remarks are especially relevant to the concept of leadership.

In his recent book, *Leadership for the Twenty-first Century,* Joseph C. Rost (1991) has proposed the following definition: "Leadership is an influence relationship among leaders and followers who intend real changes that reflects their mutual purposes." By this definition Rost is pointing out the future direction of what might be the emerging content of leadership in the twenty-first century. My own definition agrees with Rost's direction.

Alignment with Rost can be found in three of his four key words: influence (create), relation (interaction) and purpose (goals), but not change. In my opinion Rost defines creative leadership and not leadership. To resolve this issue we must first understand leadership.

Gradually I find support for my view of leadership in many recent books. Especially in Peter Vaill's *Managing as a Performing Art* (1989). (In Norway we don't distinguish between leadership and management—and I don't like the distinction.) *Fifth Discipline* (1990) by Peter Senge sees leaders as designers, as stewards, and as teachers.

More fundamentally George Land (1992) in *Breakpoint and Beyond*, in his use of the word connecting (chapters 6 and 10), explains fully what I mean by the word leadership.

NEXT GENERATION　　　　　　　　　　　　　　　*Discovering Creativity*

In the same book (chapters 6 and 8) Land clarifies the concept of creativity to include his key concept—future pull.

We are left with the basics—

BEING AND BECOMING
or
CREATIVE LEADERSHIP

where being is leadership and creativity is becoming.

References

Land, G., & Jarman, B. (1992). *Breakpoint and beyond.* New York: HarperCollins.
Rost, J. C. (1991). *Leadership for the twenty-first century.* New York: Praeger.
Senge, P. (1990). *Fifth discipline: Mastering the five practices of the learning organization.* New York: Doubleday.
Vaill, P. B. (1989). *Managing as a performing art: New ideas for a world of chaotic change.* San Francisco: Jossey-Bass.

~~~

Per Grøholt, Norwegian Center for Leadership Development, Post Office Box 75, Grefsen, 0409 Oslo, Norway. Tel: +47 2 713591. Education: Norwegian University School of Business and Administration.

TEACHING CREATIVITY BY DISTANCE LEARNING METHODS

Leslie J. Jones

Background

The Open University is one of the great success stories of British education. It is the largest and most innovative university in Britain with a worldwide reputation for the quality of its courses and the soundness of its teaching methods. Since receiving its Royal Charter in 1969, more than a million people have studied with the OU, most of them as undergraduates.

More recently the Open Business School has been formed and is expanding rapidly. It teaches management and business courses to certificate, diploma, and MBA levels. OBS students, like their undergraduate counterparts, are mainly in full-time jobs and study in their free time. Much of this is done at home using study materials provided by the OU with some local tutorials and national residential schools. The assessment system on most courses consists of 50% tutor-marked assignments and 50% final examination. All qualifications are made up of a number of courses each of which has a credit rating which may be a quarter-, half- or full-credit.

At the 1988 Greensboro conference, Jane Henry and John Martin of the OBS gave a presentation about a new creativity and innovation course which they would be running as part of the MBA program. This course, entitled Creative Management, is now nearing the end of its second year of presentation and has been an outstanding success. It has 560 students this year, compared with the 300 originally estimated by Jane and John. Many of this year's students have come as a result of personal recommendations from last year's.

The program requires about 200 hours of student work over a seven-month period and is evaluated by coursework, consisting of four 2,500-word assignments, and a final three-hour examination.

A multimedia approach is used involving textbooks, course notes, audio and video tapes, TV programs, computer disks, computer seminars, networking, written assignments, face-to-face tutorials, and residential schools.

The marking of assignments and the tutorials are undertaken by 36 tutors, of which I am one, in the 13 Open University regions within the United Kingdom.

Most of my students are senior managers in large companies or government agencies such as the National Health Service. They have to fit their studies around their workload which in some cases involves a great deal of overseas travel. What follows is the structure for the course they have developed.

Course Content

The course is broken down into four blocks for each of which the students are required to submit an assignment.

Block 1 (Perspective) starts by introducing the idea of creativity, its role in management, and the nature of creative thinking. It then develops the idea that different people and different organizations have different perspectives and different creative styles, and looks at the barriers to creativity that can arise. In this block students are asked to act as "reflective practitioners." This includes exploring their own, their colleagues' and their organization's creative style, strengths, weaknesses, and potential and considering the underlying values and metaphors. They tackle this by using inventories, mapping, feedback from peers, and other activities to help them. In the light of these analyses, they are encouraged to think of a personal course focus and to begin to set up the network that they will use in later blocks. In the first assignment they report on their analyses.

The Residential School overlaps with the second half of Block 1. It provides the foundation for Block 2 by teaching basic problem-solving techniques and skills, particularly for those that are difficult to teach by post, including face-to-face teamwork, imagery development, and certain types of computer work. It is run as a workshop, with tutors facilitating solo and small group settings in which students apply a range of basic creative problem-solving techniques (e.g., brainstorming and related methods, synectics, morphological grids, mind mapping, and evaluation and development methods) to practical issues (usually their own). It includes options such as a "software show," which allows students to examine a number of relevant software packages. Another novel aspect of the residential school is the "tutor fair" where tutors explain the approach which they intend to use in their tutor group, and students then decide which group they wish to join.

Block 2 (Techniques) builds on the Residential School to provide a resource bank of about 200 solo and team methods for various aspects of problem solving, opportunity analysis, and insight finding. It includes familiar techniques such as brainstorming, but goes well beyond these to encompass a broad range of divergent and convergent, analytic and intuitive, manual and computer-based techniques. An overall picture of the principles underlying the techniques is given in the introductory text that precedes the techniques and in a collection of video, audio, and computer demonstrations. Students select from among the techniques those which are appropriate to their needs and apply them to current problems that face them. At the same time, networking is encouraged to see how others are progressing with their chosen techniques. In the assignment they report on their experience, compare it to the experiences from their network colleagues, and try to draw conclusions to help with future applications of problem-solving techniques.

Block 3 (Innovation) is concerned with problem solving at the organizational level, focusing on how to develop and manage the creative climate for others. It considers the factors that create the need for organizational creativity, and the effects of creative management on organizational identity, ethics, culture, roles, and relationships. It then goes on to look at the different kinds and levels of innovation that top management can aim for, the targets at which it can be directed, and the tactics that can be employed. These include improving environments, facilitative management styles, intrapreneurship schemes, vision building, changes of organizational climate and culture, etc. The block contains a range of text and video case studies which illustrate some of the major themes of organizational creativity, such as changing the orientation of the organization, encouraging invention or innovation, new product development, and organizational renewal. In the assignment, students are asked to relate ideas from the block to their own situations.

Block 4 (Project) is a 50-hour practical project on a creative management issue of the students' own choice within certain broad guidelines. They take strategic issues that currently affect them and apply the course methods to these issues. This project also serves to pull together themes from all the three previous blocks and so encourage a more holistic approach to problem solving.

~~~

Leslie J. Jones, Les Jones and Associates, 30 Beryl Avenue, Tottington, Bury, Lancs BL8 3NF United Kingdom. Tel: +44 204 882950. Education: Degree in psychology; Master's degree from Manchester Business School.

CHANGE AS A CREATIVE CATALYST: A MODEL FOR A REGENERATIVE MINDSET

Joseph M. Miguez

> Every time I think I know something, life keeps on being itself, and I'm left standing on my head.
>
> Charles W. Prather,
> in an address given at the 1992 ICINC

Change, when we least expect it or feel the need for it, is often considered undesirable. Change creates, and when something new is created it creates change, and when change is created it in turn creates, which in turn creates. Change does not come in an orderly manner, but at different times from different places, in different forms, and mostly unexpectedly. George Land, co-author of *Breakpoint and Beyond*, says, "Today's change is not just more rapid, more complex, more turbulent, more unpredictable. Today's change is unlike any encountered before" (Land & Jarman, 1992). It is no longer, "Stop the world I want to get off." It is "Stop the world I want to stay on."

Change is occurring every second of our lives—all around us, for good or bad whether we want it or not. Change often goes unnoticed—the continuous seasonal changes of the deciduous trees; the transformation of ice into water; the caterpillar into a butterfly; the breathing in of new air; the constant replacement of the cells in our bodies. Matter into energy. Energy into matter.

Change is constant, and we all are resistant to change. We like to maintain the status quo. In a recent article from a newsletter published by Project Adventure of Massachusetts called "Ziplines," Tim Chorchard wrote about change. "Change! If we don't embrace it, it will knock us over. We not only have to embrace change when it comes, we have to pursue it. Change comes too fast and is too relentless. We need a fundamental shift in attitudes toward change" (Summer, 1992).

In order to support and nurture that shift to embrace the constancy of change, participants were introduced to a "Momentum Kube," a model I developed for entrepreneurs to establish a creative/regenerative mindset and bring new ideas to reality. The "Kube" is a non-threatening model that initiates a momentum that begins with change as its catalyst. Its organic energy moves participants from change . . . to awareness . . . to new thinking . . . creativity . . . risk . . . competition/completion, and returns to change. The process develops a synergy that allows participants to focus on awareness, thereby opening new insight and understanding.

The "Momentum Kube" is driven by two forces—one external, the other internal. The external force is energy that is available outside of the self imposing the change. The internal force is energy from within—purpose, commitment, and courage. The fusion of these forces provide the momentum to *change* the "Kube" *from a static to a dynamic position,* and from a *viewpoint to points of view*—the essence of a creative/regenerative mindset. This awareness brings about new thinking. Either *or* thinking is transformed into both *and* thinking. Challenges become opportunities. A brand new attitude emerges.

Different thinking leads to new connections, discovery, and creativity. A recent *New York Times* advertisement for the New York Open Center read: "Shift happens . . . when you connect with New York Open Center." My version says, "Shift happens . . . when you connect with new ideas!"

New ideas need to be put into action. There are, however, inherent risks in implementing new ideas in this very competitive world. What are the risks? What can be done to minimize them? How important is a plan of action? Listening? Being risk prudent?

Competition/completion. I choose to include both of these terms. Competition usually refers to rivalry. Today, a global economy and shrinking resources are causing a shift toward seeking to work together—cooperation—in order to compete. P. Crosby, in his book *Completeness* (1992), lists four ideas to bring about this level of cooperation. They are:

1) Treat the whole as one.

2) Build a culture of understanding.

3) Make everything understood.

4) Be complete but not finished.

This approach creates a gap in the cycle allowing momentum to carry itself on to another level of change/creation, sustaining itself for another point of departure toward one's purpose. This philosophy of completion allows for the establishment of a creative/regenerative mindset. Change create. Create change. Change create change. A paradiddle of sorts.

I use three exercises which stimulate this process:

1) A physical/mental exercise modeled from Leonardo DaVinci that requires participants to restretch their mental mindsets.

2) Participants are asked to switch their watches to the opposite wrist from which it is normally worn, and asked to pay attention to their reactions to the change.

Discovering Creativity

3) Participants are asked to read outside their normal reading material, to explore newspapers and magazines (*Omni, Scientific American, Rolling Stone, Spy, Vanity Fair, Harvard Business Review,* and the tabloid *The National Enquirer*) and record changes they found. They discussed how these changes might affect or connect with their own areas of expertise or interest.

But, what about the duck?

References

Crosby, P. (1992). *Completeness.*
Land, G., & Jarman, B. (1992). *Breakpoint and beyond.* Scranton, PA: HarperCollins.

~~~

Joseph M. Miguez, Small Business Development Corporation at Governors State University, Illinois, Post Office Box 372, Olympia Fields, IL 60461. Tel: (708) 747-2670.

LEARNING TO CREATE SHARED VISION

W. Christopher Musselwhite and Cheryl P. De Ciantis

In a shrinking and increasingly diverse world it becomes more and more important for our visions of the future to serve as an integrator of our diverse perspectives, while drawing power from our commitment to personal values. A shared vision is a shared "picture" of what we want to see in the future. This desired picture creates a tension which automatically draws us towards it and towards our shared goals.

This article chronicles the authors' efforts over two years, in widely differing settings, to learn how to facilitate the creation of shared vision, using a process for progressive integration of drawings blending individual into group visions.

The Process

Individuals, either after a guided visualization or a discussion of beliefs and values, create a drawing that captures their personal vision for their organization. Once the drawings are shared with the entire group, individuals are paired. Each pair is instructed to together create a new picture that captures the essence of their individual pictures. It is the individual's responsibility to bring what is most important from her or his original picture. Once they begin to draw, they are asked to work together without speaking. Once these drawings are completed each pair and their integrated picture is matched with another pair, and the integration process goes through another interaction. This process can continue through several iterations.

The Cases

A. The Committee of 100: The idea for the Committee of 100 was developed by the Human Relations Commission of a mid-sized Southern city in the U.S.A. Representatives were brought together from every civic, professional, and neighborhood organization in the city to work collaboratively on the city's diversity challenges. The drawing integration exercise was used during a day-long workshop with about 80 participants. Each individual was asked to draw a picture of the way he or she wanted the city to look in 20 years as it related to human relations. The integration process proceeded through four iterations until groups of eight had a common picture. Each group of eight then presented its picture to the larger group. The integration process created new levels of communication and common themes were apparent throughout the groups. The objective was not to create one pictorial representation of the group's vision for the city but to provide a sense of common direction and shared values.

B. International Consumer Products Company: A somewhat different application involved a meeting to draft a strategic plan for the corporate audit function of a multinational consumer products company. The meeting was called by the group leader, who served as general auditor and VP of Finance. The leader felt that vision building within the group would enhance its effectiveness and promote group cohesiveness in formulating the strategic plan, which the group has been struggling with over two previous meetings without success.

The group made individual drawings of their desired future state of personal involvement with work, family, career development, personal interests or hobbies, and self-development. These were shared and posted. Each participant was then asked to make a statement of the single most important thing he or she wanted to see in the strategic plan and to have reflected in the organization five years ahead. The statements were flip-charted and common key words circled to illuminate shared themes.

Working in dyads and triads, participants were then asked to draw their shared image of the organization five years into the future. These drawings were shared with the whole group. One triad was dominated by the image proposed by the group leader, who already had a personal favorite vision metaphor for the audit function. This metaphor had not been shared with the group prior to this process. The small groups were combined into two groups who were instructed to blend their drawings into one. Again, one group was dominated by the image brought by the group leader.

C. Program Design Team: An eight-member design team from an international management/leadership development organization was struggling with the design of a new program they had been brought together to develop. Each team member had to also carry on his or her regular job assignments in addition to the design effort. Commitment to this project was fragmented. In this case the individuals' pictures of a desired future result was focused on the ending of the first successful run of the program. A guided visualization was used with the group to help each person clarify the end result he or she was looking for. Individual drawings were merged in pairs. Next, pairs combined to create one drawing between four people. The two resultant drawings were presented in the larger group. Metaphors developed in each picture provided a powerful vehicle for discussion as well as forward movement for the project. Participants felt that talking during the drawing integration phases diminished the effectiveness of the drawing integration process.

D. International Electronics Manufacturing Company: This case provides an example of a group visioning process initiated by a visionary leader. We arranged to work first with the leader, the recently promoted director of training for a global communications and electronics manufacturer. We found that he already had a personal metaphor which he felt a strong connection with. The group leader used a transcript we provided of notes taken during this day to organize a personal vision presentation to his group.

The group visioning process occurred on the third day of a quarterly meeting of training managers and their immediate reports and was the first such meeting since the leader's promotion. The day began with a silent walk through a nearby prairie park. The leader chose three or four spots on the trail, places which held special meaning for him, and talked about them to the group. Next, these key themes were reviewed and flip-charted along with themes which held meaning for the individual group members from their own experience of the prairie walk. It was stated clearly to the group that the leader's vision was meant to be a starting-point or jumping-off place for the group's shared vision.

Each participant made a drawing of his or her vision for the function/organization, then wrote a one-line statement of what was most important to him or her to see in the organization. The drawings were shared in the group. Next, dyads were formed to make drawings which blended the spirit of their individual drawings. Everyone was told to make sure that what was most important to him or her to see in the organization/function going into the future was represented. The dyads were told to work non-verbally. Next, the dyads were joined into groups of four to six to share their drawings and then make a larger integrated drawing, again non-verbally. Amid much hilarity, the groups produced drawings in a remarkably short fifteen or twenty minutes. Each group presented its drawings to the large group, and were asked to give them titles as part of the presentation. The verbal presentations were flip-charted.

A detailed list of themes was derived from the drawings and flip-charted for the group to use in future vision-building. Conflict issues emerged during this process and the group voted to spend the remainder of the day in conflict airing. Two agreements arose out of the unstructured discussion: to spend more time the following day airing the identified conflict points and to devote part of the agenda of each quarterly meeting to a "gut check." No specific outcome for the day's exercise had been projected or agreed upon in advance. Continuation of the shared visioning process is still in the planning stage. It seems clear that underlying, unresolved conflict within the group will surface as a product of the picture integration process.

E. Merged School Board: Voters decided to merge three school districts in a county in the southern U.S. A new school board was elected to hire a new superintendent and carry out the merger. County politics had been highly divisive for several years. The vote to merge was close and several political factions were represented on the board. Individuals drew pictures of their desired future county-wide school system. The drawing integration exercise followed a facilitated discussion that led to a consensual identification of the board's operating beliefs. Board members were placed in groups of three (there were 12 all total) and asked to integrate their three individual pictures into one. The individuals were given time to describe their pictures and discuss the composite picture, but were not allowed to talk when the drawing started. Each person was encouraged to participate in the drawing.

Each group of three (four all together) presented their integrated picture to the larger group. Themes were identified and recorded as the pictures were presented. A mission statement was crafted. The experience of this group is best captured by one of the board members who at the end of the day stated in astonishment, "The spirit entered the room and just moved us to a higher place." This integration process could be described as transformative.

Summary of Learnings

Time: This process requires adequate time. While the creation of the actual drawing requires less time than expected (10-15 minutes for an individual drawing, 20-30 minutes for an integrated drawing), the preparation, set-up, discussion, and reflection consume even more time.

Desired Outcomes: It is critical to be clear beforehand about the desired outcomes. Visions are being shared and integrated to what end?

Conflict: Creating shared vision is not a substitute for dealing with group conflict. Conflict is not the antithesis of shared vision. The picture integration process tends to surface conflict that is residing below the surface.

Led Versus Leaderless Groups: If the group has a formal leader, then the leader's vision needs to be clarified and articulated. The leader needs to provide the baseline picture or metaphor from which to work and then to solicit input from other group members.

Non-verbal is Important: It is more effective for participants to refrain from verbal exchanges during the integration of pictures. Participants should be given time before the actual drawing integration starts to describe their pictures and plan the integration.

Stating Beliefs and Values: When the group clarifies its operating beliefs and values up front, the picture integration process is enhanced.

Individual Responsibility for Personal Vision: Shared group vision is based on personal commitment. It is essential for each person to assume responsibility for integrating what is most important from their individual drawing to the integrated drawing.

Use of Metaphor: Metaphors often emerge from the pictures and can become powerful transformative tools. Use metaphors to engage the group in a discussion of how the metaphor might change or evolve and what they mean as a picture of the organization. If metaphors are different and not easily blended, search for a new overriding metaphor that the subgroups can buy into. Do not force integration. Even though they are different, the metaphors will represent common organizational issues. Forced integration creates tension whereas a discussion of commonality leads to mutual understanding.

~~~

W. Christopher Musselwhite, Blue Ridge Resource Group, 415 Woodlawn Avenue, Greensboro, NC 27401. Tel: (910) 272-9530. Education: Master's degree in management systems engineering; Ed.D. in adult education–training and development from North Carolina State University.

Cheryl P. De Ciantis, Blue Ridge Resource Group, 415 Woodlawn Avenue, Greensboro, NC 27401. Tel: (910) 272-9530. Education: B.A. in history of art from UCLA.

"WHAT I TELL YOU TWO TIMES IS TRUE"

John Cimino

Learning is an affair of the heart as much as the mind, an activity engaging our spirits every bit as much as our digits and little gray cells. We are creatures of emotion and imagery as much as we are creatures of logic who still draw inspiration, as reflexively as we draw breath, from the natural world. Animal skins and angel wings may no longer adorn our physical bodies, but in the blinking of an eye, in that perpetual midnight behind our eyelids, we are revealed instantly to be, as we have always been, creatures of magic, dream creatures of a piece with Nature which, as William Blake reminds us, *is* imagination itself:

> To the eye of a Man of Imagination,
> Nature is Imagination itself.
> As a man is, so he sees.
> As the eye is formed, such are its powers.

So, perhaps, it may be argued that despite our hard-won sophistication and astonishing technological achievement, our most promising and practical path to the type of learning potent enough to change our thinking, perceiving, and acting may be a path through Nature, i.e., Imagination, alive with the sights, sounds, and stories of that inner world through which we explore and begin to understand our outer one. This is the journey of art, the meaning of art in our lives. No learning is complete without it. Even science is incomplete without it because *we* are incomplete without art.

> Man is unique not because he does
> science and not because he does art,
> but because science and art equally
> are expressions of his mind.
> Jacob Bronowski

As an opera singer and composer, I am no doubt biased in my perspective concerning the value in the world of art and music. I do earn much of my living performing the great masters and cultivating new audiences; I am supposed to be enthusiastic about what I do, and I am. However, I am also an unabashed lover of the sciences; my first training was in biology and physics, and I worked very enthusiastically as a teacher and curriculum developer for several years. I enjoy the mix, the juxtaposition, the complementarity. Chopin and Einstein? Mozart and Newton? From earliest memory, to me they have always seemed to go together. Even today, whenever I hear the Chopin *Preludes,* I still recall pages of Einstein's *The Evolution of Physics.* A quirk of my childhood? Perhaps. It nonetheless remains happily meaningful to me and may, in fact, betray my personal bias fairly accurately.

The organization I lead, Associated Solo Artists, Inc. (ASA), is based on this childhood notion of interdisciplinary connectedness. Since 1972, countless ASA educational workshops have explored these connections across the arts and sciences at hundreds of universities and schools nationwide. But ASA is also founded squarely on a shared belief in the power of music and art to move us, enlighten us, and orchestrate change within us. We are mindful of this unique power of our art form and make our music endeavoring to transmit more than wondrous sound. We endeavor to transmit "life," to communicate hope with our music and, thereby, to empower the spirits of our listeners.

Through special performance formats, including informances, interactive workshops, and "Concerts of Ideas," we have the privilege of exploring with our audiences a wide range of common concerns: how people learn, how we create meaning, and discover our values.

Consider for a moment our impulse to make satisfying or meaningful connections. As children we are all geniuses at creating coherent little worlds; we invent marvelously outrageous laws of physics, and people our under-the-kitchen-table universes with beings linked resolutely to each other and supremely well-attuned to the abilities granted them by their creator. We are quantum physicists and visionary poets rolled into one, co-authoring ourselves as we author our little worlds, continuously restructuring our most intimate reality.

Many of us would like to tap into this fertile frame of mind as adults, not to escape our problems but to find solutions to them. How would we do it? How would we train for it, model it? Courses abound with exercises and formulas for increasing introspection and creativity and these programs are doubtless of considerable value. I would add with emphasis, however, that *the arts offer a living, breathing counterpart to these learnings.* Rooted in emotion, imagery and inspiration, the arts are a vital second avenue of experience with which to grasp the subtlety of the creative mind. Further, I assert that the application of arts in *any* interdisciplinary context is an intrinsic enhancement of the learning process. As a counterpart experience or second-language description of a chosen subject, the arts can provide the full benefits of what the anthropologist Gregory Bateson called "double description":

> Always the multiple approach. You make two statements, and what is true of both of them is the formal truth. This is what is called explanation.

The level of meaning which Bateson calls "explanation" is derived from two differing views such as those from the arts and sciences. Taken together, the two views constitute an experience akin to "binocular vision" creating a "bonus of insight" analogous to the visual experience of "depth." The perception of "depth" is completely unpredicted by the two views taken separately. This would seem to support the assertion that arts can intrinsically enhance the learning process as a counterpart experience in *any* interdisciplinary context.

In his book, *Mind and Nature: A Necessary Unity* (1988), Bateson writes of the importance of recognizing what he calls "the pattern which connects" us to the primrose, the primrose to the crab, and the crab back to us. He describes this recognition of connection as the "essence of our sense of beauty and relationship." This recognition, like learning, is an affair of the heart as much as the mind and brings us to a level of connection which begets not only creativity but compassion. Recognition becomes self-transformation, and art—playful, potent, truthful art which prepared this recognition—becomes life.

Does it sound a bit like magic?

What I tell you two times is true.*

Summary

No learning is complete without art because *we* are incomplete without art: (a) We are creatures of emotion, imagery, and magic as much as we are creatures of logic; (b) music and art possess an uncanny power to move us, enlighten us, orchestrate change within us, i.e., to transmit life; (c) music and art add degrees of freedom to the mind and prime our native capacity to make meaningful connections.

1. The arts are a vital "second avenue of experience" with which to grasp and train the creative mind. The processes of art complement scientific approaches.

2. The arts intrinsically enhance the learning process as a counterpart experience in *any* interdisciplinary context via the full benefits of the Bateson concept of "double description."

3. Inasmuch as the arts prepare recognition of "the pattern which connects" (life forms, cultures, and systems of ideas), the experience of arts vitally begets impulses of both creativity and compassion. As recognition becomes self-transformation, art becomes life.

---

*A "double description" variant of Lewis Carroll's "What I tell you three times is true," from *The Hunting of the Snark,* Fit 1. The Landing.

Reference

Bateson, G. (1988). *Mind and nature: A necessary unity.* New York: Bantam.

~~~

John Cimino, Associated Solo Artists, Inc., 1793 Maple Avenue, Peekskill, NY 10566. Tel: (914) 736-7850. Education: Rensselaer Polytechnic Institute, biology and physics, and the Manhattan and Juilliard Schools of Music, voice.

THE TOUCHSTONE: DISCOVERING THE TRANSFORMATIVE STORY WITHIN

Cheryl P. De Ciantis

An engineer in a pharmaceuticals company arranged several objects somewhat at random on a plywood base. A spent rifle cartridge represented "my father, who taught me how to hunt." Four segments of pine twigs with the bark on them, two finger-sized twigs nestled side-by-side and two smaller twigs similarly nestled on top of them, represented his family: "This is me, my wife and children. We all sleep together." A few months later, he told me he had realized the Touchstone story he had told me was a "nice picture, but not quite true." However, in the months after he made his Touchstone, a difficult relationship with his father improved, and his family life now looks in reality more like that nice picture.

The Touchstone is an artmaking exercise which focuses on self-awareness. It was developed for the LeaderLab® program at the Center for Creative Leadership, a program which incorporates non-traditional, experiential exercises as part of its holistic approach. In the LeaderLab® context, the Touchstone becomes a tangible, symbolic representation of an individual's leadership goals—the "what I am striving for in my leadership." It also brings into focus something that artists and leaders have in common: valuing and trusting their own sense of purpose *and* being willing to commit to action in expressing it.

Artmaking is a process of personal discovery, only partly facilitated by technical ability. The ability to create metaphors with power, resonance, and beauty resides in everybody. The "stories" people have told about their Touchstones suggest that most people have access to meaningful personal imagery and metaphor to a much larger degree than they are normally aware.

The Touchstone Exercise

Participants are told they will make a sculpture, a Touchstone. They are asked to think about everything they want to remember when they are back in the midst of workplace chaos. They are told they will be asked to take the Touchstone home and put it in a place where they will "revisit" it from time to time. It can be on an office desk or in a closet, it's up to them. They are asked to use the Touchstone to: "reflect on your experiences and goals, on your sense of purpose, on your center—on *you*."

A profusion of natural materials (twigs, polished stones, shells) is available for participants to choose from in assembling the sculpture. They are invited to choose whatever they want, and as much as they want. They are asked to pay attention to the color, the shape, the size, the texture of each object they select. They are asked, when putting their Touchstone together, to think about the meaning of each thing, and the relationship of the things to the whole.

One last instruction is given: When they have finished the Touchstone, take a couple of minutes "to let it tell you its story," then take a few minutes to *write it down* in their Learning Journal. Transforming the "story" into words and recording it is an important part of the exercise.

Touchstone Symbolism

People who have made a Touchstone, and say they have not made any kind of artwork before, have told stories about their Touchstone which have detailed and highly developed symbolic content. Since the exercise itself takes only a short period of time, these stories seem all the more remarkable for their richness. Over the course of conducting the Touchstone exercise in the LeaderLab® context (in ten programs, involving 180 participants) and elsewhere, a number of themes have emerged which appear again and again in the stories participants tell about their Touchstone. Very often they depict aspirations for personal change and growth: "This is me now; this is where I want to be."

One participant, a young head of a business unit within a global finance institution, chose a piece of plywood which was an irregular rectangle as a base for his Touchstone. This rectangle was right-angled at one end, whereas the corners had been cut off the other end. At the right-angled end of the base, he placed two clam shells side by side. One was a medium-sized half of a shell, placed inner side up, or "open." This represented "my analytic side." The other was a small, whole clam shell, partly open. As a found object, this small clam shell was only slightly open. He used a small stick to pry it a little further open for his purposes. "This is my emotional side." He then selected a dried leaf, which he placed to almost completely cover the smaller shell: "My emotional side is covered up."

He then took some time to painstakingly select two more clam shells, of nearly equal size. These he placed side by side at the irregular end of the base, inner side up. "This is my analytic side and my emotional side, more in balance. This is where I'm coming from, all right angles and analytic, and this is where I want to go—away from all the right angles. But, there's something missing: how do I get there?"

He finally selected two more objects: a twisted piece of dried woodvine, which he broke to a selected length, and a smooth, straight finger-sized twig with the bark removed. He placed the smooth twig so that it touched the side-by-side shells at the right-angled end of the base and was pointing at the shells at the opposite end. Its shortness did not permit it to touch the shells at the other end. The twisted vine he placed next to the twig on the base and at a slight angle so that one end touched the smooth twig a short distance from the shells at the right-angled end of the base, and the other he reached to the shells at the other end. "There are two paths; one is pretty straight and quick, and doesn't get all the way there. The other is winding and rough and it will take awhile, but it will get there." When he had selected and placed the path elements, I asked "Is that all?" He said, "It's all I can deal with emotionally right now." He later wrote to say he added to his Touchstone, placing a series of pebbles along the paths, symbolizing the obstacles he will face in his development.

Some people have placed objects in their Touchstones without knowing "what it means yet." For people used to crunching numbers and providing an answer to every question, the comfort with "not knowing" is a quiet revelation in itself, a glimpse at something unquantifiable and ineffable in themselves and the world around them. Several people who have made Touchstones have told me they never looked at art before, and now that they do, it has meaning for them. If they can look at art differently, what else can they look at differently? Relationships? Values? Global responsibilities? What will they be able to assimilate, understand and be taught by, now that they look at the world with new eyes?

~~~

Cheryl P. De Ciantis, Blue Ridge Resource Group, 415 Woodlawn Avenue, Greensboro, NC 27401. Tel: (910) 272-9530. Education: B.A. in history of art from UCLA.

THE ART AND DISCIPLINE OF DEBRIEFING

Hedria P. Lunken

"Give a man a fish and he will eat for a day—
teach him to fish and he will eat always."

"If I hear, I forget; if I see, I remember; if I do, I understand."

We are all familiar with these quotes and the philosophy of learning inherent in them. With what regularity do we incorporate their meaning into our training and experiences? Do we test to see if we have been effective? Do we know if the participants, staff, or customers have assimilated the message on a professional or personal level so they understand their behavior well enough that change will take place? Do we question them about their understanding of what has taken place, so that we may recognize the depth of their knowledge and comprehension?

When our focus or mode of operation for future activities changes, we have truly been affected by an event. It has had an impact on us! Much thought has been given to the ways of effecting change by establishing patterns or processes to help others become aware of new insights. A tool, known as debriefing, can be used to stimulate staff and customers to gain insights that may have a profound effect or influence on future behavior or to "force an aha!"

In a workshop at the International Creativity and Innovation Networking Conference participants were asked to think of the most significant learning experience they had had. Then they were asked to write: (1) A brief description of what happened; (2) why it was important to them; (3) and how this incident had affected their future. As they shared their comments it became apparent that significant experiences are those that change or affect future behavior.

In what ways might we systematically help our staff and customers change or affect their future behavior? How can we help them understand and gain personal insight from a meeting, workshop, or activity? This can be facilitated by debriefing, the process of using skillful questioning techniques. Probing questions presented after the event, that help elicit feedback, are the keys to making a meeting, activity, or seminar experience meaningful and lasting. By sequencing the questions and processing them the facilitator is able to help participants dig deeper into the intuitive, make their own discoveries, and maximize the learning experience. "It is not the 'real' challenges presented by the situation that counts, but those that the person is aware of" (Csikszentmihalyi, 1990).

The effectiveness of debriefing is heightened by the establishment of a creative climate (Ekvall, 1971)—a climate in which the participants feel safe, are able to trust each other, know that what they say will be accepted, and where they can share their feelings and take risks. This supportive framework provides the atmosphere where participants become change agents. This creative climate allows for openness, dynamism/liveliness, playfulness/humor, debates, risk-taking, idea time, and the absence of conflicts.

Debriefing questions are presented to staff or participants in a framework that progresses from: (1) A description of the event—"WHAT HAPPENED?" to (2) What are their reactions and feelings during the event—"SO WHAT?" to (3) Seeing connections to future actions in their personal and professional lives and gleaning insight into how they may continue to effectively use the proposed changes in behavior to effect future results—"NOW WHAT?" The facilitator chooses questions from those suggested below to gather data on the activity. The questions are chosen in sequence to provide a flow of activity from reporting of the event, to uncovering feelings, to an awareness of changes in future behavior. The transferring of learning is determined by the data the participants generate, which is enhanced by the facilitator having a large and flexible repertoire of questions to stimulate, maintain, and complete the cycle.

The first series of progressive questions are needed to help the participants see the actual sequence of events, as they begin to generate ideas, the "WHAT HAPPENED?" Some examples of these questions are: What went on/happened? Could you be more specific? Can you say that in another way? What else? Who else? Who reacted differently, same?

The next section is the "SO WHAT?" These are key questions directed towards eliciting feelings, sorting the data, abstracting specific knowledge, and moving towards generalizations of behavior and feeling. Some examples of these questions are: How did you feel about that? How many felt the same? Different? What does that mean to you? How was that significant? How do those fit together? How might it have been different? Do you see anything happening there? What does that suggest to you about yourself? What do you understand better about yourself? What might we conclude from that? What did you learn/relearn?

The final group of questions are the "NOW WHAT?" These questions elicit answers that transfer to learnings in real-world situations, towards applying insights and new learnings to personal and professional lives. Some examples of these questions are: How could you apply/transfer that? How could you repeat that again? How could you make it better? What modifications can you make work for you? How was this for you? What changes would you make? What would you continue? If you had to do it over again, what would you do?

The facilitator or consultant who uses questioning techniques in a climate that is safe and trusting will find in many instances that they have helped their staff or customers discover their own "aha's." These discoveries are profound

Discovering Creativity   PARTICIPANT THEMES and result in influencing the personal and professional behavior of the participants.

Summary

How do we help people gain insights and meaning from activities, to go beyond an experience being merely exciting and involving? By using debriefing, a technique that involves asking significant and probing questions in a specific sequence, a facilitator is able to help participants make discoveries that facilitate changes and the transfer of learning into future behavior.

References

Csikszentmihalyi, M. (1990). *Flow, the psychology of optimal experience*. New York: HarperCollins.
Ekvall, G. (1971). *Creativity at the place of work*. Stockholm: Swedish Council for Personal Administration.
Project Adventure, Inc. (1991). *Adventure based counseling workshop manual*. Dubuque, IA: Kendal/Hunt Publishing Company.

Additional Resources

Gaw, B. A. (1979). *The 1979 handbook for group facilitators*. University Associates.
Kolb, D. A., & Fry, R. (1975). Toward an applied theory of experiential learning. In C. Cooper (Ed.), *Theories of group processes*. New York: John Wiley & Sons.

~~~

Hedria P. Lunken, 487 Morgan Drive, Lewiston, NY 14092. Tel: (716) 754-8406. Education: Bachelor's degree in education from the University of Buffalo; Master of Science degree in creativity and innovation from the State University College at Buffalo.

LEADERSHIP DEVELOPMENT THEORY AND A MODEL FOR INTERVENTION IN THE DEVELOPMENT OF LEADERS

Charles J. Palus and Wilfred H. Drath

Introduction

Our contribution to the 1992 International Creativity & Innovation Networking Conference consists of our definitions of the terms "leadership," "leadership development," and "leadership development program." In the following summary, we present these definitions and some of their bases and implications. We conclude with a 3-part model for considering the design, execution, and evaluation of developmental programs for individual leaders. Of course, programs for individuals are just one small aspect of leadership development (according to our definitions); a discussion of the development of individual leaders is merely a place to begin.

One of the problems in the field of leadership development is the lack of fundamental, theoretical definitions. Instead, there is a plethora of prescriptions for achieving leadership and leadership development, typically in a form something like "the 10 practices of highly effective leaders." Many of these prescriptions are based in wisdom and even research, and provide real help to practitioners. However, they tend to be context and culture bound and quite vague as to the underlying processes at work. We strongly feel that by addressing fundamental processes we can in the long run improve our practice, allowing us to better apprehend not only the trees, but the forest, and the ecology of this forest of leadership development.

What is Leadership?

In brief: Leadership is meaning making in collective experience (see Drath & Palus, 1994, for detailed treatment of this idea). Another way to say this is: Leadership is the processes by which a set of cognitive and affective responses and anticipations ("meaning")—including interpretations, metaphors, beliefs, values, relationships, norms, habits, solutions to problems, understandings, purposes, mental models, paradigms, visions, strategies, and goals—is evolved, created, nurtured, and maintained ("made") in a group of people who see, or come to see, themselves as part of a unified ("collective") endeavor ("experience").

Leadership, we maintain, is *the* basic social process through which people join together, make sense of their predicaments, and anticipate the future. In so doing, leadership forms, maintains, and evolves the arts, science, religion, politics, and popular fashion and trends, and the ways these all blend together to form what we recognize as culture. Leadership is the set of processes which move culture, and the components of culture, forward (see Schein, 1985).

Leadership makes, remakes, and maintains the fabric of meaning by which a group recognizes its collective identity and its collective work. This fabric—often a patchwork—of meaning is the social reality of the collective, the means by which the collective understands its purpose. Leadership is all about the creation and maintenance of ideas, feelings, and actions about what is real, right, important, and possible within a community.

Meaning is defined as the frameworks by which people make cognitive and affective sense of things. Meaning is fundamental to human beings, both as personal meaning (Fingarette, 1963; Kegan, 1982; Kelly, 1955) and as collective meaning (Berger & Luckman, 1966; Bruner, 1990). Meaning may be of a transcendent order, such as in one's (perhaps religious) sense of "the meaning of life." Meaning also presents in more mundane forms, such as "how these standard operating procedures organize my work," or "how the organizational chart helps me fit in," or "Hey, what just happened?"

Meaning is constructed and reconstructed, and thereafter maintained, changed, nurtured, and evolved. All this is what we mean by "making" meaning. Meaning is subject to dissolution and decay, as well as cacophony. Making meaning is the essential process of leadership. The processes of making meaning include (for example): dialogue; the learning cycle of planning/acting/reflecting; designing effective, coherent, and useful organizational structures; interpretation; problem solving; visioning; and story-telling.

Leadership requires collective experience, some sense among individuals that they are active in a unified endeavor. The first act of leadership may be to cohere collective experience. Often, leadership fails because the collective experience is fragmented, weakly unified, or ill-defined. Or leadership fails because the meaning making is personal rather than collective in nature. For example, "top management" may constitute a small collective experience aloof and apart from any other.

This definition encompasses both of what we may call the entity and process conceptions of leadership prevalent in the literature. That is, some have focused on entities: for example, leaders who have followers and visions within defined groups. Others see leadership as a mutual process: for example, leaderless activity in which leadership is shared by forging coherent interpretations within common experience.

An advantage of this definition is that it opens the discussion of leadership to various and diverse contexts and cultures. We may thus inquire as to the forms of leadership—as constituted by forms of meaning, meaning making, collectivity, and experience—one refers to when speaking of leadership in the

Discovering Creativity   *PARTICIPANT THEMES*

sciences, leadership in street gangs, leadership in families, or leadership with respect to pressing social issues.

What is Leadership Development?

The word development has come to be used as a blanket covering almost every form of growth or progress; for example, skill training, competency building, job rotation, accumulated experience, and so on. The concept of development has thus unfortunately been diluted to the point of platitude.

A more fruitful and precise view of development is the constructivist approach, based in a long and robust tradition of psychological theory and research, as exemplified in the work of Robert Kegan, George Kelly, and Jean Piaget. This approach views skills and knowledge not as modular units, but rather in terms of how they are organized into integrative structures. Any single new learning tends to become assimilated into these larger structures, although the whole sometimes has to stretch or change to accommodate a new element. When accommodation results in a new structure which is more encompassing and adaptive, we have the essential motion of development. These structures are of course meaning structures, using our prior definition of "meaning," and using the word "structure" to emphasize the way meanings typically are part of larger wholes (e.g., Kelly, 1955; Mezirow, 1991).

Examples of *personal* meaning structures include (running in rough order toward increasingly more superordinate structures): metaphors and analogies, short-term priorities, stereotypes and prejudices, internalized parental expectations, career aspirations, value systems, "the story of my life," the full sense of "who I am" (or identity), comprehensive beliefs about how the world works (or epistemology), and religious faith.

Thus, we define development as the evolution of the capacity to make more encompassing and adaptive meaning.

Leadership development is the evolution of the capacity to make more encompassing and adaptive meaning *in collective experience.*

One important way in which development happens is through a hierarchically-ordered succession of qualitatively distinct epistemological meaning structures called stages, such that each stage depends upon—but incorporates and transcends—the prior stage (Kegan, 1982; Loevinger, 1976; Perry, 1970; Piaget, 1954). A completed transition from one stage to another appears as a transformation in a person's mode of being (Boydell, 1990). One such stage model we use in our work is that of Robert Kegan (1982), in which movement between stages is a matter of coming to "hold" (objectifying) what one was once "held by" (subject to). Kegan's model is illustrated in Figure 1.

Torbert (1987) has done important conceptual and empirical work in relating the constructivist framework to organizational leadership. Most significantly, Torbert has applied the framework not only to individual development but to organizational development. We agree that leadership is a process which develops within and among stages, and that such stages may be manifest in individual leaders, as well as in other, more distributed, processes of leadership.

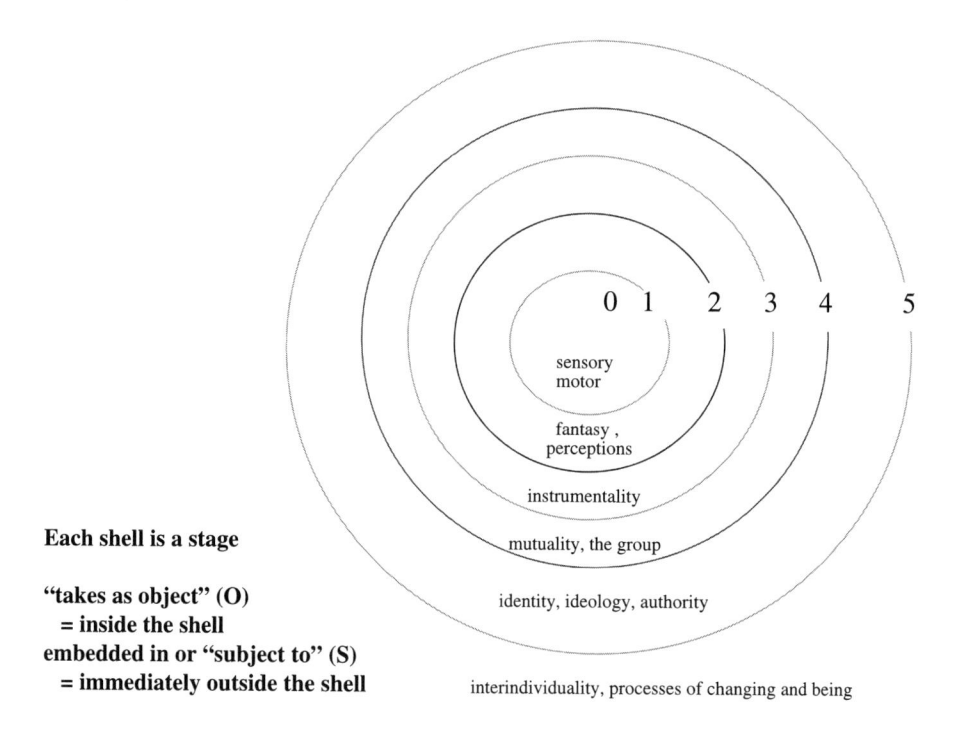

Each shell is a stage

**"takes as object" (O)
= inside the shell
embedded in or "subject to" (S)
= immediately outside the shell**

Stages (from innermost to outermost):
- 0, 1: sensory motor
- 2: fantasy, perceptions
- 3: instrumentality
- mutuality, the group
- 4: identity, ideology, authority
- 5: interindividuality, processes of changing and being

**Figure 1:
The Kegan Stage Model As An Onion**

Merron, Fisher, and Torbert (1987) found that individuals at more advanced stages of development are more able to successfully engage more technically and socially complex tasks. Table 1 shows the distribution of levels of management among the various stages reported by Torbert (1991). Table 2 presents a description of leader potential strengths and weaknesses as a function of stage (Drath, 1990).

Table 1:
Distribution of Managers By Developmental Stage Reported by Torbert (1991)

Stage (per Kegan)	1st Line Supervisors n = 37	Jr. & Mid. Managers n = 177	Senior Managers n = 66	Executives n = 104
Imperial (stage 2)	0%	5%	0%	0%
Interpersonal (3)	24	9	6	3
(transition)	68	43.5	47	43.5
Institutional (4)	8	40	33	39.5
(transition)	0	2.5	14	14
Interindividual (5)	0	0	0	0

Note. Stage labels were originally reported by Torbert according to his set of labels derived from Loevinger's (1976) work. They have been translated to Kegan's labels for clarity in this report.

What is a Leadership Development Program?

A leadership development program is therefore some intervention designed to support the evolution of the capacity to make more encompassing and adaptive meaning in collective experience.

It is important to note from what we have said so far that leadership is usually much more than an individual function. A full picture of leadership development will attend to the evolution of meaning making throughout the collective, as well as to the development of the processes that cohere the collective. For the rest of this article, however, we would like to narrow our focus to individual development as assisted by short interventions (e.g., one-week programs). The reason for this narrowing should be obvious: The full range of leadership development as defined here is simply too large a topic to be fairly treated at this time. But it would be wrong to conclude that all we mean by leadership development is the development of individuals.

There is currently no adequate description of the means of assisting the advancement of stages with respect to leadership. Even less has been done to describe how short-program interventions may accomplish this. One-week programs are the bread and butter of the Center for Creative Leadership, and we wish to be explicit in how these apparently successful programs assist (or not) in the advancement of developmental stages in individuals.

To that end we propose a three-part model for designing, executing, and evaluating leadership development programs for individuals.

The model has three parts: **readiness, developmental processes,** and **outcomes** (see Figure 2).

Table 2:
Leader Potential Competencies:
Strengths and Weaknesses as a Function of Stage Structure

Stage (per Kegan)	Strength	Weakness
Interpersonal	———— take needs and wishes as object ————	
	self-sacrifice for group	conformity
	———— ultimacy of relationships ————	
	mutual relationships	lack of identity
	loyalty to in-group	group interests primary
Institutional	———— take interpersonal as object ————	
	instrumental relationships	difficulty with intimacy
	head over heart	difficulty with emotion
	———— ultimacy of identity ————	
	drive and ambition	can't relax
	accountability	difficulty with criticism
	responsibility	difficulty seeing others' views
Post-Institutional (transitional)	———— take identity as object ————	
	systems thinking	"mid-life crisis"
	other's-perspective taking	
	true collaboration possible	
Interindividual	———— take process of identification as object ————	
	dialectical thinking	misfit in most orgs
	thriving on whitewater	a little crazy
	self-transcendence	
	spirituality	

Discovering Creativity   *PARTICIPANT THEMES*

| READINESS | DEVELOPMENTAL PROCESSES | OUTCOMES |

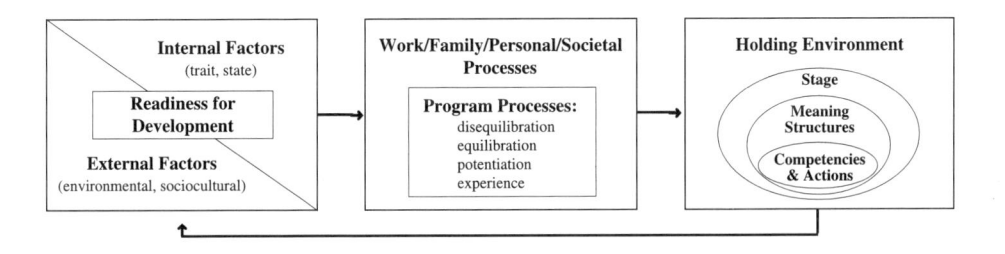

```
┌─────────────────────────┐      ┌──────────────────────────┐      ┌──────────────────────────┐
│    Internal Factors     │      │ Work/Family/Personal/    │      │   Holding Environment    │
│      (trait, state)     │      │   Societal Processes     │      │      ╱ Stage ╲           │
│  ┌──────────────────┐   │  →   │  ┌────────────────────┐  │  →   │   ╱  Meaning  ╲          │
│  │  Readiness for   │   │      │  │ Program Processes: │  │      │  │   Structures │         │
│  │   Development    │   │      │  │   disequilibration │  │      │  │ ╱Competencies╲│        │
│  └──────────────────┘   │      │  │   equilibration    │  │      │  │ ╲ & Actions ╱ │        │
│    External Factors     │      │  │   potentiation     │  │      │   ╲           ╱         │
│(environmental, sociocultural)│  │  │   experience       │  │      │    ╲_____╱          │
└─────────────────────────┘      │  └────────────────────┘  │      └──────────────────────────┘
           ↑                     └──────────────────────────┘                   │
           └─────────────────────────────────────────────────────────────────────┘
```

Figure 2:
Leadership Development Program Model

Readiness

Any developmental program designer must assume that potential clients will be differentially ready, or prepared, for developmental work. Participants will be having different experiences within the program depending on their readiness. The basic diagnostic question for readiness is, "What kind of developmental work is each person best prepared to do?"; or more simply, "Where are they and what do they need?"

We propose four types of readiness factors: trait, state, environmental, and sociocultural. Trait and state refer to a person's internal condition. Environmental and sociocultural refer to a person's external milieu. Table 3 lists selected factors which we propose in each type. We caution that the diagnosis of readiness involves a consideration of the pattern which is emergent from the totality of factors—that is, a consideration of "the whole person"—rather than of abstract factors taken only one at a time. (See Palus and Drath, in preparation, for a discussion of individual readiness factors.)

Intervention

The second part of the model deals with the deliberate attempt to foster development through some kind of programmatic intervention.

According to the model, such interventions contain four processes: experience, disequilibration, equilibration, and potentiation.

(a) Experience. "Experience" as used here refers to circumstances that fully engage the person's meaning structure, forcing the person either to (in Piaget's terms) assimilate the experience or to accommodate his or her meaning structures. Experience in this sense is something that the person cannot take in passively; rather it must be encountered, dealt with, and responded to. The

Table 3:
A Selected List of Proposed Developmental Readiness Factors

Internal

Trait	*State*
openness to experience	developmental stage
early commandments	stability
chronic psychopathology	age
	satisfaction
	life-story
	acute psychopathology

External

Environmental	*Sociocultural*
holding environments:	developmental norms
work, family, community	social milieu
job challenges	construction of diversity:
stressful events	age, gender, race, class, ethnicity
fortuitous events	

experience may be constructed completely within the bounds of the program, or it may consist of addressing material from work, family, or personal life.

(b) Disequilibration. An important role of experience in a developmental intervention is to provide some level of disequilibrium. This occurs when the person's existing meaning structures are in some way challenged and experienced as less (even greatly less) than adequate. There is a temporary sense of loss of meaning. The experience will not "digest" in the person's existing frameworks of meaning, and yet cannot be completely rejected as nonsense.

(c) Equilibration. Providing only disequilibration is unethical, unkind, and possibly dangerous. A person must be given support in recovering equilibrium in the face of whatever disequilibrium is introduced by the program—as well as in the face of the disequilibration of modern life (Kegan, 1982).

(d) Potentiation. Acquiring a new, enduring structure of meaning that allows assimilation of the experience is *not*, we believe, the most likely outcome of a developmental intervention. This degree of development typically takes place over a period of years rather than days.

The more likely way of resolving loss of meaning is that the person, upon leaving the program, will re-equilibrate within the old meaning structure. If the intervention has succeeded, the person will retain some reverberation of the disequilibrating experience. This "echo of experience" will take its place (with other such remembered experiences) at the leading edge of the movement toward a new meaning structure. In this way the program *potentiates* development toward a new meaning structure into which the program has offered a glimpse.

Outcome

In this model, the outcome of a developmental intervention cannot be satisfactorily assessed solely in terms of acquired competencies. Competencies are supported by and flow from meaning structures—"whole" new ways of knowing and acting. At the level of developmental stage, this means outcomes should be assessed by attending to epistemologies as well as competencies and to the relationships among them. Various methodologies have been described for assessing epistemology (e.g., Kegan, 1982; Loevinger, 1976).

A loss of meaning is possible as a person faces the "neutral zone" (Bridges, 1988) between meaning structures. A temporary performance decrement may actually result from a developmental experience (McCall, Lombardo, & Morrison, 1988). The failure of the developmental program to immediately transfer back to a real-world setting is an expected and anticipated part of the process to which various elements of program design and assessment are addressed.

Because development is a naturally occurring process that happens over a long period of time with multiple causes, it is hard to attribute development specifically to the intervention. In addition, any emergent competencies will be complexly related to increased effectiveness. Thus, tying a developmental intervention to increased effectiveness is doubly difficult and a ripe subject for theory building and empirical research.

References

Berger, P., & Luckman, T. (1966). *The social construction of reality.* New York: Doubleday.
Boydell, T. (1990). *Modes of being and learning* (Transform Working Paper No. 8).
Bridges, W. (1988). *Surviving corporate transition.* New York: Doubleday.
Bruner, J. S. (1990). *Acts of meaning.* Cambridge, MA: Harvard University Press.
Drath, W. H. (1990). Managerial strengths and weaknesses as functions of the development of personal meaning. *Journal of Applied Behavioral Science, 26*(4), 483-500.
Drath, W. H., & Palus, C. J. (1994). Leadership as meaning making in collective experience. Manuscript in preparation.
Fingarette, H. (1963). *The self in transformation.* New York: Basic Books.
Kegan, R. (1982). *The evolving self.* Cambridge, MA: Harvard University Press.
Kelly, G. A. (1955). *The psychology of personal constructs.* New York: Norton.

Loevinger, J. (1976). *Ego development.* San Francisco: Jossey-Bass.
McCall, M. W., Lombardo, M. M., & Morrison, A. M. (1988). *Lessons of experience.* Lexington, MA: Lexington Books.
Merron, K., Fisher, D., & Torbert, W. F. (1987). Meaning making and management action. *Group and Organization Studies, 12*(3), 274-286.
Mezirow, J. (1991). *Transformative dimensions of adult learning.* San Francisco: Jossey-Bass.
Palus, C., & Drath, W. H. (in preparation). Leadership and management development interventions: A process model.
Perry, W. G. (1970). *Forms of intellectual and ethical development in the college years: A scheme.* New York: Holt, Rinehart and Winston, Inc.
Piaget, J. (1954). *The construction of reality in the child.* New York: Basic Books.
Schein, E. (1985). *Organizational culture and leadership.* San Francisco: Jossey-Bass.
Torbert, W. R. (1987). *Managing the corporate dream: Restructuring for long-term success.* Homewood, IL: Dow Jones-Irwin.
Torbert, W. (1991). *The power of balance.* Newbury Park, CA: Sage Publications.

~~~

Charles J. Palus, Center for Creative Leadership, One Leadership Place, Post Office Box 26300, Greensboro, NC 27438-6300. Tel: (910) 288-7210. Education: Undergraduate degree in chemical engineering; Ph.D. in adult developmental psychology from Boston College.

Wilfred ("Bill") H. Drath, III, Center for Creative Leadership, One Leadership Place, Post Office Box 26300, Greensboro, NC 27438-6300. Tel: (910) 288-7210. Education: Completed graduate work in English at the University of North Carolina at Chapel Hill.

RISK-TAKING AND INNOVATION PERFORMANCE

Charles W. Prather

Why is innovation so difficult for organizations today? What is it that prevents us from turning new ideas into profitable reality? Looking into this area, I have concluded that the single biggest deterrent, and at the same time the single biggest enabler, is the organizational culture around risk-taking.

What do we mean by "risk-taking?" Certainly we DO NOT mean taking a blind chance or throwing caution to the wind and rolling the dice. What we do mean is deciding to implement a well-reasoned idea where the benefits would far outweigh the loss, should that occur. What we do mean is trying things out early, making mistakes at low cost, refining the idea, product, or process, and re-trying.

Creativity is the principle process leading to ideas, while risk-taking is the process responsible for taking ideas to a result. Most people will recognize that the latter is most often called "innovation." I equate "innovation" with risk-taking. Certainly the process of innovation requires much more than just risk-takers, but at the heart of the matter lies risk-taking. For example, every successful innovation has a clearly identified sponsor. What makes a good sponsor?—risk-taking. It is a personal risk to provide resources, encouragement, and legitimization for a team working on an idea that may never come to commercial fruition. Every successful innovation has a number of implementers who make things happen in their day-to-day work. What makes a good implementer?—risk-taking. It is a personal risk to spend working time and company resources on uncertain ideas. Because the work environment can determine whether or not risks are taken, it is of critical importance to the process of creativity and innovation.

Does Risk-taking Pay Off in Business?

In workshops on risk-taking, participants are asked to complete a survey designed to measure their individual orientation to risk-taking. From this information, I have been able to relate individual job performance to risk-taking scores on the risk assessment. The data confirms the belief that performance at work parallels risk-taking orientation; those more inclined to take higher levels of risk also received higher performance ratings. Consequently, organizations might have better performance rations as a whole if they support risk-taking.

How Organizations Handle "Mistakes"

How can you know how well your organizational climate promotes innovation? You can answer this question by asking, "How OK is it to fail in my organization?" What happens to those closely associated with ideas or projects that never quite make it? For purposes of discussion, I'm calling these events "mistakes," when what we mean is well-reasoned attempts at trying something new that didn't meet expectations. When an attempt results in a "mistake," one of three avenues of response is open.

One avenue of response is to refuse to publicly acknowledge that a "mistake" has been made. If it is a "low-level" mistake, known only to the mistake-maker, it can be concealed, and in this case, of course, there can be no organizational learning. In the safety arena this is sometimes referred to cynically as the "bloody pocket syndrome" in which the incident is covered up. If, however, the mistake occurs at higher and more visible levels, the mistake-maker can simply refuse to mention it publicly or can choose to minimize it if public silence isn't possible. Because the degree of possible organizational learning is directly related to the degree of public acknowledgment of the "mistake," organizational learning is either absent or minimized in these cases.

A second avenue of response is to acknowledge the "mistake," but rather than have the organization focus on the learning, management may choose to focus on fixing the blame. Even when learning results, blame-fixing sends powerful messages throughout the organization about how the next "mistake" will be dealt with. You can be sure that trust within the organization will be diminished as a result of the blame, making the learning process all that less likely since it will be less likely that all succeeding "mistakes" will be acknowledged in the first place. In purposeful organizations, does blame improve individual performance? Does it *really* help the business to fix blame? I am fond of saying the responsibility of management is to "manage the learning, and not the blame."

The avenue most likely to encourage learning is to acknowledge the "mistake," seek to learn from it, and share the learning broadly throughout the organization. Who is in the driver's seat? The person at the lowest organizational level who has knowledge of the situation should consider himself or herself accountable. The responsibility to support this productive response and to reinforce learning falls to those higher in organizational authority. In Du Pont, as in many other companies, there already is an excellent model to follow, and it is the model for handling safety incidents. Typically when a safety incident is uncovered, it is acknowledged, and great effort is expended to learn what went wrong and how to prevent the same incident from occurring again. The parties involved in the incident are always included in this process. The learning is communicated broadly throughout the organization, reinforcing the corporate value for safety. *The degree of organizational learning is directly related to the degree of acknowledgment and discussion of the incident and about the learning.*

The Role of Leadership

Which of the three preceding avenues of response would you like to see more of in your company? Most people would select the third avenue, in which mistakes are acknowledged and learned from. To acknowledge a mistake, individuals must believe this action will be more beneficial to themselves than not to acknowledge the mistake. This means that the organizational climate must be one in which TRUST rather than FEAR prevails, trust that being honest and admitting mistakes will not lead to personal damage. If the organizational climate is characterized by FEAR, there will be little perceived incentive for individuals to acknowledge mistakes. So the question distills to "How can we develop a climate of trust in which mistakes will be acknowledged?" Management must lead by example. What would happen if you led by example and started acknowledging your own mistakes, and led the organization to focus on the learning? Once you had set the pattern of learning, how long would it be before others in your organization began doing the same? What would happen if you categorically refused to fix blame, or listen to anyone else in your organization who attempted it? The power of this behavior is that small mistakes would be admitted early, before they turned into really big mistakes, and while they could still be remedied at very low cost.

Everyone Has a Role

Taking appropriate risks lies at the heart of excellent performance in organizations today. When managers list the risks they expect their direct reports to take as they do an excellent job, and when the direct reports list the risks they expect their managers to take as they do an excellent job, the result is a job description for the ideal manager and the ideal direct report. The key is that risk-taking should become a win-win proposition when it is understood and supported by direct reports, peers, and superiors.

Charles W. Prather, Du Pont Center for Creativity & Innovation, 1007 Market Street, D-6009 Wilmington, DE 19898. Tel: (302) 773-0205. Education: Ph.D. in biochemistry from North Carolina State University.

WORK ENVIRONMENT DIFFERENCES BETWEEN HIGH CREATIVITY AND LOW CREATIVITY PROJECTS

Teresa M. Amabile, Regina Conti, Heather Coon, Mary Ann Collins, Jeffrey Lazenby, and Michael Herron

What makes the difference between high levels of creativity and low levels of creativity within an organization? Is it possible to detect differences between high creativity and low creativity projects, differences that might be useful to managers who wish to encourage creativity? Over the past several years, there has been a growing body of research into the influence of the social environment on creativity, using experimental and non-experimental research designs. Controlled laboratory experiments have demonstrated that verbal, artistic, and problem-solving creativity can be undermined by several environmental factors, including: evaluation, surveillance, contracted-for reward, competition, restricted choice, and a focus on external motivators (Amabile, 1979, 1982, 1985, 1988; Amabile & Gitomer, 1984; Amabile, Goldfarb, & Brackfield, 1990; Amabile, Hennessey, & Grossman, 1986). Interview research with R&D scientists has suggested that many of these same environmental factors (as well as several others) importantly influence creativity in organizational settings (Amabile & Gryskiewicz, 1987). The Work Environment Inventory (WEI; Amabile, 1987) has been developed to assess these work environment factors that appear to affect creativity. Preliminary psychometric research on the WEI has been encouraging, concerning both the instrument's reliability and its validity (Amabile & Gryskiewicz, 1989). The ultimate goal of this research is to understand the influences on creativity in organizational settings, allowing organizations to assess and improve their environments for creativity and innovation.

This study investigated differences in the work environments surrounding high creativity projects and low creativity projects at a large high-tech electronics company. The primary instrument used in the study was the Work Environment Inventory (WEI), which assesses six "creativity stimulants" and two "creativity obstacles." Managers across four different divisions of the company were each asked to nominate two projects: the highest creativity project and the lowest creativity project, chosen from all the company projects over the last three years with which they were closely familiar. Sampling was done in a manner to ensure representation of both technical and non-technical personnel, nominating both technical and non-technical projects. This repeated-measures design allowed us to sample a large number of high and low creativity projects, without having to meet the difficult requirement that all projects be well-known by a single group of expert assessors. After providing some descriptive information on each project, participants completed one WEI to describe the work environment surrounding each project.

High creativity projects, compared to low creativity projects, had work environments that were *higher* on *challenging work, freedom, organizational encouragement, workgroup supports, supervisory encouragement,* and *sufficient resources*. Moreover, high creativity projects had work environments that were *lower* on *organizational impediments* and *workload pressure*. Of these eight work environment factors, five strongly distinguished between high and low creativity projects: challenging work, organizational encouragement, freedom, workgroup supports, and organizational impediments. These findings held across types of projects and participants (technical/non-technical).

A second phase of the study revealed that experts within the company rated the high creativity projects of the first phase significantly higher in creativity than they rated the low creativity projects. This provided crucial validity evidence for the first phase.

Several interesting and potentially important findings emerged from this study. In large part, these findings are compatible with those of our earlier research (e.g., Amabile & Gryskiewicz, 1989) and those of Pelz and Andrews (1966), who studied the creativity of R&D scientists. Thus, this study lends considerable support to the utility of the WEI for assessing work environment factors that affect creativity.

The highest creativity projects have work environments that stand in stark contrast to the work environments of the lowest creativity projects. It is important that, although the study was conducted in a research-oriented organization, these findings applied equally to technical and non-technical projects, technical and non-technical personnel, and large and small projects.

Although the results of this study are strong, there are some limitations in their interpretation. Most of the projects were currently ongoing; still, however, there is some room for retrospective bias in memory. Moreover, the repeated-measures design, while it controls for respondents' idiosyncratic use of the response scales, does allow for respondent bias. The positive results obtained from the expert raters in Phase 2, however, suggest that the choice of high and low creativity projects in Phase 1 was not idiosyncratic to the individual respondents. Still, further data collection (which is ongoing) will be required to validate the Phase 1 environment descriptions.

Keeping these cautions in mind, it is possible to suggest implications for management on the basis of these results. Creativity and innovation are likely to be at their highest levels when employees feel optimally challenged in their work. To some extent, of course, this sense of challenge depends on the nature of the work itself; some tasks are unchallenging for most people, and some tasks are probably overly difficult for most people. However, there is room for wide variability between these extremes. The important lesson for managers is to appropriately match employees to projects so that, whatever an employee's skill level, he or she feels challenged by and interested in the assigned project.

Several other managerial techniques may be important in promoting creativity. To the extent possible, managers should allow project team members autonomy in deciding how to carry out their work. They should attempt to form teams from individuals who communicate well with each other (even when challenging each other's ideas), combine diverse talents, and respect each other's skills. Top management should strive to encourage creative thinking through an innovative vision for the company, the fair evaluation of new ideas, and a system for hearing, recognizing, and rewarding creative ideas. Finally, attempts should be made both to reduce an emphasis on the status quo and to reduce internal political pressures, including destructive intergroup competition and harshly critical norms of evaluation.

Perhaps the most important lesson for management from the results of this study is that the environment does indeed play a clear role in distinguishing high levels of creativity from low levels of creativity in organizations. In combination with other studies, these results also suggest that there are common patterns in creativity-supporting and in creativity-killing environments across organizations.

References

Amabile, T. M. (1979). Effects of external evaluation on artistic creativity. *Journal of Personality and Social Psychology, 37,* 221-233.

Amabile, T. M. (1982). Children's artistic creativity: Detrimental effects of competition in a field setting. *Personality and Social Psychology Bulletin, 8,* 573-578.

Amabile, T. M. (1985). Motivation and creativity: Effects of motivational orientation on creative writers. *Journal of Personality and Social Psychology, 48,* 393-399.

Amabile, T. M. (1987). *The Work Environment Inventory.* Unpublished instrument.

Amabile, T. M. (1988). A model of creativity and innovation in organizations. In B. M. Staw & L. L. Cummings (Eds.), *Research in organizational behavior,* Vol. 10. Greenwich, CT: JAI Press.

Amabile, T. M., & Gitomer, J. (1984). Children's artistic creativity: Effects of choice in task materials. *Personality and Social Psychology Bulletin, 10,* 209-215.

Amabile, T. M., Goldfarb, P., & Brackfield, S. C. (1990). Social influences on creativity: Evaluation, coaction, and surveillance. *Creativity Research Journal, 3,* 6-21.

Amabile, T. M., & Gryskiewicz, N. (1989). The creative environment scales: The Work Environment Inventory. *Creativity Research Journal, 2,* 231-254.

Amabile, T. M., & Gryskiewicz, S. S. (1987). *Creativity in the R&D laboratory.* Technical Report Number 130. Greensboro, NC: Center for Creative Leadership.

Amabile, T. M., Hennessey, B. A., & Grossman, B. S. (1986). Social influence on creativity: The effects of contracted-for reward. *Journal of Personality and Social Psychology, 50,* 14-23.

Pelz, D. C., & Andrews, F. M. (1966). *Scientists in organizations.* New York: Wiley.

Teresa M. Amabile, Department of Psychology, Brandeis University, Waltham, MA 02254, Tel: (617) 736-3251 or (508) 358-4931. Education: Ph.D. in psychology from Stanford University.

Regina Conti, Department of Psychology, Brandeis University, Waltham, MA 02254, Tel: (617) 736-3286. Education: Doctoral candidate.

Heather Coon, Research Center for Group Dynamics, Institute for Social Research, University of Michigan, Ann Arbor, MI 48106-1248, Tel: (313) 747-3614. Education: Doctoral candidate.

Mary Ann Collins, Department of Psychology, Brandeis University, Waltham, MA 02254, Tel: (617) 736-3286. Education: Doctoral candidate.

Jeffrey Lazenby, 2453 Silverstrand Ave., Hermosa Beach, CA 90254, Tel: (310) 568-6245. Education: Undergraduate degree in psychology, University of California, Santa Barbara, Doctoral candidate.

Michael Herron, 3026 Kelton Ave., Los Angeles, CA 90034, Tel: (310) 568-6737. Education: Master's and Ph.D. degrees in organizational psychology from California School of Professional Psychology.

DISCOVERING THE UNSEEN LEADER

Robert C. Burkhart and David M. Horth

This paper aims to stimulate reformulation of the relationship between management and leadership by making the forms of language which uniquely characterize management and leadership more explicitly understood. Underlying this paper is the principle that the way we humans communicate corresponds to the way we look at the world. Furthermore, our expressed communications are the result of internal inquiry processes which guide our interactions with the world about us. The paper shows how our expressed communication—our language—can be analyzed in order to reveal the internal dialogue which produces it and how this understanding can be used to resolve the dilemma between management's need for efficiency and leadership's capacity for change.

The intuitive processes described in this paper constitute a behavioral definition of INTUITION. These processes can be learned and applied to meet the demands of change for our times. They offer a practical, personalized method for enhancing the essential leadership capacity for envisioning meaningful futures for our own lives and the lives of those we serve.

The concepts underlying this paper have emerged from a unique connection between the worlds of business and art. A practical application of pragmatic, analytical thinking on the one hand and holistic intuitive thinking on the other in order to address the leadership issues confronting us as we cross the threshold of the 21st century.

The Leadership-Management Paradox

Post-industrial Concept of Leadership

Joseph C. Rost (1991) defines leadership as: "an influence relationship among leaders and followers who intend real changes that reflect their mutual purposes." In response to the need for productivity and efficiency, past decades have concentrated on and institutionalized an industrial concept of leadership which called for a rational, technocratic, and linear approach and uses scientific language and method. In Rost's view this constitutes good management (p. 180). This can be characterized as a problem-solving approach—traditional management's way of achieving operational excellence. Zaleznik (1992) observes that the management approach often results in structural solutions which narrow choices and "even limit emotional reactions. . . . Managers aim . . . toward solutions acceptable as compromises among conflicting values."

J. P. Kotter (1990) asserts that "Good management controls complexity; effective leadership produces useful change." Leadership and Management thus appear to be in direct conflict with one another. The challenges posed by the current decade of change will be even more challenging in the 21st century. The change is continuous and "even the nature of change is changing" (Land & Jarman, 1992). The challenges are stimulating a rapid transition from an emphasis on efficient and effective management to the need for truly creative change leadership. A post-industrial concept of leadership is emerging to meet the demands of these turbulent times. The emerging concept must not only promote the capacity for change but also harness the creative tension that exists between the processes of leadership and management.

The Language of Leadership

Management's problem-solving approach is very different from leadership's issue-based approach. Zaleznik (1992) observes: "Where managers act to limit choices, leaders develop fresh approaches to long-standing problems and open issues to new options. To be effective, leaders must project their ideas onto images that excite people and only then develop choices that give those images substance." This is supported by Will McWhinney (1992) who proposes that "there is no greater leadership than that which creates meaning in the lives of the followers." McWhinney describes the role and change methodology of the charismatic leader in formulating long-term meaning for themselves and their communities. McWhinney's charismatic leader has a view of the world he calls the Mythic world view. One who has this world view is not constrained by what already exists and uses symbols and ideas to foster meaningful change. Leadership's language is future oriented and uses its own unique processes of communication. It is a language of visualization comprising the projection of ideas onto images used by Zaleznik's leader and the symbols and ideas of McWhinney's charismatic leader. This language emanates from the intuitive viewpoint. It is an essential capacity for leaders of change in the 21st century. During crises, intuitive communication provides a vehicle for facilitating the rediscovery of metaphors that bind organizations, communities, and society and stimulate the discovery of new metaphors to shape future societies.

Invisible Components of Management and Leadership

Managing and leading are processes in their own right. As such they can benefit from process improvement. An essential step in improving processes is to analyze and document everything that makes the process operate the way it does. This is made doubly difficult with processes such as management and leadership which have substantial "soft" components. The external manifestations of management and leadership behavior as articulated by Kotter, Rost, Zaleznik, and McWhinney have invisible components within each of us—the source of many of these intangibles. The numerous ways we communicate externally exhibit behavioral patterns that are inextricably linked to processes that go on within ourselves. These internal processes comprise the existential questions we ask ourselves in response to external stimuli provided by day-to-day living and life's dilemmas. The internal dialogues are often invisible to ourselves and even within each of us the invisible aspects of managing and leading are at odds with one other. By surveying the visual and verbal communications which characterize the invisible, implicit processes and how they interact, we can make them explicit. We can make them visible and measurable, and we can enhance them. In order to learn creative leadership we must recognize their existence and make appropriate use of them. In particular, the unseen processes of leadership are seldom recognized by ourselves and are usually not obvious to others. We are therefore apt to limit the creativity and long-term significance of our responses to crises. A taxonomy of the unique internal processes underlying our externally manifested communications is captured in the Inquiry Process Grid. To harness these inner dialogues involves each of us in a process of self-discovery: learning more about our strengths and developmental needs and the metaphors that sustain them.

The Inquiry Process Grid: Four Communication Pathways

The Inquiry Process Grid's Four Dimensions

We have identified four primary orientations or aspects of ourselves emerging from the preferred forms of questions we ask ourselves and an analysis of transcripts of our interactions with others. The forms of inquiry may be sensory, cognitive, affective, or intuitive in nature. We have found that the orientations are best understood and accounted for by using the terms REALIST, DESIGNER, EXPRESSIONIST, and INTUITIVE. The four ways of asking five fundamental questions—characterized as WHAT? WHICH? HOW? IF? and WHY?—are captured in The Inquiry Process Grid. The Grid is constructed from observable processes of behavior both visual and verbal. Each of these patterns of interaction were shown to be factorially distinct from each other in early studies done by Burkhart and reported in his book, *Spontaneous and Deliberate Ways of Learning* (1968). In this and later research done by Burkhart under the auspices of the U.S. Office of Education and the State Education Department of New York, significant correlations were found with various personality inventories: notably, instruments used in their creativity research by Frank Barron and Paul Torrance. More recently Les Jones of the Manchester Business School has developed an instrument based on an adjective checklist we had developed to describe each orientation. He has correlated this with his own instrument—The Jones Inventory of Barriers to Effective Problem Solving (JIB); Michael Kirton's Kirton Adaption-Innovation instrument (KAI); and the Myers-Briggs Type Indicator (MBTI). These are all measures which relate to leadership roles in our society.

Four Management and Leadership Language Orientations

On the basis of the significant correlations he found and the adjectives he used as test items, Jones developed concise descriptions for four archetypal viewpoints describing the different ways people tackle the various processes necessary for developing creative insights into their long-term motivations: their orientations for learning about and relating to the world. They are as follows:

REALIST: This is essentially a sensory viewpoint. It tends to focus on a factual, down-to-earth, rational approach which values tradition, decisiveness, and dependability.

DESIGNER: This is a cognitive viewpoint focusing on competence, clarity, control, and precision valuing objectivity, perfection, and playing by the rules.

EXPRESSIONIST: This is an affective viewpoint involving feelings, emotions, enthusiasm, and pleasure and values kindness, openness, loyalty, and [emotional] self-awareness.

INTUITIVE: This is a transformative viewpoint associated with an insightful, self-starting, empathic, and integrative approach which values uniqueness, flexibility, courage, and a philosophical outlook.

From Concrete to Abstract—Five Inquiry Processes

The inquiry processes we use range from defining objects and events (WHAT?), to distinguishing between things (WHICH?), to making things work (HOW?), to imagining new things or new ways of doing things (IF...THEN?), through to evaluating the significance of items or events (WHY?). The progression WHAT, WHICH, HOW, IF, WHY represents an increasing level of abstraction in the overall process of discovering long-term motivation and meaning. Five generic inquiry processes are defined as follows:

Conceptual What?
The basis on which we build a library of concepts about the external world and ourselves.

Comparative Which?
The basis on which we make distinctions to clarify objects, events, attitudes, ideas, and criteria. This focuses on what's relevant when we are making comparisons.

Procedural How?
How we go about achieving our day-to-day objectives: our operational process. This identifies our methods for achievement.

Suppositional If... Then?
How we use our imaginations to create new ways of looking at things and promote real change. Imagination is a necessary divergent process for extending our current realities in order to create new realities.

Evaluative Why?
Use of our value system to create purpose and motivation for real change. This is the foundation for envisionment of our futures and our sense of destiny.

The Inquiry Process Grid

The forms of inquiry for each orientation differs in the way they use five essential inquiry processes. The different forms of inquiry are captured in the rows (inquiry viewpoints or orientations) and columns (inquiry processes) of the Inquiry Process Grid. This is summarized in the following table. A more detailed description of the intuitive inquiry processes follows this. A more detailed version of the Grid describing the processes for all the orientations is available from the authors.

Implications of Process Inquiry Trends. The first three rows, labeled REALIST, DESIGNER, and EXPRESSIONIST, deal predominantly with our management needs. The INTUITIVE row describes the inquiry processes which deal with our visionary capacities as change leaders. The first three columns, WHAT?, WHICH? and HOW?, characterize the industrial management orientation through the last few decades. More recently, in the late 80's and the early 90's, there has been a growing emphasis on SUPPOSITIONAL (IF... THEN?) inquiry processes and most recently a dramatic shift to EVALUATIVE inquiry process (WHY?) as the concept of VISION enters our

INQUIRY PROCESS GRID

GENERIC INQUIRY PROCESS

Conceptual WHAT?	Comparative WHICH?	Procedural HOW?	Imaginative IF...THEN?	Evaluative WHY?
REALIST				
Perceive	Discriminate	Experiment	Relate	Prioritize
DESIGNER				
Comprehend	Analyze	Apply	Symbolize	Synthesize
EXPRESSIONIST				
Prefer	Appreciate	Persuade	Personify	Formulate Criteria
INTUITIVE				
Internalize	Contrast Using Paradox	Revise	Transform	Vision for a Purpose

industrial and cultural repertoire. An examination of the prevailing *zeitgeist* demonstrates these effects. In the last decade men's and women's tennis wear has shifted from simple, balanced, symmetrical designs (DESIGNER) to asymmetrical, bold, and dynamic patterns and colors characteristic of an Expressionist's SUPPOSITIONAL orientation. In commercial advertising a concrete REALIST depiction of the CAMEL on a pack of cigarettes has shifted to a large SUPPOSITIONAL personification—the dramatically distorted image of a cool and sophisticated person. Cool, sophisticated, musically-gifted camels are appearing on billboards all over the USA. In just the last two years there has been a shift away from management security values to leadership values. The trend towards the EVALUATIVE WHY? was extraordinarily evident in the 1992 USA Presidential campaign which had a focus on the adequacy of a Vision for the future. For our purposes this trend is summed up with great specificity by Göran Ekvall's trend analysis of the movement from Employee and Production-centered Management to Change-centered Leadership in modern institutions both in the USA and Europe (1991). All these are clear indicators that we are in a decade of change which places a new emphasis on IF? and WHY? and the intuitive capacities of Change Leadership.

The Language and Methods of Leadership and Management During Crises

In both our professional and personal lives the key discovery about an intuitive orientation to change is the recognition and imaginative use of the "UNSEEN LEADER" within us. The voice of our unseen leader addresses long-term issues relating to the unfolding of our future. However, a dilemma exists within all of us. Whereas the inner leader provides orientation for our creative responses to change, an intense dialogue is inevitable with the champion for stability and the status quo—the manager within us. Both within ourselves and in our organizations, an emergent change leader is resisted because change is threatening to the well-ordered pattern and comfort of day-to-day structures for efficiency and operational harmony—regardless of whether or not change leadership provides meaning for our own endeavors and the endeavors of those we lead. Meaninglessness is relentless. It eats away at individuals, organizations, and communities—demanding to be replaced by an alternative system whose purpose generates meaningful operations or a meaningful way of life. Our inner dialogue is about change to resolve issues on the one hand versus tactical problem-solving on the other. If we listen only to the manager within us we may fix the problem today only for it to emerge again—at another time and often in another guise. Eventually not addressing the issues will limit our options and our potential for growth. We are fearful of major changes. One reason we often fail to recognize our Unseen Leader is that our inner manager believes, especially in times of crisis, that we do not have the time for the luxury and confusion of a future-oriented perspective and that the tried and tested strategies will continue to work despite the changing circumstances. The opposite may be true. During crises, most of all, we need the courage to engage in the future-oriented process of intuitive inquiry essential to the determination of our future. However, in times of crisis, pragmatic management's short-term revisionism may dominate, resulting in short-sighted patching up of an inadequate system for which the long-term solutions remain undiscovered. Alone, the processes of management limit our options, trivialize our emotions, and may lead us up a blind alley. Alone, "bottom line" management mentality cannot provide for our long-term needs. Scientific management or realism is based on what exists now. Analytical, cause-and-effect problem-solving language does not reach far enough in redesigning existing operations. Nor is effective change achieved by motivational programs for change inspired by an affective orientation to problem solving. An existence based purely on

RESEARCH *Discovering Creativity*

our prevailing emotional needs may cause us and those we lead to lose sight of future realities. The need for realism, analysis, and affective motivation are all important in the total change process but most of all we need to become engaged in leadership processes which are forward-looking and visionary in their content. Managers seek orderly operation. Leaders promote change. Open planning between them ensures that the pathway to change is an orderly one.

Making Intuitive Processes Visible

This paper explores the internal processes of management and leadership by examining both the preferred language and underlying inquiry processes which characterize them. In response to the need for productivity and efficiency, past decades have concentrated on and institutionalized concrete inquiry processes—manifested as scientific language and method (see, for example, Rost, 1991). The prevailing need is for an expanded language and method more suited to handling complexity and leading to more imaginative means of envisioning our future and providing new meaning for our work and our lives. Intuitive inquiry processes provide this expanded repertoire. They are fundamental to successful change leadership in formulating visions and facilitating meaning for individuals and organizations. However, even for people enacting them, the intuitive inquiry processes they use are largely unrecognized or misrepresented. Intuitive inquiry processes are not gifts given to few people. They can be made explicit, learned, and internalized to enhance the leadership capacities of anyone wishing to discover meaning for their own lives and provide meaning for the endeavors of others.

Metaphoric Language for Leading Change

The intuitive processes of the unseen leader's language of change is observable, measurable, and reproducible. Making them explicit enables us to master the capacity to envision metaphors necessary for determining our own future and ultimately the future of those we serve. Intuitive communication enables us to discover the source of long-term motivations: "ROOT METAPHORS" which act as inner symbols for a sustaining sense of purpose and provide meaning for our life's unfolding. Metaphoric language is vitally important in the self-development leadership process. All of us carry metaphors around with us as internal compasses that guide or may even block our life's unfolding. Root metaphors are at the heart of our meaning systems. Such metaphors also exist for our organizations, communities, and nations. They are the essence of our cultures. By discovering our existing root metaphors and revising them or formulating or transforming new ones, we can enlighten the pathway of our developmental route. We need them because we and those we serve can only become what we can envision. Root metaphors are the navigation instruments of the unseen leader enabling us to discover and chart our new destinations.

Self Leadership: Creating Internal Synergy

Our leadership and management inquiry processes and their resultant language and methods provide us with two different images of ourselves. Each holds different and conflicting self concepts and opposing roles. A constant, creative tension exists between the security of our inner manager's proven operations and the risk-taking of our unseen leader's vision of the future. A loss of meaning is the result of a gap within us—a black hole—which exists between what we're doing operationally and how we envision ourselves in the future—what we would like to become. Though the outcomes of this existential dilemma are more obvious at developmental passages of our lives—for example, so-called mid-life crisis—the existential dilemma is relentless. Who we really are is constantly being questioned by who we would like to be.

The dilemma is heightened by gaps created by the cultures which fostered us and the cultures in which we now live and work. Our research in the USA demonstrates that these gaps are usually sensory, cognitive, or affective in nature. They are in sharp contrast to the language we experience in the privacy of our intuitive moments of self-insight. Here the private self-image of who we would like to be confronts the public image of who we are. Here we meet our unseen leader—often only as a fleeting shadow. By courageously engaging in the inner dialogue and confronting the gaps, we make our unseen leader visible and discover a meaningful answer to life's dilemmas. The intuitive insights which emerge about our unseen selves provides us with the motivational power to develop as leaders.

To learn this process of self-discovery we need to be aware of four different kinds of communication pathways: the Inquiry Systems we use to achieve an integrative orientation to life's many dilemmas.

The Intuitive Processes of Inquiry

Intuitive Inquiry's Distinct and Integrative Attributes

The distinctive attribute of the intuitive orientation is the capacity to shift viewpoints in order to create forms of imagery which have meaning and embody significant personal insights—touchstones, if you will. The intuitive orientation is also integrative in nature: like an umbrella to the other orientations. In invoking the inquiry processes of the other orientations, intuitive inquiry achieves a more inclusive orientation. Intuitive inquiry thus provides a unique leadership capacity to discover and share meaning derived from the complexity and ambiguity found in crisis situations. For example,

Intuitive What?
INTERNALIZING involves PERCEIVING the subject matter using the external sensory imagery of the REALIST orientation and PERSONIFYING using the internal affective orientation of the EXPRESSIONIST. Identifying with the subject matter in this way facilitates deeper aesthetic learning of and from the subject matter. This is the basis of the process used by the sculptor and the portrait artist. Learning how to portray their subjects by becoming them—posing like them.

Intuitive Which?
CONTRASTING using PARADOXES requires both the REALIST capacity to DISCRIMINATE between external aspects of the subject matter and the EXPRESSIONIST capacity for affectively APPRECIATING the internal dilemmas which emerge. The DESIGNER capacity to SYNTHESIZE is invaluable in developing images for effectively resolving conflicting elements as input to the intuitive operational inquiry process (HOW?).

Intuitive How?
REVISING existing metaphors involves the DESIGNER-oriented processes of ANALYZING and APPLYING in order to redesign and revitalize existing imagery. This is our central process of quality improvement: altering what exists in order to make it more relevant.

Intuitive IF . . . THEN?
The process of TRANSFORMING in order to embody meaning in a metaphor involves RELATING to create a convincing sensory image. The affective process of PERSONIFICATION ensures that the final image has emotional value.

Intuitive Why?
VISIONING FOR A PURPOSE creates in the present a tangible image which stands for and guides the development of a meaningful future. The image which emerges stands for a more inclusive lifestyle pattern, since the EVALUATIVE processes of all the other orientations are involved.

Applying Intuitive Inquiry for Creative Leadership Self Development

From our workshops, particularly those for helping people develop the leadership capacity for insightful writing, we have found that intuitive inquiry requires and promotes the development of DIVERGENCY. Intuitive processes are inclusive of other orientations and are able to handle more complexity in deriving or creating meaning through representative imagery. These observations suggest that engaging in intuitive inquiry is a very practical way of learning about the other—more singular—forms of communication in an integrative way. For example, we have found that intuitive writing generally includes combinations of the language constructs from the other orientations. We have also found that a form of integrative development appears to occur when people with different predominant inquiry language preferences are guided through the intuitive inquiry processes. Quite suddenly, both Suppositional and Evaluative forms of imagery emerge in their communication to represent the who they are and who they would like to be in the future. The new creative imagery is usually the product of their preferred language orientations—a kind of "Going with the Grain." It may also occur in other orientations—"Going Across the Grain." Following these kinds of development individuals begin to "speak out" more consistently and freely in their own unique voice. Their imagery comes alive. For example, their writing becomes more engaging to other people through its compelling imagery and intimacy. Our leadership instructional units are based on the five intuitive inquiry processes. We have found that each process in the sequence—INTERNALIZING–CONTRASTING–ALTERING–TRANSFORMING–VISIONING—must be mastered before the inquiry process that follows it can provide consistently high-quality breakthroughs in terms of personal insights gained—for example, in written assignments. Overall, there is ample evidence to suggest both to outside observers and more importantly to participants themselves that enhanced and useful creative capacities emerge from the application of intuitive inquiry processes. The level of quality has been remarkably uniform across each class. Analyzed samples of participants' creative output and self-assessment methods are described in a follow-up to this paper: "Structure for the Instructive Methodology for Intuitive Self Development."

Conclusion

Intuitive inquiry has enormous potential in helping us to become aware of the inner dialogue between manager and unseen leader concerning the unfolding of our lives. In order to develop as effective and authentic change leaders we need to overcome the barriers and grasp the opportunities generated by this inner dialogue: to become integrated, fully-functioning individuals with unmistakable and unique powers of creativity. Our unseen leader is our intuitive liberated self.

References

Burkhart, R. C. (1968). *Spontaneous and deliberate ways of learning.* Scranton, PA: International Textbook Company.

Ekvall, G., & Arvonen, J. (1991). Change centered leadership: An extension of the two-dimensional model. *Scandinavian Journal of Management, 7*(1), 17-26.

Jones, L. (1993). *New insights into different styles of creativity.* In S. Gryskiewicz (Ed.), *Discovering Creativity: Proceedings of the 1992 International Creativity and Innovation Networking Conference,* pp. 167-170. Greensboro, NC: Center for Creative Leadership.

Kotter, J. P. (1990, May-June). What leaders really do. *Harvard Business Review,* 103-111.

Land, G., & Jarman, B. (1992). *Breakpoint and beyond.* New York: Harper Business.

McWhinney, W. (1992). *Paths of change: Strategic choices for organizations and society.* Newbury Park, CA: Sage.

Rost, J. C. (1991). *Leadership for the 21st century.* New York: Praeger.

Zaleznik, A. (1992, May-June). Managers and leaders: Are they different? *Harvard Business Review,* 126-135.

Additional Sources

Burkhart, R. C. (1969). *The assessment revolution: New viewpoints.* National Symposium on Evaluation in Education (ERIC EDO 36485 1969 343 ERIC ED Accessories File 1966-76 Vol 1.: Burkhart).

Burkhart, R. C., & Horth, D. M. (1991). Creative self leadership: A resource book. Unpublished manuscript.

Burkhart, R. C., & Horth, D. M. (1992). Learning creative self leadership. In T. Rickards, S. Moger, P. Colemont, & M. Tassoul (Eds.), *Quality Breakthroughs: Proceedings of the 1991 International Creativity and Innovation Networking Conference.* Delft, The Netherlands: Innovation Consulting Group TNO.

~~~

Robert C. Burkhart, Professor of liberal arts, State University College–Buffalo, 1432 Amherst Street, Buffalo, NY 14206. Tel: (716) 832-0221.

David M. Horth, Center for Creative Leadership, One Leadership Place, Post Office Box 26300, Greensboro, NC 27438-6300. Tel: (910) 288-7210.

INTRODUCING A CREATIVITY IMPROVEMENT PROGRAM FOR THE FEDERAL EXPRESS I.S. ORGANIZATION

J. Daniel Couger, Pat Flynn, and Doris Hellyer

Introduction

This project of the Center for Research and Innovation was the second one concentrating on creativity improvement for an Information Systems (I.S.) organization. The first (Couger & Snow, 1990) involved a team of analysts and programmers in a small microelectronics manufacturer (United Technologies Microelectronics Center) with $20 million annual sales.

Formal creativity improvement projects are rare in the I.S. field. This is not to say that I.S. has not been creative—just that the formalization of the process can lead to a concerted effort by all individuals in a work group. The UTMC project proved the validity of such an approach, by raising the group's creative output significantly.

There are many examples of creativity improvement programs for other functional areas of the business, such as marketing, manufacturing, and distribution (see Kuhn, 1988; Nayak & Ketteringham, 1986; Rickards, 1985; Von Fange, 1959). Not only are creativity improvements rare in I.S., few articles have been written on the subject of creativity in I.S. (Couger, 1990). The development and implementation of creativity programs for I.S. has been a primary focus for the Center for Research on Creativity and Innovation (CRCI) at the University of Colorado, Colorado Springs.

This report discusses a pilot project on creativity improvement for the Federal Express Corporation, involving two groups. Each has responsibility for a major subsystem within Federal Express's package tracking system, COSMOS. One is the total custodial control subsystem and the other is the generic queuing subsystem.

Design of the Creativity Improvement Program

A two-pronged approach was utilized for the pilot program:
1. Improvement of the environment for creativity and innovation.
2. Training in specific techniques for creativity generation and evaluation.

The six-month program consisted of two phases:

Phase I. One-day workshop to ensure an environment to facilitate creativity and to teach a variety of creativity generation, evaluation, and implementation techniques.

Phase II. Reinforcement of the concepts/principles taught in the workshop, with monthly meetings to discuss application of the techniques and test the degree to which the environment for creativity had been enhanced. Additional techniques were also introduced during this period.

A survey instrument was selected to administer to each employee before the program began, to obtain perceptions on the environment for creativity and innovation. The same instrument was administered at the end of Phase II as part of the measurement of results. The instrument selected (Glassman, 1988) was chosen for two reasons: (1) It was simple to administer, requiring less than 15 minutes to complete and (2) norms had been developed from use of the instrument in other occupations. We could compare the results of the responses of I.S. personnel to the norms.

Training on Creativity Generation/Evaluation Techniques

A one-day workshop was provided to the two groups, covering both analytical and intuitive creativity generation/evaluation techniques: analogies/metaphors, Crawford blue-slip writing, 5Ws and the H (Who, When, Where, Why, What, and How), problem reversal, progressive abstraction, wishful thinking, peaceful setting, brainwriting, brainstorming, and nominal group technique. Participants were involved in exercises using each of those techniques, both to gain familiarity in use and to generate questions about applicability in the Federal Express setting.

After defining and illustrating creativity, the workshop leader gave examples—first for the business field in general and then specific to the I.S. field. Next, conceptual blocks to creativity (Adams, 1986) were analyzed. The creative problem solving (CPS) model was discussed and illustrated. The group then was led in an exercise to identify the key components for a climate that would foster creativity. Since all members of the work unit and their manager were in the workshop, they could concentrate on items specific to their work environment for climate improvement. The remaining workshop exercises dealt with applying creativity techniques to specific I.S. problem areas, such as approaches to improve the receptivity to new system methodologies, improving the quality of systems development, and improving service to users/clients. The workshop concluded with a discussion of how best to implement the new-found knowledge on creativity approaches and techniques. One effective way is to establish working dyads.

Follow-up Sessions

Reinforcement occurred two ways. First, in staff meetings, there was managerial follow-up on the use of creativity log sheets to record all creative ideas. Second, a two-hour monthly meeting was led by a facilitator from the CRCI. While the workshop had been combined for the two groups, the monthly meetings were held separately so each group could concentrate on the areas specific to its interest. In each of these meetings participants were invited to identify results of creative activity. Additional creativity techniques were introduced and illustrated—such as IWWMW (in what ways might we), forcefield analysis, progressive abstractions, and right brain intuitive approaches. There was follow-up on the factors identified in the workshop for improving the climate for creativity. Also, each group identified ways that creativity could be recognized and rewarded.

Results

Results are shown in two ways: (1) participants' views of their improvement in creativity and (2) identification of the specific creative ideas. We will review point two first, which is of course the bottom line. Participants in the program were asked to keep a log of their creative ideas. Some 40 creative ideas were recorded in the log. The large majority dealt with specific production areas. However, ideas were also generated for improving communication and procedures within the work unit.

A review of the ideas reveals that most persons were able to apply their newly learned creativity techniques to both large and small problems/opportunities, e.g., a fix that increased processing speed by a factor of 10 and an approach to simplify building on-line screens.

Concerning their own view of how much more creative they were, the post-test (using the Glassman instrument) revealed a significant improvement ($p<.01$ level of probability). For the independent variable, the participants were asked to rate the correctness of the statement, "Overall, my work unit demonstrates a great deal of creativity." For Group 1 the rating improved from a mean of 1.3 to 3.05 (on the scale of 5). For Group 2 the rating improved from a mean of 2.2 to 4.44. Both groups perceived their level of creativity to have more than doubled. Comparing these results to Glassman's norms for organizational effectiveness showed that both groups increased their effectiveness significantly (at the $p<.05$ significance level). The net improvement for Group 1 was 3.48 and for Group 2 was 4.66. However, Group 2 rated organizational effectiveness significantly higher at the start. The most important indicator of effectiveness of the program, of course, is the degree to which creative ideas are generated.

References

Adams, J. L. (1986). *Conceptual blockbusting*. Reading, MA: Addison-Wesley.
Couger, J. D., & Snow, T. A. (1990). *Case study: Introducing a creativity improvement program in an information systems organization*. Colorado Springs: CRCI Report 90-5.
Couger, J. D. (1990). Ensuring creative approaches in information system design. *Managerial and Decision Economics, 11*(5), 281-295.
Glassman, E. (1988, October). Are your workers as creative as they could be? *Management Solutions,* 29-31.
Kuhn, R. L. (1988). *Handbook for creative and innovative managers*. New York: McGraw-Hill.
Nayak, P. R., & Ketteringham, J. M. (1986). *Breakthroughs!* New York: Rawson Assoc.
Rickards, T. (1985). *Stimulating innovation*. New York: St. Martin's Press.
Von Fange, E. K. (1959). *Professional creativity*. Englewood Cliffs, NJ: Prentice-Hall, Inc.

Additional Sources

Amabile, T. M., & Gryskiewicz, N. D. (1989). The creative work environment scales: Work Environment Inventory. *Creativity Research Journal, 2*(4), 231-253.
Kirton, M. J. (1989). *Adaptors and innovators*. New York: Routledge.
Miller, W. (1988). *Validation of the innovation styles profile*. Mill Valley, CA: Global Creativity Corp.

~~~

J. Daniel Couger, University of Colorado at Colorado Springs, Post Office Box 7150, Colorado Springs, CO 80933-7150. Tel: (719) 593-3403. Education: Ph.D. from the University of Colorado, Boulder.

Pat Flynn, Federal Express Corporation, 5550 Tech Center Drive, Colorado Springs, CO 80919. Tel: (719) 599-4700.

Doris Hellyer, Federal Express Corporation, 5550 Tech Center Drive, Colorado Springs, CO 80919. Tel: (719) 599-4700.

CREATIVITY IN PROJECT WORK: A LONGITUDINAL STUDY OF A PRODUCT DEVELOPMENT PROJECT

Göran Ekvall

Project cycles are generally said to have four phases: *initiation, preparation, execution* or *implementation,* and *delivery.* These phases are then broken down into a series of steps. The preparatory stage appears to be the most crucial to the subsequent outcome. By the end of this phase a detailed product specification and a detailed plan for timing and manpower requirements should have been produced. From then on the concept of the product should be "frozen" (Bruzelius & Hansen, 1986), and no further changes made. In other words, it ought now to have been established what functional qualities the product is to have, and what the cost is to be in time and money. During the execution stage the opportunities for creativity are thus restricted. The characteristics of the end result have been carefully specified; it is to fulfill certain requirements, neither more nor less. If it does not fulfill these requirements it will fall short of expectations and the client will be dissatisfied. If the product exceeds the demands, the costs are likely to burst the budget, and again the client will be unhappy.

A quick survey of the relevant literature—manuals as well as theoretical studies of project work—reveals two factors as being particularly important to success. These are structure (organization, planning, control) and the existence of a stimulating and creative work climate. Ander and Karlsson (1989) claim that a "project methodology" and "an atmosphere and work climate that can stimulate creative collaboration" are both necessary.

Thus a work climate that encourages creative behavior in the participants, combined with clear structure and control over the project, is thought to be the desirable aim. But there is a hitch in this argument. A palpably creative climate and strict control do not go together. The creative climate means freedom, risk-taking, and an abundance of ideas (Ekvall, 1990). But freedom and order pull in opposite directions. If order is imposed with the help of detailed instructions, rules and routines, then freedom is inevitably diminished.

Project work can be regarded as a process of extended problem solving—and any element of creativity will depend on the nature of the result being sought, on how conventional or original it is supposed to be. It could therefore be useful to consider how far our knowledge and theories about problem solving and creative thinking can help to explain what happens in projects. Theories and methods relating to group problem solving are of particular interest, since projects are usually undertaken by several people working together.

The similarities between the two models are obvious. The creative problem-solving process (Parnes, Noller, & Biondi, 1977) includes the four main phases of the project process. But there is one important difference: When a project is run strictly according to the model, the functional requirements and related criteria are exactly specified and established at the preparatory stage. The nature of the solution and the way in which it is to function are largely determined in advance, which means that there is little room for experimentation or search for new types of solution when the project is actually being carried out. In the creative problem-solving model this kind of intentional "freezing" at an early stage in the task is avoided. When the execution phase starts, the question is still pretty open so that different suggestions for solutions can still be presented and tried. Only after ideas have been generated are exact criteria introduced and evaluations made. This is in line with the fundamental brainstorming principle of deferred judgement, i.e., criticism and evaluation of ideas occur after ample time has been allowed for free idea generation.

Thus project work could be defined as a problem-solving process extended over time and undertaken by a group of people in collaboration. But the strict planning and control introduced into the process mean that it does not altogether accord with the methods of creative problem solving, where the idea instead is to allow more freedom during the execution phase.

Thus there are certain built-in contradictions and traps in the theories and models of project management and project administration. Project management methods, as generally taught and aspired to, diverge in important ways from the widely recognized principles of creative problem-solving cycles—even though creative results are still expected. Rigorous structures and control mechanisms are adopted; at the same time it is assumed that a stimulating climate—one that will inspire creativity—is necessary.

The company in which this project was conducted is in the electronics industry and is part of a multinational European corporation. It is located in Stockholm. The project was being carried out in a division for defense materials, more specifically in a department for basic technology. It could be described as a combined technology-led and market-led project. It was known as Operator Station.

The project had a dual goal. On the one hand it was to develop a new technology for future use, to produce a generally useful basic system of components and modules for the hardware and software. On the other, it had to see that the product as a whole fulfilled a specific marine order.

The goals for the work on the Operator Station project were vague from the start, owing to poor communications between this project and the product department. The engineers in Operator Station were engaged to design a highly innovative product capable of general application and with future potential. The project department wanted to get exactly what their customer had asked for, neither more nor less. But this difference in goals was never made clear, and no specific agreement was reached. In this confused situation the Operator Station people had set their technological sights high. They aimed to develop a technologically leading-edge product.

The climate in the Operator Station project was what the project management manuals would have described as favorable; it had a stimulating effect on motivation and creativity. The project's structure and control mechanisms, on the other hand, had several weaknesses when judged against the generally accepted prescriptions for "ideal" project management. The goal was not clearly specified, coordination between the internal customer and the project was poor, coordination within the project was equally poor—so planning and follow-up were not as strict as prescribed, and so on.

Evaluations of the finished project, Operator Station, differed markedly, depending on the organizational base of the speaker. Representatives of the internal customer who had ordered the product said that it did not fulfill the specified requirements and was therefore something of a failure. Representatives of Operator Station itself and of the basic technology unit, on the other hand, maintained that the product represented a successful investment in the future; it was absolutely first-class in technological terms; it incorporated several original solutions.

A follow-up three years after completion of the project revealed that the product had been successful. It had proved possible to use it in new orders for defense systems. The technological standard was regarded as good. The earlier internal criticism had simmered down.

If we wanted to, we could claim that the project management manuals were right. The project went wrong because structure and control were both weak. The product was not finished in time and it cost much more than expected. But in terms of creativity, things look different. The climate encouraged creative thinking and the final product—the finished Operator Station—was technologically advanced and embodied several original solutions. It also proved to be a product with a future. This result was achieved largely due to the weak controls. The members of the project could set their goals, without being hampered by specifications which would have inhibited their ambitions. They were able to enter upon the execution phase with their minds open to different solutions, just as the models for creative problem solving prescribe. The agreement between the engineers' high technological ambitions and the opportunities provided by the project made for creative motivation and commitment, with the result that the level of creativity continued to rise in the course of the job. It would not have been possible to achieve this level of motivation if strict control had been exercised to tie the project to the customer's lower-level requirements, and if this control had been strong enough to determine the direction of the project.

References

Ander, I., & Karlsson, R. (1989). *Battre projekt*. Lund, Sweden: Studentlitteratur.

Bruzelius, L. H., & Hansen, O. R. (1986). *Styrning av utvecklingsprojekt*. Stockholm: Norstedts Forlag.

Ekvall, G. (1990). *Ideer, Organisationsklimat och Ledningsfilosofi*. Stockholm: Norstedts Forlag.

Parnes, S. J., Noller, R. B., & Biondi, A. M. (1977). *Guide to creative action*. Charles Scribner's Sons.

~~~

Göran Ekvall, FAinstitute Stockholm and University of Lund, FAradet, Box 5042, S-102 41 Stockholm, Sweden. Tel: +46 8 666 68 00.

MBTI AND KAI BIAS ON CREATIVITY COURSES

Jane Henry

Abstract

This paper presents an analysis of Creative Management MBA students' responses to the KAI and MBTI. Results over a two-year period show a marked bias towards NT on the MBTI and the innovator end of the KAI scale. Although these results are in the expected direction, the degree of bias is substantial. Possible social desirability and atypical sample characteristics explanations are explored.

Introduction

The student sample described in this paper is comprised of Open Business School students who have opted to study an MBA course on Creative Management. This is probably the largest organizational creativity course in the world, and currently has over 600 registered students per year. Most of the students are engaged in full-time work and study part-time. They are distributed throughout the U.K. and increasingly throughout Europe and range in age from their twenties to fifties. Sixty percent work in the private sector and forty percent in the public sector. Eighty percent are male and twenty percent female. The Creative Management course addresses development, problem solving, climate and innovation issues and currently introduces two inventories—the Myers-Briggs Type Indicator (MBTI) and the Kirton Adaption-Innovation Inventory (KAI).

Myers-Briggs Type Indicator. The MBTI purports to measure bi-polar preferences derived from Jung's theory of personality types: Extroversion E, Introversion I, Sensing S, Intuition N, Thinking T, Feeling F, Judging J, and Perceiving P. Various studies have associated intuiting N and perceiving P preferences with creativity (see Myers & McCaulley, 1988, who offer a fuller description).

Kirton Adaption-Innovation Inventory. The KAI is a measure of creative style. It aims to assess preferred thinking style in respect to creativity, problem solving, and decision making. Briefly, Adaptors are characterized by having a preference for improving existing practice, i.e., doing things better, whereas Innovators are characterized by a preference for doing things differently. See Kirton (1987) for a fuller description.

Results

Compared to KAI norms our sample shows considerable bias towards the innovation end of this scale, with an average of 113 compared to the norm of 95 in both 1991 and 1992. Our students also show a marked bias towards N and P on the MBTI, with forty percent NPs in 1991 and nearer fifty percent of the sample in 1992 (compared to a U.K. norm for managers of fifteen percent). Around seventy-five percent are intuitives (the U.K. norm is nearer fifty percent). We also have an above-average number of thinkers (eighty percent of the sample), even given the male bias towards this preference. The sample is also slightly more introverted than expected (Henry, 1991).

Table 1
1991/2 Creative Management MBA Students' MBTI Results

	1991 (360)	*1992* (430)		*1991* (360)	*1992* (430)
E	42%	42%	I	58%	57%
S	27%	20%	N	73%	80%
T	88%	83%	F	12%	16%
J	53%	46%	P	47%	54%

Discussion

Our students' KAI sample mean score of 113 is very high. It is well above the mean of 105 obtained by Fleenor and Taylor (in this volume) among 12,000-odd Center for Creative Leadership attendees, and at the top of averages obtained in 33 U.K. studies of various occupational groups quoted in the KAI Manual (Kirton, 1987). It is also 13 points above the figure of 100 Kirton recorded for MBA students (M. Kirton, personal communication, 1990), though Jones (L. Jones, personal communication, 1992) quotes 108 for MBS MBAs. Our samples' percentages of introverts, intuitives, and perceiving types is towards the top end of the many hundreds of occupational groups shown in the MBTI manual (Myers & McCaulley, 1988), and the percentage of thinking types is higher than the 180 or so studies quoted there. Two possible explanations for this bias are a social desirability effect and atypical sample characteristics.

Social Desirability. Any social desirability effect might be expected to be particularly acute in creative management students, as novices often have more positive associations with innovation than adaption, though Kirton (1987) reports studies to suggest that the KAI is not particularly subject to social desirability. In addition, the positive relationship previously found between innovation on the KAI and intuition (r = .4) and perception (r = .5) on the MBTI (Carne & Kirton, 1982) shows in our data. This suggests that unless the MBTI is also subject to a major social desirability effect we need to consider characteristics of the sample as an explanation for the atypical profile.

Sample Characteristics. Perhaps creativity courses attract "creative" people, who one might expect to score at the innovator end of the KAI and come out high on the intuitive N preference. Anecdotal evidence from trainers supports this idea (e.g., S. Levers, personal communication, 1992). However, in 1991 our MBA students had few courses to choose from, and Creative Management was the only "soft" option, and seventeen percent took it for want of a preferred alternative (Henry, 1992b). In 1992, when further options came on stream and their selection represents a real choice, the skew in the KAI scores and the E-I dimension on the MBTI show little change, though as might be expected, the sample did shift slightly further towards N, P, and F. Jones (personal communication, 1992) suggests the bias towards innovation he has found among Western senior management (with KAI means of 109 to 113) may also be a contributing factor (this assumes that MBA students are relatively senior). The author is following up KAI and MBTI profiles for samples studying other management options.

Conclusion

If the degree of bias shown in our sample is typical of other creativity courses (and not the result of some social desirability effect) we may need to fundamentally redesign creativity courses to emphasize the skills of convergence and address the weaknesses associated with an innovative, intuitive, thinking orientation. See Henry (1992a) for a fuller account of this paper.

References

Carne, G., & Kirton, M. (1982). Styles of creativity and test-score correlations between Kirton Adaption-Innovation Inventory and the Myers-Briggs Type Indicator. *Psychological Reports, 50,* pp. 31-36.

Henry, J. (1991). *Creative management.* Milton Keynes, UK: Open University Press.

Henry, J. (1992a). Creative style. In L. Novelli, Jr. (Ed.), *Collected research papers: International Creativity and Innovation Networking Conference.* Greensboro, NC: Center for Creative Leadership, pp. 52-60.

Henry, J. (1992b). *Creative management evaluation.* Milton Keynes, UK: Open University IET Project Report No. 32.

Kirton, M. (1987). *Adaption-Innovation Inventory Manual* (2nd ed.). Hatfield Herts: Occupational Research Centre.

Myers, I. B., & McCaulley, M. H. (1988). *Manual: A guide to the development and use of the Myers-Briggs Type Indicator.* Palo Alto, CA: Consulting Psychologists Press, pp. 214-215.

~~~

Jane Henry, Open University, Walton Hall, Milton Keynes MK7 6AA, United Kingdom. Tel: +44 908 65 29 13.

AN INQUIRY INTO CROSS-CULTURAL CREATIVITY TRAINING: RESULTS FROM A FIVE-WEEK STUDY TOUR IN BERGEN AND BRATISLAVA

Scott G. Isaksen and K. Brian Dorval

As a result of the growth of interest in creativity and innovation, there has been a sharp increase in the emergence of centers, conferences, journals, and professionals in the creativity field focusing on the study, training, and application of creativity (Isaksen, 1987). In particular, organizations have demonstrated a growing interest in cross-cultural creativity given their multi-national and cross-functional teaming activities (Adler, 1991). Many of these organizations have identified cross-functional and cross-cultural teams as an effective strategy for developing a substantial competitive advantage. Despite increasing interest in understanding cross-cultural aspects of creativity, deliberate and explicit inquiry concerning the cross-cultural challenges and opportunities facing creativity researchers and practitioners is very rare. Given the need to facilitate effective understanding and application of creativity across cultures, more extensive cross-cultural creativity research is necessary (Isaksen & Murdock, in press).

This paper summarizes the results of an exploratory research project which examined the cross-cultural challenges associated with creativity research and training. It included a five-week European study tour, as well as numerous training programs conducted in Belgium, Czechoslovakia, Denmark, Norway, and the United States. The primary source of the data collection was in the planning, delivery and follow-up of two-day training programs presented in Bergen, Norway, and Bratislava, Czechoslovakia, and based on those programs presented in Buffalo, New York.

Similarities Across Cultures

There were similarities found across cultures associated with such topics as providing training while focusing on real problems and challenges associated with an intact working team; having a positive outlook on creativity; and the promotion of positive interaction and effective teaming. More specific similarities are identified below.

The current version of CPS was viewed as valuable. Taking the descriptive view of Creative Problem Solving (Isaksen & Treffinger, 1991; Treffinger & Isaksen, 1992) as three components in which there was no set order or sequence in which they were applied was seen as valuable in all the cultures.

The Level-Style distinction was viewed as relevant. The difference between level of creative ability and style or kind of creativity was found to be a productive and important distinction to hold in learning and applying CPS across cultures.

Having a research-based program was worthwhile. Having a consistent program design which has been tested and validated on a variety of levels (i.e., use of instrumentation, participant feedback, CPS training impact studies, etc.) increased the ability of the training team to build linkages to other contexts, as well as the credibility of the program and training team.

Differences Between Cultures

There were a number of differences found between cultures. However, it is interesting to note that the similarities found between cultures outnumbered the differences. The differences tended to focus on such issues as the effective communication of information during training; that nature of the social interactions of participants before, during, and after training; and differences in the level of emphasis on cognitive and emotional aspects of problem solving. Specific examples of these differences are identified below.

Language differences may be challenging. Learning a specialized vocabulary around CPS and creativity was a challenge. It took additional energy and time to develop a common understanding of some of the main concepts examined during training.

Social role differences appeared. There were observable differences in the expectations participants held for the leadership roles within the groups. Of particular interest were the differences found in level of assertiveness-submissiveness exhibited by females during male-female interactions.

Varying levels of cognitive emphasis were observed. Both the Bergen and Bratislava groups had a deeper concern for the personal aspects of creativity and pushed beyond the relatively strong and rather traditional cognitive focus to the training of the Buffalo groups.

Key Learnings and Implications

The following key learnings and implications were identified from this exploratory examination of cross-cultural creativity training. In planning and facilitating the teaching and learning of CPS across cultures it is important to:

Start with a search for similarities. As a result of our search for similarities and differences across cultures, we found some of the core constructs and principles of CPS to be supported. These fundamental "building blocks" for creativity training can be used as a starting place for developing and tailoring creativity training programs.

Know your participants. The ability to visit individuals' homes and to interact with them on a social level provided a much clearer picture of the program participants and their potential learning needs.

Consider the emotional component of creativity. Given that different cultures express emotions concerning CPS in different ways, it is important to be ready to address different levels of emotional involvement for the specific nature of the problems addressed during the program.

Carefully position the use of assessment. Since cultures have different experiences with testing and assessment, it is important that these types of tools be fully explained and their purpose communicated prior to training.

Build a common language. To overcome language differences between cultures, it is helpful to build a common and simple language around the training content which leans more heavily on the use of graphics, pictures, and symbols in combination with verbal information.

Future Considerations for Examining Cross-cultural Creativity

It is evident from this study that creativity is a multicultural concept and that creativity researchers and practitioners can benefit from understanding the impact of culture on the learning and application of CPS. This study also sparked some questions for future inquiry into cross-cultural creativity. Some of these questions include: What are the specific creativity-related skills which transcend cultural boundaries to reside more centrally in the person? How do perceptions of environments which are conducive to creativity differ across cultures? What are the attributes of individual preferences for characteristics of creative outcomes across cultures? As our ability to understand what CPS techniques work best for whom under what circumstances (including cross-culturally), we will be in a better position to recognize, predict, and enhance creative behavior in all cultures.

References

Adler, N. J. (1991). *International dimensions of organizational behavior.* Boston, MA: PWS-Kent Publishing Company.

Isaksen, S. G. (1987). Introduction: An orientation to the frontiers of creativity research. In S. G. Isaksen (Ed.), *Frontiers of creativity research: Beyond the basics* (pp. 1-26). Buffalo, NY: Bearly Limited.

Isaksen, S. G., & Murdock, M. C. (in press). The emergence of a discipline: Issues and approaches to the study of creativity. In S. G. Isaksen, M. C. Murdock, R. L. Firestien, & D. J. Treffinger (Eds.), *Understanding and recognizing creativity: The emergence of a discipline.* Norwood, NJ: Ablex.

Isaksen, S. G., & Treffinger, D. J. (1991). Creative learning and problem solving. In A. L. Costa (Ed.), *Developing minds: Programs for teaching thinking* (rev. ed., Volume 2; pp. 89-93). Washington, DC: Association for Curriculum Development and Supervision.

Treffinger, D. J., & Isaksen, S. G. (1992). *Creative Problem Solving: An introduction.* Sarasota, FL: Center for Creative Learning.

Authors' Note: For a more complete version of this paper, please contact the authors.

~~~

Scott G. Isaksen, Center for Studies in Creativity, 1329 North Forest Road, Suite D-15, Williamsville, NY 14221. Tel: (716) 689-2176. Education: Bachelor of Science in education; Master of Science in creativity from Buffalo State College; doctorate in curriculum planning from the University of Buffalo.

K. Brian Dorval, Creative Problem Solving Group–Buffalo, 1329 North Forest Road, Williamsville, NY 14221. Tel: (716) 689-2176.

THE DYNAMIC NATURE OF CREATIVE PROBLEM SOLVING

Scott G. Isaksen, K. Brian Dorval, Ruth B. Noller, and Roger L. Firestien

Creative Problem Solving (CPS) is a flexible and dynamic system that is designed to assist individuals, groups, and organizations to solve problems, meet challenges, or capitalize on opportunities. Although its origin and popularization began with Alex Osborn, the founder of the Creative Education Foundation and the originator of brainstorming, there are now many different techniques, methodologies, and approaches which call themselves "creative problem solving." Many of these are really nothing more than modifications, specifications or build on brainstorming, or only focus on the element of idea generation. The growth within the field and increased demand for effective strategies to improve the creative thinking and problem-solving abilities of individuals and groups within the context of various organizations is creating some confusion regarding what is meant by creative problem solving. In the midst of this chaotic growth and activity there are a few organizations which have chosen to commit to build on an established CPS tradition while working to constantly improve the framework of CPS theory and practice.

We use the term Creative Problem Solving (CPS) to refer to a specific framework for dealing with challenges and opportunities which are novel, ambiguous, or complex. It is important to understand that our view of Creative Problem Solving is not a singular unidimensional approach, but a dynamic framework from which different individuals and groups can draw and design helpful "social technology."

The purpose of this paper is to provide a brief history of the early Osborn-Parnes or the "Buffalo" tradition of Creative Problem Solving, trace the development of the CPS model, and report some of the new key developments on the CPS process as utilized in various settings. Rather than holding rigidly to an old tradition, we have found it much more productive to build on a fifty-year tradition of research and empirical validation to continue development of both scientific and practical approaches relating to CPS.

Early Developments 1953-1982—The First 29 Years

In the 1953 edition of *Applied Imagination,* Osborn first described a seven-stage version of CPS that consisted of: Orientation, Preparation, Analysis, Hypothesis, Incubation, Synthesis, and Verification. This work was designed to be the first comprehensive description of CPS based on his career within the advertising field.

In the revised 1967 edition of *Applied Imagination,* Osborn modified his conception of CPS and condensed the seven-stage process into three, more comprehensive, stages. These stages included: Fact-Finding, Idea-Finding, and Solution-Finding. Osborn considered this three-stage view to be more productive in light of his experiences with the seven-stage process identified in 1953.

First, working with Alex Osborn and then continuing after his death in 1966, Sidney Parnes, in collaboration with other creativity professionals, developed a modification of Osborn's approach. This revised five-stage model was tested through an experimental program called the Creative Studies Project at Buffalo State College. Parnes' adaptation of Osborn's work formed the foundation for what is commonly called the Osborn-Parnes tradition of CPS. This process consisted of five steps: Fact-Finding, Problem-Finding, Idea-Finding, Solution-Finding, and Acceptance-Finding.

Until this point, most of the descriptions of CPS were verbally based. One of the first visual or graphic depictions of CPS appeared in Parnes' (1967) workbook. This image became the first in a series of graphic depictions of CPS and provided the initial break from the dominant verbal description of CPS.

Ruth Noller worked with Parnes to revise this earlier work and helped to develop an alternative graphic depiction of the five-step CPS model. This depiction is illustrated in Figure 1.

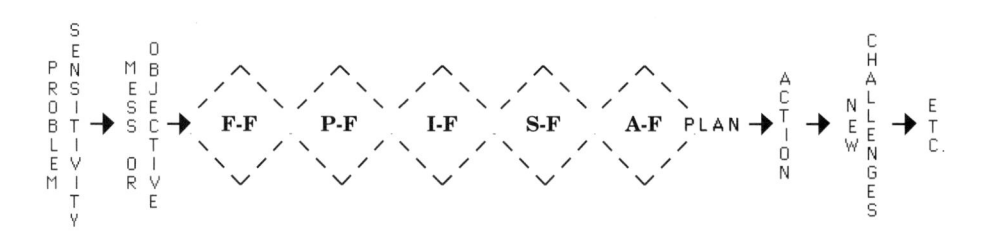

Figure 1

The advantage of this new depiction of process was that it illustrated the alternate divergent and convergent thinking inherent in the CPS process. However, the depiction also conveyed an image of the creative process as a neat, linear, and sequential series of stages in which a person started with a mess or objective, worked through each stage in its entirety, and ended with an action plan ready for new challenges. Although this appeared to be one possible image of the creative process, it also seemed a limited depiction of natural creative problem-solving behavior. As a result, this view of process was well received by some and seen as having limited value by others.

Discovering Creativity   *RESEARCH*

The 1980s: Additional Stages and a New View of Process

Treffinger, Isaksen, and Firestien (1982), working with this widely diffused, validated framework, focused on building a more deliberate balance of CPS techniques. Most existing techniques and instructional activities focused on divergence. They began to expand their work in the development of convergent technologies for CPS. Additionally, they learned about the importance of the client or problem owner during convergence (Firestien & Treffinger, 1983).

From their experiences with business and educational groups, Isaksen and Treffinger (1985) modified the process to be more easily learned and applied. First, a sixth stage called Mess-Finding was added. The purpose of this stage was to examine the personal and situational factors involved in learning and applying CPS. Second, they redefined the Fact-Finding stage as Data-Finding. They asserted that effective problem solving considered more than simply facts as relevant inputs to the problem-solving process. They suggested feelings, impressions, observations, and questions were also important. Third, Isaksen and Treffinger emphasized the importance and need for having a dynamic balance between divergent and convergent thinking in the process. As a result, they developed deliberate critical-thinking guidelines and techniques to balance those which had already been created for divergent thinking.

Along with these changes in the CPS process, Isaksen and Treffinger found it necessary to modify the graphic depiction used to communicate CPS. Mess-Finding was added to the "front end" of the process and the graphic was rotated to a vertical position. Text was also added to help explain some of the key functions involved in the different stages (see Figure 2, next page).

To emphasize the flexible application of CPS, Isaksen and Treffinger developed an analogy of the six stages as "buckets." They suggested that each stage was a bucket containing methods and techniques which could be used to assist people with their problem-solving efforts. This analogy also suggested that the six stages or buckets could be rearranged, excluded, or included as necessary based upon specific problem-solving needs.

Although Isaksen and Treffinger emphasized the flexible nature of CPS in its description, the graphic depiction used to communicate the process continued to have its challenges. This particular view seemed to present an image of CPS as a one-way process in which problems were dropped in the "top" of the process and solutions were received at the "bottom."

It became apparent that tension was building between the description of CPS as a flexible process identifying stages of creative thinking, and the graphic depiction of CPS as a linear framework prescribing a pre-set series of stages or steps.

DIVERGENT PHASE	PROBLEM SENSITIVITY	CONVERGENT PHASE
Experiences, roles and situations are searched for messes . . . openness to experience; exploring opportunities.	**Mess-Finding** (Diverge / Converge)	Challenge is accepted and systematic efforts undertaken to respond to it.
Data are gathered; the situation is examined from many different viewpoints; information, impressions, feelings, etc., are collected.	**Data-Finding**	Most important data are identified and analyzed.
Many possible statements of problems and sub-problems are generated.	**Problem-Finding**	A working problem statement is chosen.
Many alternatives and possibilities for responding to the problem statement are developed and listed.	**Idea-Finding**	Ideas that seem most promising or interesting are selected.
Many possible criteria are formulated for reviewing and evaluating ideas.	**Solution-Finding**	Several important criteria are selected to evaluate ideas; criteria are used to evaluate, strengthen, and refine ideas.
Possible sources of assistance and resistance are considered; potential implementation steps are identified.	**Acceptance-Finding**	Most promising solutions are focused and prepared for action; specific plans are formulated to implement solution.

NEW CHALLENGES

Figure 2

1987: Breaking the Process Apart

In 1987 Isaksen and colleagues continued to work with the new process modifications but very quickly found that adding more explicit emphasis on the "front-end" of CPS, as well as the social roles of facilitator, client and resource group, made it nearly impossible to "run through" or "perform" the entire process. This finding was also confirmed when they examined how people actually applied CPS in real problem-solving situations. They found that people did not generally apply all six stages in sequence; they were instead used according to how they most naturally fit together to deal with a specific problem, challenge, or opportunity. As a result, Isaksen noticed that people tended to use CPS to clarify their understanding of problems, generate ideas, and plan for taking action. He concluded that the six stages of CPS could in fact be broken up into these three components of problem-solving activity and worked with Treffinger to name these new components.

As a result, in 1987 the description and depiction of CPS was changed to include three main components and six specific stages. Component titles—Understanding the Problem, Generating Ideas, and Planning for Action—were added. In 1989, colors and dashed lines were used to graphically distinguish the components from each other.

Although the new depiction of CPS had a component focus, the process graphic continued to emphasize a somewhat linear series of stages. However, reactions to teaching and learning CPS improved with the addition of components. The image of CPS as three components marked a transition away from a linear, six-step approach toward a more flexible componential approach. It is interesting to note that this direction was consistent with the view of CPS held by Osborn in 1967.

The 1990s Alternate Depictions of CPS

The Center for Studies in Creativity continues to focus on maintaining a current understanding of CPS and its application. Publications such as Isaksen and Treffinger (1991) and Treffinger and Isaksen (1992) are examples of this process of ongoing refinement and improvement.

Additional research has continued on developing alternate ways to view CPS. For example, in 1989, deliberate research was begun to examine the challenges surrounding the graphic depiction of CPS. A study was conducted which examined the way in which people naturally solved problems. Participants and students from a variety of programs and classes were asked to recall a problem they successfully solved and to draw or illustrate the process they used to solve it. Pershyn (1992) analyzed over 150 illustrations to determine the similarities and differences between natural approaches to problem solving.

The illustrations were synthesized into general graphic depictions based on the similarities and differences found in the drawings and then arranged along a continuum ranging from processes characterized as linear, orderly and targeted at one end, to random, spontaneous and complex at the other. It is interesting to note how similar the historical depictions of CPS are to those processes located on the linear, sequential side of the continuum.

These findings suggested that effective problem solving took on a variety of forms and that any process graphic which attempted to describe natural problem solving needed to take this into consideration. The research on graphic depictions of natural approaches to problem solving validated the need to take a different approach to representing CPS. Given the dynamic nature of natural problem solving, it was important that the new depiction be more representative of a wider array of problem-solving approaches.

From our experiences with studying CPS, as well as from being involved in its teaching and learning, we have found that identifying a common set of graphic depictions and language useful for sharing and discussing creative problem solving may be more appropriate than trying to identify or depict THE creative process. It was with this in mind that Isaksen and Dorval (1992) developed the current graphic depiction of CPS. The graphic included separate symbols for each of the three main components of activity: Understanding the Problem, Generating Ideas, and Planning for Action. These graphics were designed to illustrate the dynamic relationship between components and stages. Each component is characterized as having specific "inputs," "processing," and "outputs" which assist in the understanding of when and how to use the different elements of the process. This is shown in Figure 3 below.

COMPONENTS OF CPS

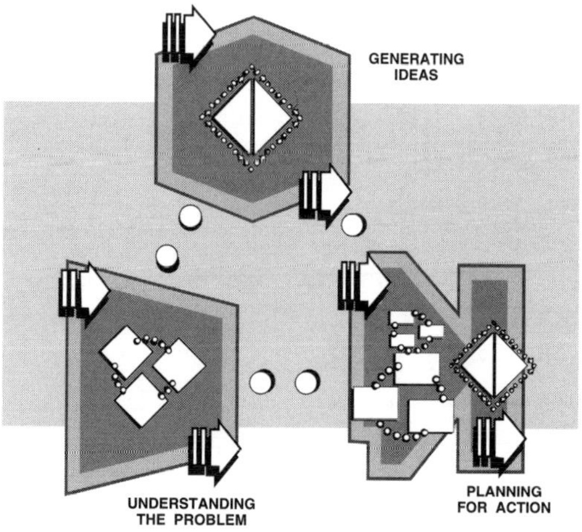

Figure 3

We present this view of CPS to create a common set of symbols and terminology which we can use to effectively learn and apply CPS. As we have noted earlier, to capture the complex and dynamic nature of natural problem-solving behavior in one graphic is a very difficult task.

This paper has attempted to summarize some of the major historical changes that have occurred on the CPS process. In our work with CPS, we believe it is important to emphasize that the purpose of having a model of the CPS process is not to replace participants' natural process, but to help enhance their natural approaches to problem solving. Research and development continues to find ways to make CPS more accessible and valuable to users. Although there has been a great deal of dynamic development over the past fifty years, we are pleased to be able to build upon a very rich tradition. Our future efforts should continue to be dynamic as we work to bridge theoretical creativity research from the behavioral, social, and cognitive sciences while striving to validate and extend the practical applications of CPS.

References

Firestien, R. L., & Treffinger, D. J. (1983). Ownership and converging essential ingredients of creative problem solving. *The Journal of Creative Behavior, 17*(1), 32-38.

Isaksen, S. G., & Dorval, K. B. (1992). *Creative approaches to problem solving.* Buffalo, NY: The Creative Problem Solving Group–Buffalo.

Isaksen, S. G., & Treffinger, D. J. (1985). *Creative problem solving: The basic course.* Buffalo, NY: Bearly Limited.

Isaksen, S. G., & Treffinger, D. J. (1991). Creative learning and problem solving. In A. Costa (Ed.), *Developing minds. Volume II: The programs* (pp. 89-94). Alexandria, VA: Association for Supervision and Curriculum Development.

Osborn, A. F. (1953). *Applied imagination.* New York: Scribner's.

Osborn, A. F. (1967). *Applied imagination.* New York: Scribner's.

Parnes, S. J. (1967). *Creative behavior guidebook.* New York: Scribner's.

Pershyn, G. (1992). An investigation into the graphic depictions of natural creative problem solving processes. Unpublished master's project, Buffalo State College, Buffalo, NY.

Treffinger, D. J., Isaksen, S. G., & Firestien, R. L. (1982). *The handbook of creative learning, Volume 1.* Williamsville, NY: Center for Creative Learning.

Treffinger, D. J., & Isaksen, S. G. (1992). *Creative Problem Solving: An introduction.* Sarasota, FL: Center for Creative Learning.

Scott G. Isaksen, Center for Studies in Creativity, 1329 North Forest Road, Suite D-15, Williamsville, NY 14221. Tel: (716) 689-2176. Education: Bachelor of Science in education; Master of Science in creativity from Buffalo State College; doctorate in curriculum planning from the University of Buffalo.

K. Brian Dorval, Creative Problem Solving Group–Buffalo, 1329 North Forest Road, Williamsville, NY 14221. Tel: (716) 689-2176.

Ruth B. Noller, 1040 Sylvan Drive, Sarasota, FL 34234. Tel: (813) 365-1935. Former codirector of the Center for Studies in Creativity in Buffalo.

Roger L. Firestien, Ph.D., Center for Studies in Creativity, Chase Hall 218, 1300 Elmwood Avenue, Buffalo, NY 14222. Tel: (716) 878-6223. Education: B.A. from the University of Northern Colorado; M.S. in creativity from Buffalo State College; Ph.D. in communication from the State University of New York at Buffalo.

PROFILING CREATIVITY: NATURE AND IMPLICATIONS OF A NEW RESEARCH PROGRAM

Scott G. Isaksen and Gerard J. Puccio

Introduction

This paper describes the nature of the major research initiative underway at the Center for Studies in Creativity, called the Profiling Project. This research initiative takes an ecological approach to understanding the dynamics of creativity (Harrington, 1990). The underlying methodological approach to this research initiative is an interactionist one. More specifically, the purpose of this research is to understand how aspects of the four fundamental domains of creativity (person, process, product, and press) interact to yield creative performance. The practical implications of this research initiative are described.

Rationale for the Profiling Project

Many scholars (MacKinnon, 1978; Mooney, 1963; Rhodes, 1961; Stein, 1968) agree that creativity research can be organized within four domains. Rhodes (1961) described these domains as the "four Ps" of creativity, namely person, process, product, and press (environment). Although Rhodes noted that creativity involves the simultaneous interaction of aspects from all four Ps, past investigations have tended to involve variables from a single facet. In a sense, past investigators have dealt with the multifaceted nature of creativity by separating it into more manageable areas of investigation. This separatist approach enabled researchers to focus their attention solely on variables within a specific facet, without concern for potential interaction effects created by other variables outside that particular facet. Where this historical approach to the study of creativity allowed researchers to more effectively manage the dynamic nature of creativity, this research did not reflect the multifaceted nature of this phenomenon (Isaksen, 1987; Murdock & Puccio, in press; Puccio, 1990). Put in other words, few investigators have explored how aspects of the person, the processes they use, the qualities of the products they create, and the nature of the environments in which they work interact to yield varying levels and styles of creative productivity. The absence of research that has examined the interaction of the four Ps limits practitioners' ability to effectively enhance individuals' creative potential.

Profiling Creativity: Definition and Implications

In a psychological sense, the term profiling is generally limited to a summary or sketch of an individual's abilities and traits. Typically, a profile evokes an image of a series of scores on various personality measures that have been linked to enhance their meaningfulness. However, for the proposed project the term profiling is defined more broadly. The intent of the proposed project is to move beyond the person facet when profiling creativity and to consider aspects from all four Ps. Thus, the following definition represents a conceptual starting point for this research project: *Profiling refers to the development of a framework that takes into consideration a constellation of personality characteristics, product qualities, dimensions of climate and culture, and process behaviors that help to understand, predict, and facilitate creative problem-solving performance.* A number of other writers have also argued for an interactionist or ecological approach to studying creativity (Harrington, 1990; Helson, 1988; Rhodes, 1961; Stein, 1975). However, the point of departure for the present research initiative is an explicit focus upon Creative Problem Solving (CPS). As the above conception of profiling suggests, this project will take into consideration aspects of each of the four Ps as they relate to CPS. The numerous tools and principles of this well-validated process offer a rich and well-defined foundation upon which to build the Profiling Project (Treffinger & Isaksen, 1992).

Implications of the Profiling Project

It is easy to anticipate many positive implications from the studies to be carried out within the Profiling Project. The following is an initial attempt to summarize some of these implications for practice.

Bridge between theory and practice. Perhaps the broadest implication associated with this multifaceted approach to creativity research is the explicit bridge it makes between theory and practice. By developing a profile of the four Ps, researchers will be examining interactions that occur in real situations. The separatist approach to the study of creativity focused on one facet and ignored the potential interaction effects between the variables isolated for study and others found in the four Ps. Despite researchers' previous efforts, the reality is that variables from the four Ps do not exist in isolation. Therefore, the explicit effort researchers will make in the Profiling Project to examine interaction effects will better represent the nature of creativity in real contexts.

Enhance transfer of research outcomes. The enhanced external validity of the research efforts carried out within the Profiling Project will, in turn, increase the degree to which research findings can be applied to real situations. Since the interactionist methodology employed in the Profiling

Project will better reflect the nature of creativity in natural settings, it should therefore be much easier to apply these findings to real situations. If this research shows, for example, what kinds of process approaches work best for what kinds of people and under different circumstances, then it should be much easier to predict and facilitate creativity in settings where these variables are present.

Stimulate further development of CPS. Knowledge concerning the various influences that interact with CPS will undoubtedly stimulate further development of this process model. For instance, information that suggests that CPS is particularly relevant and useful to individuals who work in certain environments and possess particular characteristics may foster the development of techniques or modifications that are useful for others in different circumstances. In short, findings from the Profiling Project will lead to a more comprehensive and flexible process framework and approach.

Improve transfer of CPS training. Findings from the Profiling Project will act as a powerful tool to help individuals transfer and apply their training in CPS. If individuals, for example, are aware that their problem-solving preferences increase the likelihood that they will produce certain kinds of products, and they currently face a problem that requires a different solution, they can then consciously select CPS techniques that will help them to meet the demands of that situation.

Enhance effective facilitation of CPS. Armed with information about various interaction effects among the four Ps, individuals will be able to better design and lead CPS sessions. Facilitators will be able to use information about the people to be involved in their sessions, the products they produce, and the nature of environments they work in to develop more effective process plans. This approach will likely lead to enhanced process outcomes, as well as more satisfied participants.

As previously noted, these implications do not represent an exhaustive list. The writers believe that they represent a few of the many implications that will be derived from the Profiling Project. The writers invite our colleagues in the field of creativity to react to this research program. Your suggestions will assist us in further developing this initiative.

References

Harrington, D. M. (1990). The ecology of creativity: A psychological perspective. In M. A. Runco & R. S. Albert (Eds.), *Theories of creativity* (pp. 143-169). Beverly Hills, CA: Sage.

Helson, R. (1988). The creative personality. In K. Grønhaug & G. Kaufmann (Eds.), *Innovation: A cross-disciplinary perspective* (pp. 29-64). Oslo, Norway: Norwegian University Press.

Isaksen, S. G. (1987). Introduction: An orientation to the frontiers of creativity research. In S. G. Isaksen (Ed.), *Frontiers of creativity research: Beyond the basics* (pp. 1-26). Buffalo, NY: Bearly Limited.

MacKinnon, D. W. (1978). *In search of human effectiveness.* Buffalo, NY: Bearly Limited.

Mooney, R. L. (1963). A conceptual model for integrating four approaches to the identification of creative talent. In C. W. Taylor & F. Barron (Eds.), *Scientific creativity: Its recognition and development* (pp. 331-340). New York: Wiley.

Murdock, M. C., & Puccio, G. J. (in press). A contextual organizer for conducting creativity research. In S. G. Isaksen, M. C. Murdock, R. L. Firestien, & D. J. Treffinger (Eds.), *Understanding and recognizing creativity: The emergence of a discipline.* Norwood, NJ: Ablex.

Puccio, G. J. (1990). Person-environment fit: Using Kirton's Adaptor-Innovator theory to determine the effect of stylistic fit upon stress, job satisfaction, and creative performance. Unpublished doctoral thesis, University of Manchester Institute of Science and Technology, Manchester, England.

Rhodes, M. (1961). An analysis of creativity. *Phi Delta Kappan, 42,* 305-310.

Stein, M. I. (1968). Creativity. In E. F. Boragatta & W. W. Lambert (Eds.), *Handbook of personality theory and research* (pp. 900-942). Chicago: Rand McNally.

Stein, M. I. (1975). *Stimulating creativity: Group procedures—Vol. II.* New York: Academic Press.

Treffinger, D. J., & Isaksen, S. G. (1992). *Creative Problem Solving: An introduction.* Sarasota, FL: Center for Creative Learning.

~~~

Scott G. Isaksen, Center for Studies in Creativity, 1329 North Forest Road, Suite D-15, Williamsville, NY 14221. Tel: (716) 689-2176. Education: Bachelor of Science in education; Master of Science in creativity from Buffalo State College; doctorate in curriculum planning from the University of Buffalo.

Gerard J. Puccio, Center for Studies in Creativity, State University College at Buffalo, Chase Hall 244, 1300 Elmwood Avenue, Buffalo, NY 14222. Tel: (716) 878-6223. Education: Bachelor of Arts in psychology; Master of Science in creativity from Buffalo State College; doctorate of philosophy in organizational psychology from the University of Manchester, England.

NEW INSIGHTS INTO DIFFERENT STYLES OF CREATIVITY

Leslie J. Jones

The Burkhart/Horth Model

In their paper (see "Discovering the Unseen Leader" in this book, pp. 127-138) Robert Burkhart and David Horth discussed the forms of communication and inquiry which characterize management and leadership. They described the Inquiry Process Grid which looks at the processes used in different ways by people who have different backgrounds and personality characteristics and hence different ways of looking at the world. They spoke of the four primary orientations which form part of their Inquiry Process Grid and which they have labelled as follows:

> REALIST—is essentially a Sensory viewpoint and tends to focus on a factual, down-to-earth, rational approach which values tradition, decisiveness, and dependability.
> DESIGNER—is a Cognitive viewpoint which focuses on competence, clarity, control, and precision and which values objectivity, perfection, and playing by the rules.
> EXPRESSIONIST—is an Affective viewpoint involving feelings, emotions, enthusiasm, and pleasure and values kindness, openness, loyalty, and self-awareness.
> INTUITIVE—is a Transformative viewpoint associated with an insightful, self-starting, empathic and integrative approach which values uniqueness, flexibility, courage, and a philosophical outlook.

My own research set out to devise an instrument to measure these four orientations and to compare the results with those from other inventories measuring similar characteristics.

Development of an Instrument

In their explanation of the model Burkhart and Horth listed self descriptors for each of the four orientations. The author took twenty adjectives from each of these four lists and presented them as an alphabetical listing of eighty words from which respondents were required to select the twenty items which best described themselves. The inventory was then completed by 41 MBA students at a residential school for the Open University's Creative Management course. The respondents also completed the Kirton Adaption-Innovation Inventory (KAI) and the Jones Inventory of Barriers to Effective Problem Solving (JIB). The two inventories measure individual differences in the way people approach the problem-solving and decision-making processes, respectively.

The JIB is an instrument for investigating psychological barriers to problem solving. It looks at four different types of barriers, with a high score suggesting that an individual is blocked on that particular barrier. Strategic Barriers are connected with the individual's preferred approach to the problem-solving process and include aspects such as imagination, ability to tolerate uncertainty, and openness to new ideas. Values Barriers reflect personal values, beliefs, and attitudes and the degree of flexibility displayed in applying them. Perceptual Barriers indicate sensual acuity and awareness of the environment. Self-image Barriers relate to preparedness to assert oneself and make use of the resources available.

The KAI is a well-validated and widely used measure of problem-solving and decision-making style and describes the way in which individuals are likely to behave in problem-solving situations. People with low scores have been described by Michael Kirton as Adaptors and those with high scores he calls Innovators. The types of behavior associated with each of these is described below:

The Adaptor—Seeks solutions to problems in tried and tested ways. Maintains accuracy and attention to detail over long periods of time. Rarely challenges rules; is well able to use the space within them. Prefers to work within given structures; may find it hard to break out.

The Innovator—Queries definition of problems and their assumptions. Is easily bored and quick to delegate routine tasks. Has little respect for past custom. Creates own structures but it may be hard to get others to accept them.

The results of the Burkhart/Horth inventory were then discussed with each student after explaining the Inquiry Process Grid. In the vast majority of cases it was seen to represent a true picture of the preferred approaches of each individual.

Development of Hypotheses

In terms of the internal relationships between the four orientations it was my expectation that there would be a significant negative correlation between the Intuitive and Expressionist categories, on the one hand, and the Realist and

Designer categories on the other. I did not expect that there would be any significant correlation between either Intuitive and Expressionist or Realist and Designer.

In relation to the JIB, I expected, on the basis of comparisons with other measures of creativity and thinking styles, to see significant positive correlations between both Strategic and Self-image Barriers and Realist and Designer scores, less significant positive correlations for the Values Barrier and virtually no correlation for Perceptual Barriers. For the Intuitive and Expressionist scores I would expect a similar pattern but correlated negatively.

For the KAI, in the light of a very wide range of comparisons with other personality and creativity measures, I would expect significant positive correlations between KAI scores and Intuitive and Expressionist scores and negative correlations between KAI and Realist and Designer.

Experimental Data

The data from the three instruments were collected and correlated with each other using the Pearson Product-Moment Correlation method. The results are shown below:

	JIB			KAI		BURKHART/HORTH		
	Values	Perceptual	Self-image	Total	Realist	Designer	Expressionist	Intuitive
Strategic	0.33	0.47	0.42	-0.53	0.41	0.51	-0.38	-0.54
Values		0.03	0.08	-0.17	0.12	0.18	-0.11	-0.18
Perceptual			0.36	-0.23	0.14	0.35	-0.21	-0.27
Self-image				-0.29	0.40	0.36	-0.36	-0.43
KAI Total					-0.36	-0.48	0.38	0.44
Realist						0.15	-0.60	-0.51
Designer							-0.60	-0.52
Expressionist								0.10

Significance Levels
Probability	<0.1	<0.01	<0.001
Value of r	0.26	0.40	0.47

Discussion of Results

As predicted Realist and Designer are negatively correlated with Intuitive and Expressionist at the 0.001 level, even on so small a sample as 41. Less predictable was the distinction between the sub-categories within these groups. The very low correlations of these subdivisions demonstrates the accuracy and thoroughness with which Burkhart and Horth have chosen their descriptors for the four orientations.

The correlations with KAI were all significant in the directions predicted though the degree of correlation was not as great as expected.

With JIB, the Strategic and Self-image correlations were as expected but the Values, though in the predicted direction, had no significant correlation with any category. Conversely, the Perceptual Barrier had an unexpectedly significant correlation with Designer and Intuitive, both in the direction any correlation might have been expected.

The overall effect of these results is to suggest that Realists and Designers are likely to be blocked on Strategy and Self-image. They are likely to prefer proven methods, operate best within clear structures and guidelines, and have a low tolerance of ambiguity. They may also lack assertiveness, be undemonstrative, and be unwilling to seek help from others. Intuitives and Expressives are unlikely to be blocked in the above-mentioned areas and will prefer looser structures, be happier to try out new ideas, and are likely to treat life less seriously. They are also more likely to ensure that their views are heard, disclose their feelings more easily, and be more prepared to involve others.

Conclusions

This model is different from most which are used to categorize behavior and personality in that it defines the processes people use rather than their fixed personality attributes. Another attractive aspect of the Inquiry Process Grid is that it is not just a theoretical model tested out on a suitable group of subjects. It is a practically grounded model deduced from observation and analysis of the different ways that writers set about their work. I am satisfied from the results obtained that this model has face, content, and concurrent validity and that the concepts will transfer unchanged into managerial problem-solving and decision-making strategies.

Leslie J. Jones, Les Jones and Associates, 30 Beryl Avenue, Tottington, Bury, Lancs BL8 3NF United Kingdom. Tel: +44 204 882950. Education: Degree in psychology; Master's degree from Manchester Business School.

MANAGING CREATIVE PEOPLE AT WORK

Will McWhinney

The purpose of this article is to identify the characteristics of highly creative scientists in order to suggest how to best support and manage their efforts. Differences that are important to this purpose can be grouped into those which describe
- the way in which a person works,
- the way in which he or she interacts with the environment,
- the ways in which a manager can both improve the creative person's effectiveness and manage his or her performance.

The table on pages 172-173 presents characterizations of the modes of creativity in scientific work that are derived from theoretical considerations, empirical studies, and observations. Its purpose is heuristic, aimed at helping us more accurately assess these qualities and their variations. Eight characteristics of the creative modes are presented.

TYPES OF CREATIVE WORK

Each creative task calls on a particular mode of work as described in this article. A manager needs to pay attention to the match between the task mode and that which is most appropriate to the creative abilities of the individual worker—scientist, designer, mathematician, etc.

CREATIVE WORK PROCESSES

The typical work processes of each of the modes is described, comparing them to the accepted theories of creative behavior, looking particularly at differences in the use of material, time involved in reflection and incubation, the right-left mind dominance, and patterns of learning.

PEOPLE WHO EXEMPLIFY THIS MODE

People of note whose work epitomized achievement in each of these modes are listed to give the reader an image of this mode of work at its best.

PSYCHO-SOCIAL DYNAMICS

Perhaps the most important set of characteristics the manager needs to know about a creative worker is the psycho-social dynamics that drive a person's engagement with the creative effort.

DESIRED TASK ENVIRONMENT

Our understanding of the likes and dislikes of scientific personnel for various spatial arrangements, privacy, settings, and facilities is still mostly

CHARACTERISTICS OF FOUR CREATIVE MODES

Mode & Type of Creation	Creative Processes	Sample Creators	Psycho-social Dynamics
Mythic Grand schemes; fundamental new designs working from metaphors & ungrounded ideas. ONTA: Symbols	Intuitive, working out of 'primary processes' Uses classic creative sequence. Long incubation periods (up to 20 years) Imaging (in 3/4 dimens.) Right Mode Thinking Learning style: mixed* *Knock upon silence for an answering music*	Goethe† Nikola Tesla Heisenberg Richard Feynman Picasso† Blake W. B. Yeats Mozart	The effective creator is integrated, has access to intuition, the feminine*, generally individuated Unaware of others and their values
Logic Mathematics, Logical systems Architecture/Organization of abstract elements ONTA: Relations	Heavy use of formal metaphors and patterns to gain instant insight; long incubation periods, strong drive for elegance Learning style: Assimilator	Euler (1707-1783) Einstein† Weierstrass Bach Turner (English painter) Mark Rothko	Typically accepting of authority, but isolated from social engagement Emotionally dependent, low individuation, not conflicted Relatively isolated from social exchange
Dialectic Resolution of design issues, contradictions Value aspects of scientific issues ONTA: Relations (mixed)	"Breaking rules" Violations of assumptions Learning Style: Divergent, Problematic Right & Left Mode Thinking	Gödel Charles S. Pierce Nietzsche Gênet Andy Warhol	A dis-integrated person, in conflict with authority Mood not easily predictable Likely to be concerned with rights and values Less well connected to intuitive (rt. mode) than the mythic, but good at spotting contradictions and anomalies
Design Physically realizable systems Architectures ONTA: Relations/Objects	Constructive Learning Style: Convergent Particularly attuned to organizing/combining ideas and elements into a working whole Left Mode Thinking evaluative	John Roebling (Brooklyn Bridge) Carl Sagan	More adaptable than those using the other modes and more constrained in their thinking Masculine orientation, literal Sensation oriented Socially effective
L&C: Creat.Char. Jan 88 WMcW	* Following Kolb's Learning Style Indicator (1987)	†These people obviously transcend classification!	* Whether male or female, the mythic creator needs access to the feminine.

Discovering Creativity   RESEARCH

Desired Task Environment	Incentive & Career	Training	Supervision & Team Play
Varied, high stimulus Richly provided resources Conversation, exchanges Variable/unprogrammed incubation periods Free from institutional constraints	Praise from power people, particularly from outside of the organization Control of resources and people used in work Freedom from controls and direction Visible perks CAREER†: Episodic & Spiral	Self-esteem, affirming Dream/Fantasy work Contact with high-level ideas Journals and story telling; metaphor play Reading history Pacing: meditation	The less the better; desires sole leadership of project Can work well with administrator who 'controls from beneath' Not budget conscious Almost completely avoids teamwork, except as an occasion to excel
ISOLATED, quiet, clear of interruptions Occasional intense conversations with peers Free of time pressures and institutional demands Often so highly focused as to be able to work anywhere	Peer and professional recognition Occasions to publish and discuss work Quality work space CAREER: Steady-State	Developing patterns in movement, e.g., martial arts, music and design Formal games, metaphors and puzzles	Almost meaningless; deeply self-directed in response to the problem Not bothered by rules which do not interfere with work; may even enjoy compliance if there is some degree of closure attained Some can be excellent team players, sometimes
Similar to the mythic, more engagement with peers; less incubation	Praise and support from colleagues and authorities Visible perks Attention from management even if constraining Opportunities to 'work the system' CAREER: Episodic & Linear	Design of games Dialectical exercises, puns, riddle solving Personal therapy to gain access to unconscious	Finds authorities and budgetary controls difficult Often tests rules and directives Teamwork is competitive, perhaps enlivening
Structured spaces with tools of the required types Easy communication with others; organizational support facilities Easy access to information on new materials, processes, and competitive designs	Organizational power & rewards; credit within the organization Material advantages Having supervision over work groups CAREER: Steady-State & Linear	Modelling of objects and processes Visualization Knowledge about material and their uses Sharpening sensory discrimination	Accepts authority if not overly confining Works well with colleagues in programs—if well managed Enjoys being a supervisor or manager Works well within resource and time budgets
	†See Appendix I for a description of Career styles		

RESEARCH *Discovering Creativity*

anecdotal though some experimental work has been reported on the role played by the environment in enhancing creativity. The preferences are often unexpected as well as critical for achieving high productivity.

INCENTIVES AND CAREERS

A central element of a person's psychodynamic makeup is what one feels best rewards his efforts and provides expectations of a continuingly satisfactory work situation. Lacking this knowledge of the creative staff, a manager often makes critical mistakes in the design of the organization, work assignments, and promotions.

TRAININGS

The immediate concern that led to this study was the recognition that much of the training in creativity given industrial scientists, as well as almost every other person doing creative work, is designed without recognition of differences in styles and needs. Such mismatch of trainings and modes of work clearly inhibits creativity.

SUPERVISION AND TEAM PLAY

The style of supervision produces sharply differing impacts according to the creative mode of the staff. There also are significant differences in the way the creative person works in teams, as would be expected from their psychosocial dynamics.

The entries in the table are a mixture of empirical data, extrapolation from related studies, and best estimates based on a few cases. Its best use, at this point, is a base for further research and suggestions for those who have to manage groups of creative scientists while we wait for the results.

The Training and Management of the Creative Scientist

The incentive for the exploration reported here was a need to find the most supportive ways to manage scientists in a laboratory setting (at Sarnoff and Bell Laboratories). From early discussions it was apparent that those who provided supervisory and educational support had insufficient understanding of the ways in which creative people work. Many of them made the same assumption about managing creative people as others have made about creativity—that all creative people are alike. Those scientists and managers who appear to be most successful use widely differing approaches, but the variations in their success is not accounted for simply by differences in their supervisory skills. Rather, we hypothesized, the variations were linked to how well are matched the leadership, mentoring, motivating, and training of those who were attracted to each of the different sorts of work in the laboratories.

One of the first inferences from the theory of change I have developed for large-scale social change in *Paths of Change: Strategic Choices for Organizations and Society* (McWhinney, 1992) is that if the creative process differed between the people and disciplines as much as was apparent in this laboratory, then the training and support given the laboratory's management staff should be differentiated accordingly. The strongest evidence for this conclusion is deduced from the combination of data that demonstrate well-established differences in personalities of the scientists. These differences can be clustered to some degree by the kinds of research problems; and, these research issues themselves call for different responses for their resolution. The outcome of this investigation is encapsulated in the qualities identified in the table. It provides a guide to developing programs for enhancing both the creativity and the management of creative people.

This view of creativity indicates that the differing creative regimes call on such divergent skills that people using them should have quite different programs of training and *enhancements*. For example, the designer needs practice at seeing what is, while the mythic must go beyond what is to what is not yet. Similarly, the logician is looking for what is necessary in the system, while the dialectician is looking for what is there but is not necessary (or consistent).

The support of creative people requires diverse arrangements. The promotion to a managerial position, which so enhances the world of the designers, simply invades the creative work of the logicians and locks the mythics into a structure that they deny even exists. The logicians use management as an umbrella; the mythics use management as an instrument to manifest their ideas; the dialecticians view management as a counterpoint in a struggle to unfold tangled complexities. The creative person's supervisor may also play different roles. In the typical industrial organization the manager and workers are rewarded by their contributions to the firm. In the research world, the creative workers are rewarded as much by their creation (intrinsic motivation) as by reward from the organization. The manager is in a different role system; just as the coach works for his athletes, so the manager must support his scientists.

The managing of creative people is a creative task, for all creative people are not alike. The creative person—his or her uniqueness—must be considered in order to maximize the expectations of the organization and the individual. It is my belief that the four creative modes reported here provide some insight into the uniqueness of creative people and their management.

Reference

McWhinney, W. (1992). *Paths of change: Strategic choices for organizations and society.* Newbury Park, CA: Sage.

~~~

Will McWhinney, Fielding Institute, 589 Grand Boulevard, Venice, CA 90291. Tel: (310) 392-1343. Education: Doctorate in industrial administration from Carnegie-Mellon University.

A WORLD OF IDEAS: AN INNOVATIVE RESEARCH APPROACH FOR BUSINESS

Kelly B. Morgan

Four years ago I embarked on a journey of inquiry and exploration that revealed an enlightening world of ideas. Through the eyes of many talented people from a broad spectrum of interests and concerns (such people as poet and essayist Wendell Berry, anthropologist Mary Catherine Bateson, historian Page Smith, sculptor Richard Hunt, and educator John W. Gardner) I examined and reexamined corporate America's most cherished beliefs and prevailing practices. My findings are presented in the forthcoming book, *Beyond Potential: A Revolution in Management Thought.* This book offers a new philosophy of work that is designed to enable individuals and companies alike to reach their potential and beyond. Combining history, critique, analysis, and strategies for action, it identifies how we can turn corporate America around for the benefit of employees as well as for the betterment of our economy and our society.

The first step was to identify management problems based on the views and experiences of talented employees. Over three years, I interviewed nearly 200 well-educated, intellectually ambitious, and highly motivated professionals who work in a variety of fields, such as banking, marketing, and law. Their strong indictment of the status quo, combined with their surprisingly high levels of discontent and dissatisfaction, led me to realize that we need to *rethink our entire system of work.*

Along with other noted intellectuals, David Bohm, a quantum physicist, asserts that for any system in distress, solutions can never be found within the system itself. "You have to go outside the system to see the inconsistencies, the incoherence. There's no solution to the problem within the system because *the system* is the problem" (D. Bohm, personal communication, February 14, 1991). Following this advice and keeping the concerns and frustrations of talented employees in mind, I set out to explore the larger world of ideas. I consulted the written work of such thinkers as Sir Isaiah Berlin, George Orwell, philosopher Hannah Arendt, historians Barbara Tuchman and Richard Hofstadter, and journalist David Halberstam. I also interviewed David Bohm and 50 other intelligent and talented people involved in a variety of endeavors. Throughout this process, I learned valuable lessons about conducting research:

Approach a Research Project as an Artist Approaches a Painting: Mihaly Csikszentmihalyi, a psychologist, has found that when artists are working, they rarely talk about the results—that is, creating something beautiful. Instead, they talk about and concentrate on the process itself, such as coming to grips with the canvas. In this manner, they produce greater works of art. Thus, in my research efforts, I focused on the process rather than on the outcome.

Look for Insight Wherever It Can Be Found: The painter and sculptor, Izhar Patkin, shared this advice with me: "As an artist, you're always working. You're always sucking in ideas—you're like a sponge. Whether you are watching TV, eating, talking to somebody, traveling, looking at other people's work, or whatever, you are constantly filling up your memory bank."

Challenge the Underlying Assumptions: Throughout my investigations, I followed David Bohm's advice. Whereas most business research focuses on senior management's viewpoint, I found that by asking employees what they think, many otherwise overlooked inconsistencies were readily revealed.

Consider the Gestalt: The prevailing tendency of our time is toward increasing specialization, but this penchant can greatly hinder our ability to understand the whole. By taking a generalized rather than a specialized view, I was able to find connections between seemingly unrelated topics and to address the increasing complexities of business in a more realistic way.

Abandon the Model-company Approach: In the early 1980s, Tom Peters and Robert Waterman examined successful U.S. corporations to find out what traits they had in common. They documented their findings in the best-selling *In Search of Excellence* (Peters & Waterman, 1982). While this approach proved enlightening at the time, I found that it no longer provided adequate insight, especially given the fact that the employees I interviewed said that there are no "model" companies.

Seek Out Feedback: One of the greatest strengths of my research effort was the feedback I received from others, people who represented a variety of opinions and backgrounds. Some of my reviewers, who ranged in age from 28 to 75, had little or no business experience. Others had run their own companies or were senior executives. Yet others represented the "subject" of my book—talented, professional employees.

Focus on the Qualitative, Not Only the Quantitative: It's all too easy to focus on those factors that can be measured and to dismiss those that defy precise enumeration. How often we hear the refrain, "Show me the numbers!" This bias leads to many problems: it encourages us to ignore what can't be measured; it limits our ability to respond to emerging trends; and it often encourages us to simplify reality rather than to deal with it in all its complexity.

Welcome Subjectivity: Too often we prefer the objective over the subjective. But the value of welcoming subjectivity—that is, recognizing that in most situations there is no *absolute* right or wrong answer, is considerable. First, it enables us to appreciate a broader range of views, making us more open and flexible. Second, it provides us with greater psychological freedom to accept or reject the opinions of others—as well as our own.

Don't Look for Solutions: In many cases, we set out to solve a "problem" when no solution to it exists. Jacques Barzun (1991), the scholar, teacher, and critic, observes:

> A problem is a definable difficulty; it falls within certain limits and the right answer gets rid of it. But the difficulty—not the problem—the difficulty of making a living, finding a mate, keeping a friend who has a jealous, cantankerous disposition cannot be dealt with in the same way—it has no solution. It calls for endless improvisation, some would say "creativity." (p. 47)

Similarly, because there is no solution to the ongoing difficulty of running a business, setting out to find the solution is folly. The best we can do is to look endlessly for new alternatives—better ways to address current difficulties.

References

Barzun, J. (1991). Television and the child . . . but not what you think. In M. Philipson (Ed.), *Begin here: The forgotten conditions of teaching and learning.* Chicago: The University of Chicago Press.
Peters, T. J., & Waterman, R. H., Jr. (1982). *In search of excellence: Lessons from America's best run companies.* New York: HarperCollins.

~~~

Kelly B. Morgan, 1213 Judson Avenue, Evanston, IL 60202-1316. Tel: (708) 869-3690. Education: B.S. degree in commerce from the University of Virginia.

BRIDGING THEORY AND PRACTICE: DISCIPLINARY IMPLICATIONS FOR THE FIELD OF CREATIVITY

Mary C. Murdock, Scott G. Isaksen, Suzanne K. Vosburg, and Dave A. Lugo

Issues surrounding the necessity, value, and impact of identifying creativity as a discipline are controversial (Magyari-Beck, 1991; Treffinger & Isaksen, 1992). Who should determine such a move and what process would be appropriate? What criteria should be used? What are the implications of such a step?

Background

Murdock, Isaksen, Vosburg, and Lugo (in press) noted that, "regardless of whether or not one agrees with the necessity to describe creativity as a discipline, the need to further organize, develop and structure inquiry in our field is now and has been of concern." In response to this concern, plenary and small group discussions and data were analyzed during the four-day 1990 International Working Creativity Research Conference held in Buffalo, New York (Lugo, in preparation; Vosburg, 1992).

Twenty-nine invited scholars from nine countries convened to discuss and debate the current conceptual status of the creativity field. The conference provided an opportunity to structure a forum to examine the disciplinary potential of the field.

After the conference, transcribed data of conversations and interaction among the scholars in both the plenary and working groups were analyzed within the framework of Phenix's (1962) criteria for a discipline. Phenix proposed three criteria by which to examine disciplinary rigor:

- Analytic Simplification refers to how effectively a discipline simplifies understanding through a conceptual system that provides a common framework of ideas;

- Synthetic Coordination refers to how effectively a discipline is interconnected through its identifiable significant patterns and relationships; and

- Dynamism refers to the degree to which a discipline contains the principle of growth by inviting further synthesis and analysis.

Data from this analysis indicated that elements of all three criteria, although manifested in different ways and in varying degrees, were present (Lugo, in preparation; Murdock, Isaksen, Vosburg, & Lugo, in press; Vosburg, 1992). In relation to Phenix's criteria, the answer to the original question "Can creativity be called a discipline?" posed by Isaksen and Murdock (1990) should be "yes." Developing creativity as a discipline could increase the social acceptance, or legitimacy, of creative studies. It also could provide a means to more effectively educate or instruct and guide the organization and evaluation of conceptual development within the field. Perhaps the most important outcome of this process would be the development of a common vocabulary for the field of creativity.

Results

In order to rigorously develop the disciplinary potential that has been identified in the field of creativity, further steps must be taken to strengthen a deliberate synthetic coordination. The challenge is where to begin and how to focus energy toward identified common issues that need coordination. Data from the 1990 conference proceedings indicated five areas that need strengthening to improve disciplinary rigor. Not surprisingly, each of these broad issues contained sub-issues.

Five Disciplinary Issues and Sub-issues

1. Developing a framework or reference point that will effectively organize the domain of creativity. Sub-issues include:
   - Designing a framework that is unique to creativity.
   - Organizing and sorting existing frameworks within the broader one, so that each maintains its identity.
   - Locating a common point of reference for professional interchange and interaction around new and existing frameworks.

2. Effectively organizing research to increase deliberate theory development in the field. Sub-issues include:
   - Structuring the multifaceted aspects of creativity so that their theoretical similarities and differences can be productively used.
   - Achieving general acceptance for research frameworks.
   - Allowing for research frameworks to be broad enough to integrate previous work.
   - Preserving and using theoretical concepts from former research.

Within this issue of theory development are two other topics: cross-cultural research and psychometrics (El-Aasar, in press; Raina, in press; Runco, in press; Wechsler, in press). Sub-issues here concern:
- Exploring the nature and nurture of creativity in the cultures of all countries.
- Improving the current level of psychometric rigor in creativity assessment.

3. Identifying, using, developing, and communicating methods and models that are robust. Sub-issues are:
   - Identifying appropriate models that stem from, relate to, or enhance creativity concepts.
   - Operationalizing models in a variety of contexts.
   - Developing new methods and models for targeted use in creativity studies.

4. Effectively blending theory and practice in the design, delivery, and transference of creativity concepts (Novelli, in press; Talbot, in press). Sub-issues include:
   - Selecting appropriate models for training/teaching environments.
   - Accessing the impact of creativity training.

5. Developing effective collaborative structures. Sub-issues include:
   - Identifying the ways that a network or invisible college in creativity studies could and ought to function.
   - Strengthening use of shared time.

Each issue depends upon the clear communication of ideas which would be facilitated by common language.

Conclusion

Regardless of whether or not one agrees with the importance of the disciplinarity for creative studies, using criteria for a discipline can assist us in getting our conceptual house in order. Deciding how to plan for effective action around the issues that have been identified in the conference proceedings data is no simple matter. Even with the brief overview provided in this paper, the implicit integration of identified disciplinary issues is clearly, in and of itself, a challenge to effective action.

How do we, as creativity professionals, take action on these data? We would suggest several ways to begin. There is no set priority for tackling the issues that have been identified—they *all* need attention. First, set a priority that will be both practical and appropriate to your own situation and interests. Find something in which you can invest. Second, no one issue is the purview of any particular individual, group, or organization. They are all the purview of any person who identifies him- or herself as a creativity professional.

In examining the issues and sub-issues from the conference data, however, there is one theme present in each issue: the need for a common, shared language and even terminology that will increase effective internal and external communication. Acting on that theme necessitates a commitment to the development of a common language. It is beyond the scope of this paper to elaborate on the semantic challenges that would be involved, but we would suggest that effort in this area is an important first step which can be taken immediately by conscientious creativity professionals in their activities. The semantic issues noted in the conference data not only provide a point for reflection, but also a challenge for change—if not for the sake of developing creativity itself as a discipline, then for the sake of the self-discipline that mastery in a field demands of a professional.

References

El-Aasar, S. (in press). Human potential: An exploration of the role of creativity from an Arab perspective. In S. G. Isaksen, M. C. Murdock, R. L. Firestien, & D. J. Treffinger (Eds.), *Understanding and recognizing creativity: The emergence of a discipline.* Norwood, NJ: Ablex.

Isaksen, S. G., & Murdock, M. C. (1990). The outlook for the study of creativity: An emerging discipline? *Studia Psychologicia, 32,* 53-80.

Lugo, D. (in preparation). Unpublished master's project, Center for Studies in Creativity. Buffalo State College, Buffalo, New York.

Magyari-Beck, I. (1991). Dignity of creative studies. *International Creativity Network Newsletter, 1*(3), 1-2.

Murdock, M. C., Isaksen, S. G., Vosburg, S. K., & Lugo, D. (in press). The progress and potential of an emerging discipline: An analysis of the proceedings of the 1990 International Working Creativity Research Conference. In S. G. Isaksen, M. C. Murdock, R. L. Firestien, & D. J. Treffinger (Eds.), *Understanding and recognizing creativity: The emergence of a discipline.* Norwood, NJ: Ablex.

Novelli, L. (in press). Using alternative perspectives to build more robust theories of organizational creativity. In S. G. Isaksen, M. C. Murdock, R. L. Firestien, & D. J. Treffinger (Eds.), *Understanding and recognizing creativity: The emergence of a discipline.* Norwood, NJ: Ablex.

Phenix, P. H. (1962). The disciplines as curriculum content. In A. H. Passow (Ed.), *Curriculum crossroads: A report of a curriculum conference* (pp. 57-65). New York, NY: Teachers College Press.

Raina, M. K. (in press). Ethnocentric confines in creativity research. In S. G. Isaksen, M. C. Murdock, R. L. Firestien, & D. J. Treffinger (Eds.), *Understanding and recognizing creativity: The emergence of a discipline*. Norwood, NJ: Ablex.

Runco, M. A. (in press). Cognitive and psychometric issues in creativity research. In S. G. Isaksen, M. C. Murdock, R. L. Firestien, & D. J. Treffinger (Eds.), *Understanding and recognizing creativity: The emergence of a discipline*. Norwood, NJ: Ablex.

Talbot, R. (in press). Creativity in the organizational context: Implications for training. In S. G. Isaksen, M. C. Murdock, R. L. Firestien, & D. J. Treffinger (Eds.), *Understanding and recognizing creativity: The emergence of a discipline*. Norwood, NJ: Ablex.

Treffinger, D. J., & Isaksen, S. G. (1992). *Creative Problem Solving: An introduction*. Sarasota, FL: Center for Creative Learning.

Vosburg, S. K. (1992). The progress and potential of an emerging discipline: An analysis of the proceedings of the 1990 International Working Creativity Research Conference. Unpublished master's project. Buffalo State College, Buffalo, New York.

Wechsler, S. (in press). Issues on stimulating creativity in the schools: A South American perspective. In S. G. Isaksen, M. C. Murdock, R. L. Firestien, & D. J. Treffinger (Eds.), *Understanding and recognizing creativity: The emergence of a discipline*. Norwood, NJ: Ablex.

~~~

Mary C. Murdock, Center for Studies in Creativity, State University College at Buffalo, 218 Chase Hall, Buffalo, NY 14222. Tel: (716) 878-6223. Education: Bachelor of Arts in English from the University of North Carolina at Greensboro; Master's of education in gifted education; doctorate in educational psychology from the University of Georgia.

Scott G. Isaksen, Center for Studies in Creativity, 1329 North Forest Road, Suite D-15, Williamsville, NY 14221. Tel: (716) 689-2176. Education: Bachelor of Science in education; Master of Science in creativity from Buffalo State College; doctorate in curriculum planning from the University of Buffalo.

Suzanne K. Vosburg, Department of Cognitive Psychology, University of Bergen, Sydneshaugen 2, Bergen, Norway N-5007. Education: Bachelor of Arts in music from the University of Michigan, Master of Science degree in creativity and innovation from Buffalo State College.

Dave A. Lugo, Creative Education Foundation, 1050 Union Rd. #4, West Seneca, NY 14224. Tel: (716) 675-3181. Education: Currently completing Master of Science degree in creativity and innovation at Buffalo State College.

CRITICAL THINKING: AN ESSENTIAL INGREDIENT FOR EFFECTIVE LEADERSHIP

Luke Novelli and Sylvester Taylor

The premise presented is that new concepts of leadership need to evolve in order for organizations to keep pace with the rapidly changing environments. An important part of that evolution is the challenge of incorporating critical thinking into leadership processes so that people can mold tomorrow's institutions and organizations in ways that are simultaneously efficient, effective, humane, and just.

In this paper, we argue that "environmental turbulence" and high degrees of interdependence create dilemmas, paradoxes, and opportunities for organizations. Since critical thinking is a primary tool for dealing with dilemmas and paradoxes, the support and encouragement of critical thinking is a key characteristic of effective leadership processes. First the context of current and future leadership challenges is explored. The authors' approach to leadership is described, relating critical thinking to leadership. Ideas about developing leadership for the future context and examples are provided.

Contextual Features

Environmental Turbulence

Change appears to be progressing at an increasing rate throughout multiple levels of society. Since post World War II, the connotations of "Made in Japan" and "Made in America" have become nearly reversed, epitomizing a slide in U.S. manufacturing prowess that would have been unbelievable in the recent past. The illicit drug phenomenon continues to grow, and appears to be an intractable problem that increasingly threatens various segments of society. The rapid spread of a virulent disease such as AIDS clearly did not seem possible in the modern era of medical "wonder drugs." The events that have transpired in Eastern Europe were inconceivable to most people as recently as two years ago.

Many futurists and trend trackers describe profound changes that will directly affect organizations (Attali, 1991; Celente, 1991; Harman, 1991; Naisbitt & Aburdene, 1985; Ohmae, 1990; Toffler, 1980). For example, organizations are moving from a local to a global orientation, from being solely competitive to being more collaborative, from structures based on hierarchy to flexible structures, and from emphasis on individuals to emphasis on teams.

Harman (1991, p. 24) sums up the nature of these environmental and organizational changes: "We are not referring to more change of a familiar sort, but to trend-breaking change of a kind that is unknown in our life experience—a shift of an entire society's mind-set."

Interdependence

Until recently, organizational theories viewed organizations as entities unto themselves (Aldrich, 1979). The key element of dominant organizational-design theory was buffering core production processes from external disturbances (Galbraith, 1977; Thompson, 1967). The term "decouple" was used in organizational literature to suggest a way that organizations could cope with complexity. These theories have become increasingly out of touch with the highly interdependent, tightly-coupled world within which organizations exist. It is becoming less possible for any single organization to "go it alone" (Lei & Slocum, 1991; Lewis, 1990; Lorange & Roos, 1991). Emerging network forms of organizational structure reflect recognition of the need to cope with and to capitalize on interdependence (Mills, 1991; Snow, Miles, & Coleman, 1992).

Paradox

The combination of turbulence and interdependence creates paradoxical situations for organizations (Miller, 1990; Quinn & Cameron, 1988). In the past, manufacturing organizations made a basic strategic choice between balancing costs and quality. The low-cost approach led to manufacturing strategies that focused on "economies of scale," and efficiency of capital utilization. The recent ascendance of Japanese manufacturing has been based on low cost *and* high quality. As customers began to become accustomed to better price/quality ratios in Japanese products, they also came to expect the same from U.S. manufacturers. From the U.S. manufacturers' perspective, producing high quality at low cost was paradoxical.

The solution for U.S. manufacturers was to move to manufacturing approaches that were radically different from those they had been using (Hayes & Wheelwright, 1984; Schonberger, 1986). For example, many manufacturers adopted Just-In-Time (JIT) inventory systems. In the old system, low inventories were bad and something to be avoided, a sign of poor management. In the JIT system, low inventories are desirable, something to reduce to the absolute minimum, a sign of good management. In essence, global competition required changing U.S. manufacturers' understanding of basic manufacturing principles. Successful refinement and implementation of the old principles had led to significant rewards, but these principles became impediments to effectiveness.

Leadership

Most of what we currently know about leadership was learned in the context of hierarchic-bureaucratic structures. Embedded within this form of organizational structure is an ideology that supports sharp gradations of power and authority, and a centralized decision-making apparatus (Gemmill & Oakley, 1992). This allowed a unified, coordinated response to directions from the apex. The limitation of this approach was decreased ability to respond quickly to market changes. We are not denigrating or diminishing this understanding of leadership. It is appropriate and effective for the relatively stable environments that spawned hierarchic-bureaucratic organizational designs. However, for many organizations, those conditions either no longer exist or are rapidly fading.

Currently, there is confusion regarding the leadership concept (Rost, 1991). One source of the confusion is a function of the unexamined ideology that has been carried forward from the bureaucratic age (Gemmill & Oakley, 1992). This ideology legitimates the power and control vested in those who hold senior positions. In fact, they are often called "superiors." It is difficult for many people to think of leadership in any other way than as a synonym for leader. Leadership means the people at the top of the organizational pyramid. In spite of the frequent reference to leadership as a process, leadership is still frequently thought of as a set of characteristics possessed by a person in a position of formal authority. Rost (1991), with disappointment, summed up the 1980's leadership scholarship as "leadership recast as great men and women with certain preferred traits influencing followers to do what the leaders wish in order to achieve group/organizational goals that reflect excellence defined as some kind of higher-level effectiveness" (p. 91).

A second source of confusion is the conceptual intermingling of a variety of functions important for organizational success. These functions are management, authority, and leadership (Burns, 1978; Rost, 1991). The management function involves ensuring efficient and effective operations. The authority function is about controlling operations. The core of the leadership function is maintaining orientation. In hierarchic-bureaucratic organizations, all three functions are located in a single organizational role, and the role incumbent has discretion about how the three functions are enacted. Accountability is attached to the role, regardless of how the functions are "delegated."

If we can strip away the constraining perspective of the dominant ideology and the confusion over functions, it frees us to examine leadership as a constellation of processes, functions, and roles that are necessary for organizational effectiveness rather than viewing leadership as a person. When thought of in this way, creating effective leadership processes is a design issue. It enables us to ask meaningful questions and to make choices about what functions are important, what roles are necessary, who will play what roles, and who will make the choices. The selection of questions and perspectives used for looking at such issues is a key component in the leadership process. This questioning and choosing can be strengthened through critical thinking.

Critical Thinking

Previously in this paper, we argued that there is a need for a different sort of leadership, the sort required by a world that is changing rapidly and one that is presenting us with more "ill-structured" problems than ever before. In "well-structured" problems the relevant variables are known, and algorithms for relating the variables in ways that generate appropriate solutions are also known. Launching and recovering the Space Shuttle is an example of a well-structured, although very complex, problem. In contrast, an ill-structured problem is one for which it is not even clear what the relevant variables are, let alone how they can be arranged or manipulated to arrive at a solution. Reducing drug abuse is an example of an ill-structured problem. Ill-structured problems often present themselves as paradoxes or dilemmas (Quinn, 1988).

Understanding situations from competing perspectives is a key to coping with these paradoxes and dilemmas. A primary mechanism for gaining this understanding is through critical thinking. For our purposes, critical thinking can be defined as rationally evaluating ideas from multiple perspectives—from a "multilogical" point of view (Hitchcock, 1983; Huff, 1978; Paul, 1990). This multilogical view is achieved only by acknowledging and embracing divergent and conflicting perspectives. Without it there can be no comprehensive view (Mitroff, 1987).

How we view a situation determines what features become salient and how we interpret what we see. Problems such as what to do about the AIDS pandemic or how to become an effective member of a global marketplace receive unitary and insufficient answers when viewed from only one perspective. Such problems have multiple important features that concurrently determine appropriate responses. When we use only one perspective for viewing a complex problem, there is a danger of embracing a partial or even an erroneous solution. A single perspective leads to an incomplete and therefore inadequate analysis of the problem. Critical thought yields a number of alternative perspectives from which to view situations and enhances the possibility of accurate understanding. Critical thinking facilitates casting problems in ways that point to non-obvious solutions. It facilitates illuminating poor choices based on prejudice or on erroneous presupposition. It highlights various aspects of a situation and causes us to ignore or downplay other aspects. It aids us in sense making.

Using multiple perspectives can provide an enriched understanding of a situation and a broader pool of problem definitions (Bolman & Deal, 1984,

1991; Linstone, 1989; Mitroff, 1983; Paul, 1990; Shrivastava & Schneider, 1984). Critical thinking is directly associated with the ability to generate and operate from multiple perspectives that inform a multilogical view. In short, using a multilogical view is crucial for dealing with complex situations.

Creating conditions that support the development and use of multilogical thought and action is an important leadership function, especially in turbulent environments. Leadership processes that create a monological focus on problems cannot facilitate the framing and reframing that must take place if we are to adequately deal with current and future challenges.

Developing Leadership

In hierarchic-bureaucratic organizations, the leadership development task emphasizes the development of individual leaders so that they possess more of the appropriate characteristics necessary for effective action when they are promoted to senior positions. Currently, the task and person of the senior leader is defined in heroic proportions (Bradford & Cohen, 1984). Developmentally, this seems to require creating super humans.

Evidence is emerging that the developmental task is truly daunting. Kaplan, Drath, and Kofodimos (1991) indicate that the development of leaders requires that individuals' basic character must be addressed. Kets de Vries (1980) indicates that therapeutic interventions are necessary to overcome dysfunctional behaviors. Torbert (1987) suggests that movement to an advanced developmental stage, one few people reach, is needed by effective leaders.

Our approach emphasizes creating conditions that allow people in organizations to learn what the most appropriate combination of leadership processes, functions, and roles are for the given circumstances. When conceived as a process, leadership functions may be performed in a variety of ways by individuals, groups, or even systems. In this way, a leadership process may be designed that reduces the burden on "leaders." It also is easier to change a process than to change key characteristics of a person. Since organizational conditions will be changing more rapidly, leadership processes will also need to be capable of rapid change. Widespread critical thinking abilities will be a key mechanism for learning how to invent appropriate leadership processes.

An effective leadership process will need to support critical thinking. A learning perspective can help us think about the leadership function of supporting the development and use of critical thinking. There are at least three types of learning that might occur (Argyris & Schon, 1978; Bateson, 1972). First-order learning involves improving the efficiency of current practices. Second-order learning involves examining the congruence of values and the objectives sought with the approach taken to accomplishing these objectives. Third-order learning involves improving the learning potential of the contexts within which the other two types of learning take place. We believe an increasingly important leadership function is supporting and enhancing the quantity and quality of third-order organizational learning.

It also requires that the leadership process itself contains means by which leadership is the subject of all three levels of learning. At the level of first-order learning the leadership process can be subjected to the principles of continuous improvement. At the level of second-order learning, the leadership process can be assessed for fit with values and effectiveness. At the level of third-order learning, the leadership process must create conditions that enhance learning about the contexts within which learning about leadership processes can best occur. For this kind of learning to occur, high levels of critical thinking ability need to be widely distributed throughout an organization.

However, more than the abilities are required. The kinds of learning we are describing occur when the results of critical thinking are put into action along with appropriate feedback mechanisms. The leadership process needs to encourage action taking and support developing appropriate feedback mechanisms.

In the remainder of this section we will describe some first steps in elaborating our understanding of how to develop effective leadership processes. There are some efforts underway at the Center for Creative Leadership in Greensboro, North Carolina, that shed light on some of the issues. These projects and programs are used for illustration purposes and to hopefully shed light on some elements of how we may develop organizations that invent appropriate leadership. They are not meant to be definitive.

Interorganizational Learning Networks

We are using interorganizational learning networks to study the three levels of learning described above. Regional networks have been formed that are designed to bring people together from sites that are implementing some form of the self-managed work team concept (Novelli & Koester, 1989). The networks have met annually for the past four years. The premise behind the networks is that everyone knows something about implementing teams but no one knows everything. In return for people sharing what they know, they stand to gain the accumulated learnings of all the others who attend. Typically, 40-50 people attend, representing various levels within a site from team member to site manager. The bulk of the meeting is spent in discussion groups composed of individuals interested in a particular issue or a problematic aspect of teams.

In another effort, high-level managers from materials companies who are responsible for new business development have formed an "Idea Alliance" group (Novelli & Gryskiewicz, 1992). The participants are exploring whether they can invent a process for sharing promising new ideas in a way that is more effective than current idea-sharing processes. This group has met twice and has scheduled a third meeting.

Our initial efforts in this area have revealed that people have great difficulty engaging in second-order learning. They seem to have difficulty moving beyond first-order considerations to use other participants' perspectives as sources of alternative understandings of an issue. In the case of the learning networks, we are experimenting with ways to help people examine their ability to engage in learningful dialogues when they come together to discuss a common problem (Novelli, Beard, & McLeod, 1992).

The success of the Idea Alliance rests on whether or not the group can reframe their concepts of competition and collaboration sufficiently to allow the emergence of creative alternatives to the ways they currently share ideas with each other (Novelli & Gryskiewicz, 1992). This process strikes at the heart of value and belief systems. There have been glimpses of reframing occurring, but the tendency to revert the traditional practice of making "deals" for idea exchange has dominated.

The value of these learning networks, from a research point of view, is that they have been experiments in third-order learning—we are trying to improve our ability to create contexts for participants to engage in more effective first- and second-order learning. These efforts are driven from a perspective that is based on principles of democratic dialog (Gustavsen & Engelstad, 1986) and models of collaborative action inquiry (Cooperrider & Srivastva, 1987; Emery & Emery, 1977; Reason & Rowan, 1981). The learning networks have provided us an opportunity to learn from our actions in attempting to create leadership processes that promote learning. They allow studying leadership in contexts where authority and management processes can be disentangled from leadership processes. In addition, we believe these projects provide a reasonable simulation for the participants of the previously described leadership task that tomorrow's organizations will face. This will be especially true for the "networked" organizations which will rely more heavily on horizontal relationships and less on the traditional hierarchical controls than is the case today (Mills, 1991; Snow, Miles, & Coleman, 1992).

A Leadership Program

In another development, a course has recently been developed at CCL that aims to help individuals, acting from a deep sense of purpose, to understand what is called for in their work situation and to take effective action that simultaneously improves the work situation and moves them towards their purpose. The course content focuses on three areas. The first area is developing a set of complex leadership skills: systems thinking, personal interactions, decision tradeoffs, coping with disequilibrium through emotional balance, and cognitive and behavioral flexibility. Cognitive and behavioral flexibility is most related to critical thinking ability. The second content area is learning from workplace experience. The focus is on both how to improve leadership practice and how to improve personal learning capabilities. The third area is uncovering a deep sense of purpose that can be carried out through their work.

This training course seeks to prepare individuals to take effective action within their organizations, *regardless of their formal position or authority*. Furthermore it emphasizes learning from experience, a key component in our conception of the leadership process. There is an intense research effort occurring within this program to learn more about its impact. In short, the course designers are engaging in third-order learning—understanding how the context the course presents affects participants' learnings. We would suggest that the staff associated with this course are engaged in developing leadership processes that will become crucial for tomorrow's organization.

Summary

The scope and quantity of major global problems present in the world today indicate that the effective resolution of these problems does not lie solely in improving the personal character of individuals in leadership positions. Rather, there is a need for higher quality leadership processes and for more leadership spread over a wider base. Critical thinking and learning are not separable, both are required simultaneously for effective leadership processes. Once leadership is thought of as a process that contains functions and roles, continuous improvement methods can be applied to achieve incremental gains. Second-order learning can also be applied to a leadership process to attempt a quantum improvement. Neither of these can occur if leadership is associated with the characteristics of individuals in positions of authority. Given the world's problems, not reinventing and improving leadership processes can have disastrous consequences in the not-too-distant future.

References

Aldrich, H. (1979). *Organizations and environments*. Englewood Cliffs, NJ: Prentice-Hall.

Argyris, C., & Schon, D. A. (1978). *Organizational learning*. Reading, MA: Addison-Wesley.

Attali, J. (1991). *Millennium: Winners and losers in the coming world order*. New York: Random House.

Bateson, G. (1972). *Steps to an ecology of mind.* New York: Ballantine.
Bolman, L. G., & Deal, T. E. (1984). *Modern approaches to management.* San Francisco: Jossey-Bass.
Bolman, L. G., & Deal, T. E. (1991). *Reframing organizations: Artistry, choice, and leadership.* San Francisco: Jossey-Bass.
Bradford, D., & Cohen, A. (1984). *Managing for excellence: The guide to developing high performance in contemporary organizations.* New York: John Wiley & Sons.
Burns, J. M. (1978). *Leadership.* New York: Harper & Row.
Celente, G. (1991). *Trend tracking.* New York: Warner Books.
Cooperrider, D. L., & Srivastva, S. (1987). Appreciative inquiry in organizational life. R. W. Woodman & W. A. Pasmore (Eds.), *Research in organizational change and development, 1,* 129-169. London: JAI Press.
Emery, F. E., & Emery, M. (1977). *A choice of futures.* Leiden, The Netherlands: Marinus Nijhoff.
Galbraith, J. R. (1977). *Organization design.* Reading, MA: Addison-Wesley.
Gemmill, G., & Oakley, J. (1992). Leadership: An alienating social myth. *Human Relations, 45,* 113-129.
Gustavsen, B., & Englestad, P. H. (1986). The design of conferences and the evolving role of democratic dialogue in changing working life. *Human Relations, 39,* 101-116.
Harman, W. (1991). 21st century business: A background for dialogue. J. Renesch (Ed.), *New traditions in business: Spirit and leadership in the 21st century* (pp. 19-32). San Francisco: New Leaders Press.
Hayes, R. H., & Wheelwright, S. C. (1984). *Restoring our competitive edge: Competing through manufacturing.* New York: John Wiley.
Hitchcock, D. (1983). *Critical thinking: A guide to evaluating information.* Toronto: Methuen.
Huff, A. S. (1978, August). *Multilectic methods of inquiry.* Paper presented at the 38th annual meeting of the Academy of Management, San Francisco.
Kaplan, R., Drath, W., & Kofodimos, J. (1991). *Beyond ambition: How driven managers can lead better and live better.* San Francisco: Jossey-Bass.
Kets de Vries, M. (1980). *Organizational paradoxes: Clinical approaches to management.* New York: Tavistock Publications.
Lei, D., & Slocum, J. (Winter, 1991). Global strategic alliances. *Organizational Dynamics, 19*(3), 44-62.
Lewis, J. (1990). *Partnerships for profit: Structuring and managing strategic alliances.* New York: Free Press.
Linstone, H. A. (1989). Multiple perspectives: Concepts, applications, and user guidelines. *Systems Practice, 2,* 307-331.
Lorange, P., & Roos, J. (1991). Analytical steps in the formation of strategic alliances. *Journal of Organizational Change Management, 4,* 60-72.
Miller, D. (1990). *Icarus paradox: How exceptional companies bring about their own downfall.* New York: Harper.
Mills, D. Q. (1991). *Rebirth of the corporation.* New York: John Wiley.
Mitroff, I. I. (1983). *Stakeholders of the organizational mind.* San Francisco: Jossey-Bass.
Mitroff, I. I. (1987). *Business not as usual: Rethinking our individual, corporate, and industrial strategies for global competition.* San Francisco: Jossey-Bass.

Naisbitt, J., & Aburdene, P. (1985). *Reinventing the corporation: Transforming your job and your company for the new information society.* New York: Warner Books.

Novelli, L., Beard, K. M., & McLeod, P. L. (1992). Mining videotapes for evidence of learning: A research dialogue. *Journal of Management Inquiry, 1,* 119-129.

Novelli, L., & Gryskiewicz, S. S. (1992). The idea alliance: Helping competing organizations learn to collaborate in developing business ideas. In T. Rickards, S. Moger, P. Colemont, & M. Tassoul (Eds.), *Quality breakthroughs: Proceedings of the 1991 International Creativity and Innovation Networking Conference* (pp. 43-49). Delft, The Netherlands: Innovation Consulting Group TNO.

Novelli, L., & Koester, N. (1989). N. H. interorganization learning networks to assist advanced manufacturing implementations. Third Quality of Life/Marketing Conference. Blacksburg, VA.

Ohmae, K. (1990). *The borderless world: Power and strategy in the interlinked economy.* New York: Harper Perennial.

Paul, R. W. (1990). *Critical thinking: What every person needs to know to survive in a rapidly changing world.* Rohnert Park, CA: Center for Critical Thinking and Moral Critique, Sonoma State University.

Quinn, R. E. (1988). *Beyond rational management: Mastering the paradoxes and competing demands of high performance.* San Francisco: Jossey-Bass.

Quinn, R. E., & Cameron, K. S. (Eds.). (1988). *Paradox and transformation: Toward a theory of change in organization and management.* Cambridge, MA: Ballinger.

Reason, P., & Rowan, J. (Eds.). (1981). *Human inquiry: A sourcebook of new paradigm research.* Chichester: John Wiley.

Rost, J. C. (1991). *Leadership for the twenty-first century.* New York: Praeger.

Schonberger, R. J. (1986). *World class manufacturing.* New York: The Free Press.

Shrivastava, P., & Schneider, S. (1984). Organizational frames of reference. *Human Relations, 37,* 795-809.

Snow, C. C., Miles, R. E., & Coleman, H. J. (Winter, 1992). Managing 21st century network organizations. *Organizational Dynamics, 20*(3), 5-20.

Thompson, J. (1967). *Organizations in action.* New York: McGraw-Hill.

Toffler, A. (1980). *The third wave.* New York: William Morrow.

Torbert, W. (1987). *Managing the corporate dream: Restructuring for long-term success.* Illinois: Dow Jones-Irwin.

~~~

Luke Novelli, Center for Creative Leadership, Post Office Box 26300, Greensboro, NC 27438-6300. Tel: (910) 288-7210. Education: B.A. from the University of Washington; M.B.A. from San Diego State University; Ph.D. in organizational behavior from the University of Southern California.

Sylvester Taylor, Center for Creative Leadership, Post Office Box 26300, Greensboro, NC 27438-6300. Tel: (910) 288-7210. Education: Bachelor of Science degree in economics and industrial relations from the University of North Carolina, Chapel Hill.

CREATING TOGETHER: WHO OR WHAT GENERATES THE CREATIVE ENERGY IN A COLLECTIVE EFFORT?
(Reflections relating to a study of two dramatic productions for television)

Kurt Possne

Each and every one of us is endowed with some creative talents from birth—an ability to make things, put things together, to solve problems, to break new paths, and to invent something new and different out of "old" ideas and achievements.

But, is this creative energy freely flowing and accessible at all times? Most likely not. There are factors that keep it from emerging, both within the individual and within groups of individuals working together. Creative energies must somehow be awakened, activated, or encouraged to take visible form.

The present study seeks to answer the question: *What factors stimulate, and what factors interfere with the creative process in groups?* To try to answer this question, let us consider some aspects of a study of two dramatic productions for Swedish Television that is now nearing completion. The programs were produced in 1990 and aired in 1991.

How Can We Grasp the Creative Process in a Group of Some Thirty Participants?

Our principal methods are these:

In collaboration with Göran Ekvall, University of Lund, Sweden, we have applied his scales for measuring the creative climate. Inspired by Stanley S. Gryskiewicz, Center for Creative Leadership, Greensboro, North Carolina, and Teresa M. Amabile, Brandeis University, Waltham, Massachusetts, we have conducted critical incident interviews with participants to trace and explain positive and negative factors in the creative process.

We have applied these measures during 1991/92 to two of our dramatic productions. Sixteen interviews and climate "readings" were undertaken in connection with an intimate drama of 60 minutes' length. A 90-minute operatic production was similarly followed up through 28 interviews and climate readings.

The work of Susan P. Besemer, State University of New York College at Fredonia, and Karen O'Quin, State University of New York College at Buffalo, has also inspired us to develop a scale for assessing the creative product—a television program—in terms of degree of "sensation" (degree of response), originality, and formal finesse. This work is currently under way.

The critical incident interviews cover all phases of the production. All the key personnel participating in the project—pre-production dramatists, production technicians, actors, singers, and musicians, as well as post-production technicians—were included.

Let us first consider the creative process. There are perhaps more links than one might think. The first of these is early in the conceptual phase, when the choice of topic or play begins to take form. This process may have started as much as five to six years before the production gets under way, and it is therefore difficult to assess this first phase in the study.

We encountered a similar difficulty at the other end of the "chain." Does the creative process end when the final version of the program leaves the editing table or mixer? Not quite—the "final product" is the production *as experienced by the viewer.*

When we consult research on audience reactions to one of our programs, the intimate or psychological drama, we find that a great deal of creativity takes place in the mind of the viewer. Viewers are reminded of experiences in their own lives; they process elements in the story and adopt them into their own personal outlook on life (or reject them).

My operative point of departure, then, is the following (a priori) model of the process:

An *assignment* is successively transformed into a finished product, a *television program*. The process takes place in a *climate*, which is more or less conducive to creativity, depending on *organizational features*, the *individuals* involved, and the nature of the *assignment*.

Is Our Object of Study One Single "Creative Climate," Common to All?

Do the various actors work in the same organizational climate, or are they in "worlds of their own"? When we examine the picture of the creative climate reflected in the climate rating scales, we find that some features apply across the board. But some individuals' ratings diverge markedly. What one professional finds a challenge with minimal risk may be quite the opposite for his colleague.

When we differentiate the perceptions by occupational group, we find that the respective groups do indeed operate to some extent in "worlds of their own." It would appear that each group of professionals perceives the world through their own eyeglasses, i.e., from the perspective of the specialized functions its members perform in the common enterprise, the production process.

Stimuli

Let us consider some data from critical incident interviews with 25 persons in the production phase of a musical drama. The interview data fell naturally into a number of groupings, with the organizational variable turning up in two main areas.

At first glance, the factors said to stimulate creativity raise some question-marks. The *assignment* itself appears to be the most stimulating variable of all. Is this the key that unleashes participants' creative energies? It does seem to be decisive in attracting the "right" people to the project. The assignment—i.e., a description of what the project should result in or achieve—defines participants' anticipations about what they will experience and what they may hope to learn from the project. It follows, then, that participants appreciate *clearly defined goals*.

Interaction with *co-workers* is the next-most frequently mentioned factor. Colleagues are stimulated by others' ideas, "foreign" ways of thinking that call for a certain amount of problem solving when they are to be fused together with one's own ideas. Influences should be exerted in mutual interaction, in a process of give-and-take. It is equally important to be seen, to be accepted as "one of the gang," to be relied on.

Ignoring for the moment the importance of leadership, *organizational factors* seem to exert surprisingly little influence. The organization's main contribution is most probably to shelter, to provide resources and define the project's territoriality—its "turf." It is not so surprising, then, that the organization is not explicitly mentioned as a stimulating factor. Rather a "hygienic" factor, in Hertzberg's nomenclature.

"Results" seem more important, on the other hand. Being able to see the fruits of one's labor (so far) surely serves several positive functions: It is a stimulus, a reward; it emphasizes the teamwork aspect, while it also forms a concrete starting point for the creative work to come.

Leadership, finally, is important in respect of its personal presence and relationships with the members of the team. And in problem solving. Other favorable leadership qualities are an ability to foresee future needs regarding such things as staffing and a "vision" of the final product and its audience.

Hindrances

The factors that hinder creativity are not merely a mirror image of factors that stimulate. The assignment is no longer dominant, whereas *organizational factors* play a much greater role. Faults in the steering system, insufficient resources, and an unsatisfactory physical environment clearly hinder creativity.

As in the case of stimuli, co-workers are also frequently mentioned. Situations in which the individual does not feel accepted as "one of the gang" or relied on by his or her mates are worst. Incompetence on the part of co-workers comes next.

A "Constructive Balance"?

It should be noted that stimulating factors and hindrances co-exist, side by side. Is perhaps the mix of "plus" and "minus" itself a condition that favors creativity? "When a production goes on without a hitch, all you have to do is go by the book," one respondent commented. "It's only when you run up against a problem that you have to be creative and come up with something entirely new and different."

Somewhere, however, there is a balance point, beyond which the hindering factors can defeat creative energies, and the result is an uninteresting product.

To be successful, leadership and active participation have to work side by side throughout the production process. Aiming for excellence seems to be the most powerful motivating force that will bring a group together and develop a sense of teamwork.

The creative energy is there. The trick is to find it and put it to work.

~~~

Kurt Possne, SverigesTelevision, S-105 10 Stockholm, Sweden. Tel: +46 8 784 00 00. Education: Bachelor of Arts degree in education.

THE RELATIONSHIP BETWEEN THE KIRTON ADAPTION-INNOVATION INVENTORY AND THE MBTI CREATIVITY INDEX

Sylvester Taylor

The purpose of this study was to examine the relationship between the Myers-Briggs Creativity Index (MBTICI) and the Kirton Adaption-Innovation Inventory (KAI). Data were obtained from 12,115 participants attending leadership development programs at the Center for Creative Leadership in Greensboro, North Carolina. The results of the data analyses yielded significant associations between the index and the overall Kirton score. There were also significant associations between the index and the three subscales of the Kirton. The mean creativity score as measured by the index for individuals characterized as innovators was significantly different from and higher than the score for adaptors. A number of researchers have studied the relationship between the MBTI and creativity. Representative studies can be found in Burt (1968); Erickson, Gantz, and Stephenson (1970); Gryskiewicz (1982); Ruane (1973); Stephens (1975); and Whittemore and Heimann (1965). The earliest research with the MBTI and creativity was conducted at the Institute for Personality Assessment and Research (IPAR) by Donald MacKinnon and his colleagues (Gough, 1976, 1981; Hall & MacKinnon, 1969; Helson, 1971; Helson & Crutchfield, 1970; MacKinnon, 1962). Gough (1981) reported a series of samples ranked by an experimental MBTI Creativity Index based on a program of creativity research at IPAR that began in the 1950s. In the IPAR studies 17 different samples were ranked based on their scores on the Creativity Index. Samples of creative people were selected by peer nomination from professions judged to be creative. Individuals judged creative tended to have higher scores on the experimental creativity index (Thorne & Gough, 1991).

The purpose of this study was to examine the relationship between the Myers-Briggs Creativity Index (MBTICI) and the Kirton Adaption-Innovation Inventory (KAI) measure of creative style. Specifically, this was an exploratory study designed to determine the nature and extent of the association between the KAI and the MBTICI. An additional purpose of this study was to extend the data base of creativity-related research with the MBTI by providing descriptive and normative data for a large sample of practicing managers in business and business-related professions.

Method

Sample

Data were obtained from a dataset of 12,115 participants attending leadership development programs at the Center for Creative Leadership (Fleenor & Taylor, 1992). The sample contained more men (77.4%) than women (22.6%). They represented six different organizational levels across a wide range of functions including: administration, education, human resources, manufacturing, marketing, R&D, and sales. The average age was 41.

Instruments

Participants were selected for inclusion in the study based on availability of useable scores from both the MBTI and the KAI. The Myers-Briggs Type Indicator is a self-report inventory to measure personality preferences. The development and use of the MBTI is given in Myers and McCaulley (1985). The Kirton Adaption-Innovation Inventory is a self-report inventory to measure creative style. The development and use of the KAI is given in Kirton (1987). Gough's experimental creativity index was derived from a regression analysis using MBTI continuous scores. Mean scores in the CAPT MBTI data base range from a high of 365.44 to a low of 221.07. The median value was 301.40 with a standard deviation of 96.83. The equation for the index is: MBTI Creativity Index = 3SN + JP - EI - .5TF (Gough, 1981). Table 1 shows the experimental Creativity Index scores from the MBTI data bank.

Table 1
Experimental Creativity Index Means and Standard Deviations from the CAPT MBTI Data Bank

Group	N	Mean	SD
Form F females	32,731	232.55	100.36
Form F males	23,240	239.54	99.79
Form G females	16,880	232.70	98.07
Form G males	15,791	238.75	95.69

Results

Tables 2 through 4 summarize the data. Table 2 presents summary statistics on the MBTI Creativity Index, the overall KAI score, and the three KAI subscales: Sufficiency of Originality (SO), Rule Group Conformity (RC), and Efficiency (EF).

Table 2
Summary Statistics on the MBTI Creativity Index and KAI Variables

	Mean	SD
KIRTON	104.8	17
RC	37.5	8
SO	48.5	8
EF	18.8	5
MBTICI	256.2	107

Table 3 presents the correlation between the MBTI Creativity Index and the overall KAI score, and the three KAI subscales: Rule Group Conformity, Sufficiency of Originality, and Efficiency. There is a direct relationship between the MBTICI and the overall KAI score. There is also a direct relationship between the MBTICI and all three KAI subscales.

Table 3
Pearson Correlation Coefficients Among the MBTICI and KAI Variables

	MBTICI	RC	SO	EF
Overall KAI Score	.61	.49	.54	.41

all correlations significant at p <.01

In order to determine whether mean creativity score as measured by the index for individuals characterized as innovators was significantly different from the score for adaptors, a median split was performed on the sample to yield two groups. For the group characterized as adaptors (n=1990) KAI scores ranged from 44-87 with a mean KAI score of 79. For the group characterized as innovators (n=2084) KAI scores ranged from 122-160 with a mean KAI score of 130. After testing the overall model, the differences between means were analyzed by use of an F test. Differences in the MBTICI score accounted for nearly 42% of the variance in the KAI score. Table 4 presents the means and standard deviations of the MBTICI by KAI preference. The mean MBTICI for innovators was statistically different from and higher than the mean MBTICI for adaptors.

Table 4
Means and Standard Deviations for the MBTICI,
the KAI Variables by KAI Preference

	Adaptors		Innovators	
	Mean	*SD*	*Mean*	*SD*
MBTICI	158*	90	352*	79

Summary

The results of this study indicate that there is a direct relationship between the Myers-Briggs Creativity Index (MBTICI) and the Kirton Adaption-Innovation Inventory (KAI). The results of the data analyses yielded significant associations between the index and the overall Kirton score and between the index and the three subscales of the Kirton. The mean creativity score as measured by the index for individuals characterized as innovators was significantly different from and higher than the score for adaptors.

References

Burt, R. B. (1968). An exploratory study of personality manifestations in paintings. (Doctoral dissertation, Duke University, 1968). *Dissertation Abstracts International, 29*, 1493B. (University Microfilms No. 68-14, 298)

Erickson, C., Gantz, B. S., & Stephenson, R. W. (1970). Logical and construct validation of a short-form biographical inventory predictor of scientific creativity. *Proceedings of the 78th Annual Convention of the American Psychological Association, 5*(1), 151-152.

Fleenor, J., & Taylor, S. (1992). [Myers-Briggs Type Indicator and Kirton Adaption-Innovation Inventory data for managers attending Center for Creative Leadership programs.] Unpublished raw data.

Gough, H. G. (1976). Studying creativity by means of word association tests. *Journal of Applied Psychology, 61,* 348-353.

Gough, H. G. (1981). *Studies of the Myers-Briggs Type Indicator in a personality assessment research institute.* Paper presented at the Fourth National Conference on the Myers-Briggs Type Indicator, Stanford University, CA.

Gryskiewicz, S. S. (1982, January). *Creative leadership development and the Kirton Adaption-Innovation Inventory.* Paper delivered at the 1982 Occupational Psychology Conference of the British Psychological Society: "Breaking Set: New Directions in Occupational Psychology."

Hall, W. B., & MacKinnon, D. W. (1969). Personality inventory correlates of creativity among architects. *Journal of Applied Psychology, 53*(4), 322-326.

Helson, R. (1971). Women mathematicians and the creative personality. *Journal of Consulting and Clinical Psychology, 36*(2), 210-220.

Helson, R., & Crutchfield, R. S. (1970). Creative types in mathematics. *Journal of Personality, 38*(2), 177-197.

Kirton, M. J. (1987). *Kirton Adaption-Innovation Inventory (KAI) manual, 2nd edition.* Hatfield, UK: Occupational Research Centre.

MacKinnon, D. W. (1962). The personality correlates of creativity: A study of American architects. In G. S. Nielsen (Ed.), *Personality Research, Proceedings of the XIV International Congress of Applied Psychology, 2*, 11-39. Copenhagen: Munksgaard Ltd.

Myers, I. B., & McCaulley, M. H. (1985). *Manual: A guide to the development and use of the Myers-Briggs Type Indicator.* Palo Alto, CA: Consulting Psychologists Press.

Ruane, F. V. (1973). An investigation of the relationship of response modes in the perception of paintings to selected variables (Doctoral dissertation, Pennsylvania State University, 1973). *Dissertation Abstracts International, 34,* 5031A. (University Microfilms No. 74-4285)

Stephens, W. B. (1975, April). *University art department and academies of art: The relation of artists' psychological types to their specialties and interests.* Paper presented at the National Art Education Association Conference, Miami, FL.

Thorne, A., & Gough, H. G. (1991). *Portraits of type: An MBTI research compendium.* Palo Alto, CA: Consulting Psychologists Press.

Whittemore, R. G., & Heimann, R. A. (1965). Originality responses in academically talented male university freshmen. *Psychological Reports, 16,* 439-442.

~~~

Sylvester Taylor, Center for Creative Leadership, One Leadership Place, Post Office Box 26300, Greensboro, NC 27438-6300. Tel: (910) 288-7210. Education: Bachelor of Science degree in economics and industrial relations from the University of North Carolina, Chapel Hill.

CREATIVITY EAST AND WEST: INTUITION VS. LOGIC?

Jacquelyn Wonder

The difference between Eastern and Western approaches to creativity is often described as being the difference between "intuition" and "logic." The Eastern approach is usually regarded as being more spontaneous and free-flowing, the Western approach, more systematic, and well-organized. We contrasted the two theories in an attempt to discover if one approach leads.

In order to facilitate the comparison, we looked for a working theory of creativity—one about how new ideas are generated.

The basic theory we chose was: change a fact/change the pattern. This phrase is shorthand for an epistemological theory of creativity—that is, how we "know" what we know is inextricably tied to how we "know" new ideas, i.e., how we are creative.

We arrived at this theory the way most theories are discovered—mostly by accident. We began with the following simple optical illusion:

introducing the square

o   o

o   o

No doubt the most common reaction to seeing four dots arranged as if they were the corners of a square is to visualize the dots as connected by four straight lines. This reaction is reinforced by the title, "introducing the square."

Yet if we carefully analyze the mind's process with even such a simple example it's readily apparent that what's "really there," the raw data, is, in fact, only four dots on a page. The title, "introducing the square," is not a part of the design itself, but rather something that has "predisposed" the mind to "see" a square. The dots, however, do not necessarily require that they be connected, nor, if they are connected, that they are connected by four straight lines. What the mind sees is, most basically, four dots and white space. If the mind begins to make assumptions about how the dots might be connected (i.e., what they "stand for"), it might also envision the dots connected by curved lines to form a circle, or the figure tilted to form a kite (with straight lines not only on the exterior, but also crossing in the middle to form a cross, representing the stays of the kite).

If we, in this way, begin to take apart the thought process, it quickly becomes apparent how many assumptions are involved every time we use even the simplest word, let alone a word representing an abstract concept.

Because, as the mind learns, the process of organizing facts into a pattern happens so quickly, we assumed, for the purposes of our research, that the mind forms these patterns automatically. Thus, in terms of creativity, a person can consciously decide to add new facts, or to challenge existing assumptions and existing patterns, but the mind's process itself is automatic. As a result, the way to become "creative" is to add a new fact to the data base, or to delete an old fact.

Once we started to look at the creative process as being similar to the process of acquiring information, we were able to use this theory to find subtle differences, but also significant similarities, between the two approaches. Perhaps our most interesting discovery was that our working hypothesis did in fact describe or explain both approaches. As a result, we were able to conclude that both Eastern and Western approaches to creativity are similar in that they are different methods for testing information and looking for new patterns.

In short, the Eastern approach has favored a more "passive" approach. The Eastern view is to try to forget the patterns that have been learned before. One Zen koan asks the student to try to remember his face before he was born. This could be an analogy to encourage the student to "forget" all that he thinks he knows, his old assumptions, and to try instead to look at things as they really are—not as he thinks they are. There is, obviously, difficulty in this. If one has always viewed the world through rose-colored glasses, for example, it is a real challenge to imagine a world that is not rose-colored.

The Western approach, by contrast, is typically more "active." The Western approach encourages the student to break down the image before him, to list or figure out what assumptions he has made, and then to methodically test each one.

The principal value of our investigation lies in the realization that both approaches rely on the discovery of a new pattern to produce the creative flash or inspiration. This "Aha" experience comes when we see the second or third possibility in an optical illusion, when we become aware of the possibility of a new pattern. The actual physical sensation is probably the result of a physiological event, perhaps the formation of a new electromagnetic connection somewhere inside the brain. But, although the process, East and West, is, in this one sense, the same—the preferred methodology is diametrically opposed. The East tries to utilize a "forgetting" process to get beyond the old pattern and to find the new, the creative point of view, and the West, preferring more of a "learning" approach, tries to learn new patterns, new possibilities.

An awareness that, at least on some basic level, the two approaches appear to be similar, should lead to an increased ability to facilitate the creative process by consciously shifting between methods or exercises which emphasize analysis and those which emphasize letting go of old assumptions.

~~~

Jacquelyn Wonder, Denver Center for Creativity, University of Denver, 2625 East Third Avenue, Denver, CO 80206. Tel: (303) 320-1334. Education: Ph.D. in educational psychology.

CREATIVITY RESEARCH AT THE DELFT UNIVERSITY OF TECHNOLOGY
A Report on Work in Progress

Jan Buijs and Kees Nauta

The Delft University of Technology is the oldest university of technology in the Netherlands. It has a total staff of about 5,000 people, and more than 15,000 students. Besides traditional schools (in Holland we call them faculties) like mechanical engineering, civil engineering, and architecture, we have a couple of faculties which are unique for the Netherlands, like aeronautical engineering, mining, and industrial design engineering. This last one is unique in the world; this faculty combines engineering sciences, social and cultural sciences, and management sciences with the arts. It teaches students to become product designers, product managers, or innovation managers.

It has existed for more than twenty-two years now; it has 220 staff members and 1,200 full-time students. In July 1992 the 1,000th alumnus was celebrated, and this last September 1992, 350 first-year students were welcomed.

The Faculty of Industrial Design Engineering is organized in four departments:

1. aesthetics (the traditional industrial design and arts subjects);

2. engineering design (mechanical engineering);

3. ergonomics (both the traditional anthropometric subjects and the more recent user-interface design approaches); and

4. new product development (the management sciences).

Those four departments are each responsible for one quarter of the curriculum. To emphasize that industrial design engineering is the integration of those four, the teaching of product design (about 30% of the total study time) is the responsibility of an interdepartmental task force (whose members work part-time in teaching in addition to their job inside one of the four departments).

All four departments have research programs. Usually this research is within the "mother-discipline" of the department. For example, the Department of Engineering Design concentrates on new materials and Computer-aided Design (CAD). The ergonomics department would look at anthropometric data of the elderly people. The aesthetics department concentrates on visual perception, etc.

Although stimulating creativity is an important characteristic of the curriculum, specific research on creativity has been more or less neglected—partly because of political reasons (a soft subject like that doesn't fit into the hard world of technologists), partly because of the faculty's emphasis on teaching, and partly because traditional engineering subjects are easier to investigate. But I think the most important reason for neglecting creativity as a separate research subject is our history. Traditionally, within the domain of product design, there was and still is a research emphasis on design methodology. Design methodology focuses on all aspects of product design, including creativity techniques, evaluation techniques, and decision making. The core of design science aims at the cognitive and rational aspects of design. Creativity techniques were just one of the minor subjects, and most famous designers and architects are not really interested in the investigation of "their" successes.

When we look back, creativity techniques were seen as one of the many tools a designer could use. And because as a designer in actual life you have to make decisions, both divergent thinking and convergent thinking were treated as equal (Jones, 1970; and see for the most recent state of the art: Cross, Dorst, & Roozenburg, 1992).

Research at the Faculty of Industrial Design Engineering is organized in four programs. One is on CAD, another is on product reliability, the third is on user-product interfaces, and the fourth is on management subjects. Each program has a program leader and an officially approved program. Within the theme of the program various specific research topics are dealt with. The size of the programs varies a little, but on the average they include 15 full-time researchers. The latest research program is oriented towards environmental issues in relation to product design. This program is sponsored by the Ministry of Economic Affairs and the Ministry of Housing, Environment and Health.

Within the program on management subjects we concentrate on topics such as market research, product introduction strategies, conjunct analysis (Stokmans, 1991), and concept-testing (de Bont, 1992). But besides these more traditional subjects we also concentrate on innovation management and design methods—mostly on the rational and logical ones, but recently researchers are trying to deal with the more intuitive and creative tasks of product designers and innovation managers.

Since my appointment at the university in 1986 (my official chair is Management of Innovation and Creativity), creativity is accepted as an official and separate research topic. It took a couple of years to get started, but now we are seeing some results. I will summarize the most important ones:

- The use and effectiveness of creativity techniques in the Netherlands industry. This project was executed in cooperation with the national research organization TNO (Mica, 1990).

- The role of knowledge (both domain and creativity knowledge) within the product design process and its relationship with the quality (in terms of more or less creative) of the resulting product designs (Christiaans, 1992).

Besides these, a number of projects are starting at the moment:

- An investigation on visioneering in industry, the scope of visions in organizations, the language in which they are created, made explicit and communicated (figures, plain language and/or metaphors), and its effects on long-term change (Tassoul, 1992).

- An inquiry into the effects of specific interventions in improving creativity in settled R&D environments (Buijs & Nauta, 1989).

- The role and importance of intuition in R&D and new product development (Groeneveld, 1992).

- Computer-assisted creativity education, a project aimed at identifying the obstacles in using computer assistance when teaching creative problem solving and developing useful solutions (Donkers, 1993).

All these projects are empirically based. Sometimes we do research in close collaboration with industrial organizations, but more and more we are doing experimental work in our Design Research Lab. In this lab we are able to execute thinking-aloud experiments. This so-called protocol-analysis enables us to investigate the problem-solving strategies of both experienced and inexperienced designers and managers. Because thinking aloud is a limited way of investigation, we also videotape every experiment. The combination of explicit thinking (expressed in the words of the subjects) and the link with what is actually done (shown by the drawings and sketches) gives us a good view on these strategies—especially because design thinking has a large amount of visual and spatial reasoning.

Besides these creativity-oriented research projects, we are also dealing with some very interesting design research projects. One is on the integrative aspects of design: how to balance all the different and often conflicting aspects of a product design. Are these aspects dealt with simultaneously or more in a sequential way (Dorst, 1993)? Another project focuses on using artificial intelligence methodology to investigate the design process (Kruger & Wielenga, 1993). In both projects the researchers investigate creativity, both as a personal aspect of the subjects, but also as a measurement of the quality of the end result (the product/design). The joint research meetings and the informal organization of our research team stimulates lively discussions for its members.

There are more projects coming, but we want to concentrate on these, and we want our results to influence the scientific community. Hopefully we can offer more concrete results at the next networking conference on creativity and innovation.

References

de Bont, C. J. P. M. (1992). *Consumer evaluations of early product-concepts.* Delft, The Netherlands: Delft University Press.

Buijs, J., & Nauta, K. (1989). Creativity training at the Delft School of Industrial Design Engineering. In T. Rickards, P. Colemont, P. Grøholt, M. Parker, & H. Smeekes (Eds.), *Report of the Second European Conference on Creativity and Innovation: Learning From Practice.* Drachten, The Netherlands: Innovation Consulting Group TNO.

Christiaans, H. H. C. M. (1992). *Creativity in design, the role of domain knowledge in designing.* Lemma, Utrecht.

Cross, N., Dorst, K., & Roozenburg, N. (1992). *Research in design thinking.* Delft, The Netherlands: Delft University Press.

Donkers, B. (1993). *Computer assisted creativity education.* M.Sc. thesis, Delft University of Technology.

Dorst, C. H. (1993). The structuring of industrial design problems. In *Proceedings ICED '93,* The Hague, The Netherlands.

Groeneveld, R. P. (1992). *Effectivenes of a creative problem solving course.* M.Sc. thesis, University of Amsterdam.

Jones, J. C. (1970). *Design methods, seed of human futures.* London: Wiley-Interscience.

Kruger, C., & Wielenga, B. (1993). *Methods for idea-generation in industrial design engineering, an empirical study.* Working paper, Delft University of Technology.

Mica, A. (1990). *Creativity techniques in the Netherlands.* Unpublished M.Sc. thesis, Delft.

Stokmans, M. J. W. (1991). *The relative importance of product attributes: Consumer decision theories in new-product development.* Delft, The Netherlands: Delft University Press.

Tassoul, M. (1992). *Learnings from selection.* In Proceedings 1992 ICINC, Greensboro, NC, USA.

~~~

Jan Buijs, Delft University of Technology, Faculty of Industrial Design Engineering, Department of New Product Development, Jaffalaan 9, 2628 B Delft, The Netherlands. Tel: +31 15 783068. Education: Master's degree in industrial design engineering; Ph.D. in organizational behavior.

Kees Nauta, Delft University of Technology, School of Industrial Design and Engineering, Jaffalaan 9, 2628 B Delft, The Netherlands. Tel: +31 15 784993.

ON BECOMING A FACILITATOR: DISCOVERING ONESELF

Jan Buijs and Kees Nauta

Stimulating creativity is a major activity throughout the whole curriculum at the Faculty of Industrial Design Engineering at the Delft University of Technology in the Netherlands. We offer a four-year program of 1,700 student-hours per year (42 weeks of 40 hours) which leads to a master's degree in industrial design engineering. In reality most students take up to six years to complete their study.

Creativity is taught throughout the program, starting from the very first week, and is further stimulated during the design projects. One of the things we teach them right from the beginning is, for instance, that if they want to present their idea for a new product-concept to one of the teachers, they have to present at least three different ideas (not just variations on a theme, but three different and distinct principles). In this way we teach them to think in alternatives.

In the first year we concentrate on experiential learning as the main creativity teaching method. In the second year we offer a compulsory course on design methodology. Here we offer them theoretical backgrounds and again, practical experience is offered during the design projects. In the third year we offer some in-depth teaching in creativity techniques within a course on innovation management. And finally, for those students who want to specialize in creativity, we offer an optional course in facilitating. The participating students have by then completed all the above-mentioned courses and projects. We have offered this course for four consecutive years now. The staff consists of Jan Buijs, Kees Nauta, and Marc Tassoul (a former student in the first course). Originally open to 20 students, this year the number of participants doubled.

The program is quite simple: the students have to study a book on creativity (we have used Bill Miller's *The Creative Edge*, Michael Ray and Rochelle Myers' *Creativity in Business,* and Vincent Nolan's *The Innovator's Handbook*). In this way, we provide for a common starting point which is mainly experience based. Then we have two full days to teach and study specific subjects, sometimes presented by guest lecturers (e.g., Iris Dorreboom on mind mapping or "draw your problem" by Patrick Colemont).

The program ends with a four-day (and night) intact program, executed outside the university in a rural setting. The students have to design their own session plans, sometimes they invite their own problem-owners, sometimes we provide both problems and owners. The basic rules during these four days are: Everything is allowed, experiment as much as possible, and respect each other's ideas and feelings. The role of the teaching staff is to facilitate these experiments, to help them organize "unusual" experiments, and to assist them with the debriefing of the sessions. (Another important task of the teaching staff is to do the cooking.)

Each participating student has to facilitate at least one session. This includes everything: the process, the methods and techniques they are going to use; the chemistry of the group; the physical environment, etc. Each session is set up with a real problem-owner (who should be satisfied with the results) and is recorded by an observer (one of the students). During the plenary debriefing, the facilitators share their experiments and experiences with the entire group; the observers come up with their stories and we add our comments. During these days one can see the students grow, because they discover their own strengths and weaknesses, their own feelings and limits. And usually these limits are much further away than they thought beforehand!

After these exhausting and exciting days the students have two more things to do. First they have to create a report about all the events that happened during the course, including a summary of the book they studied, the guest lectures, and the outdoor experiences. Again they are free in terms of format, form, and medium. The design of this "report" is actually one of the problems for which they have to find a solution together. This collective problem-solving activity ends two months later in a plenary get-together that includes a lot of fun, in which they present their "report" to each other and the staff. We share photographs, slides, videotapes, and emotions.

The final thing they have to do is to facilitate problem-solving sessions with the freshmen during an introductory project in their first week of the program. Now they become the facilitators (and teachers) for the new students, and their learning loop is closed. Some of the real "afficionados" specialize more and do their master's thesis on creativity. Among them, Andrea Mica, one of our alumni, spent a year in Buffalo (Center for Studies in Creativity) and Greensboro (Center for Creative Leadership) to get in touch with the founding fathers after completing his thesis on creativity. Marc Tassoul, another alumnus, did extra training in Antwerp, Belgium, at the Center for the Development of Creative Thinking (COCD). Finally, there is now a lively network of facilitators continuing to do sessions to sharpen their newly acquired tools after finishing their study.

To confront the students with their own and different styles of problem solving, we have used the Kirton Adaption-Innovation Inventory in the courses of '91 and '92. We had them fill in a KAI form at the start of the course and again some two months later after course completion. In '91, the mean of a group of 20 shifted from 105 to 110.8; in '92, the mean of a group of 40 shifted from 104.4 to 111.1. If the KAI is a measurement of style and not influenced by social desirability, it would appear that our courses influence participants to be more innovative.

To evaluate the course an inquiry was carried out by the groups of '89, '90, and '91. The inquiry was done this summer by André Liem, a student who had not taken part in the course. The response for each group was about 70%.

The creativity course was generally taken in the fifth year of their study. Most of them now have graduated and work as industrial designers or innovation consultants. Over a period of two years (average) most have participated in 4 or 5 sessions and some in as many as 25. About two-thirds of the group actually facilitated sessions and about one third of them more than 5 times. About half the respondents went on reading about creativity and read an average of three books; some 15% also took other courses on creativity.

Of those working in-company, initiatives to use Creative Problem Solving (CPS) in their organization were welcomed and supported. The amount of support correlates better with the atmosphere in their working environment than with the score on "usefulness of applying CPS." Some 60% actually took part in CPS sessions within their function.

To support the assumption of the existence of a living network, half of the respondents say they would ask peers to assist them if they were to do a CPS session. Of course this correlates with the frequency of contacts with peers. All of them would be willing to facilitate a session if they were asked by a peer. The eagerness to do so, however, depends more on the amount of experience than on the contact frequency.

The unexpected advice that half of the group gave to future students is: "Just do it." Other advice was something like, "Let go and make the best of the given opportunities." What they liked most about the course was the educational concept of experiential learning and teamwork, the stimulation of initiatives, the open atmosphere, and the intensity of the week-long course. As the most important learning experience, next to recognizing the power of CPS and learning how to use it, they claim they improved on leading and working with groups. They evaluate their own quality as facilitators as knowing how to use several techniques, how to control the process, and most of all how to get group members involved, enthusiastic and working effectively together.

If we were to offer a follow-on proficiency course, 85% would want to participate. The emphasis of the course should be on building more experience by practical training, extra techniques and experimenting, and some more about fundamentals. Some 20% stated that they simply would like to retake the same course.

In conclusion, we can say that the participants not only like the course as it is, most of them get really interested in CPS and use it actively once they leave. Within the context of the course, the students probably initiated long-lasting professional contacts and developed the ability and confidence to act more innovatively.

~~~

Jan Buijs, Delft University of Technology, Faculty of Industrial Design Engineering, Department of New Product Development, Jaffalaan 9, 2628 B Delft, The Netherlands. Tel: +31 15 783068. Education: Master's degree in industrial design engineering; Ph.D. in organizational behavior.

Kees Nauta, Delft University of Technology, School of Industrial Design and Engineering, Jaffalaan 9, 2628 B Delft, The Netherlands. Tel: +31 15 784993.

INNOVATION IN THE U.S. MILITARY

Dale W. Clauson

Innovation programs in the United States military began in the United States Air Force (USAF) as a response to a concern expressed in 1984 by the Chief of Staff that the USAF was becoming somewhat bureaucratic and stagnant. He initiated an Innovation Task Force to look at how the service could best prepare itself for the future, up to the year 2025. After 18 months of study, the task force recommended seven areas that the USAF should concentrate on to prepare itself for 2025. The seventh was Sustaining Innovation.

The Chief of Staff, in early 1986, sent a letter to all of his subordinate commanders noting that innovation was to become a long-term strategy of the USAF, and encouraged them to initiate an innovation program in their organization. One of the best programs was in the Electronic Security Command (ESC). ESC adopted the following strategy: Build a climate in ESC to foster and support innovative thinking and make ESC the most innovative, forward-thinking command in the Air Force. Our goal was to push the program to the grassroots of the command and empower those individuals such that they came up with better ways of doing their job. A two-man Innovation Center that reported directly to the Vice-Commander was created to be the catalyst for innovation command-wide.

Our marketing effort emphasized that a new era of management philosophy was starting in the United States due to the pressure of competition, and that it was in ESC's best interest to become a leader and set the example for the rest of the Air Force. This meant that ESCers needed to institutionalize innovation as a mindset. Our challenge was to change the ESC culture from one that perceived taking a risk as setting oneself up for possible failure to one that saw risk taking as an opportunity to make something good happen.

We pushed people to have an idea-capturing technique, noting that the problem with mental notes is that the cerebral ink fades so quickly, and that ideas not captured and acted upon within 24 hours were very rarely ever implemented! We suggested that people share ideas, that ideas breed ideas, and that they could piggyback and enhance their ideas by working together. We told them to look for ways of combining seemingly disparate ideas.

We particularly pushed the notion of using BlueSlips, a modified Crawford Slip Writing technique, as an idea-capturing technique, noting they were a good tool for conferences, creativity, consensus building, and brainpower mobilization, and they were anonymous. We showed them that BlueSlips could be easily "storyboarded," that is, visually integrated to show the relationships between ideas.

An immediate challenge was that these ideas rarely surfaced in a totally useable form. They needed some polishing in order to be fairly evaluated. We required the idea originator, as the initial advocate of the idea, to actively participate in the idea's development on the belief that if he or she wasn't interested enough to work the idea, then neither were we. We made it very clear in our marketing that we weren't a place to send a concept to be fleshed out; that we would help idea originators develop their ideas, but we had no intention of doing this ourselves.

We pushed the PIN concept for idea evaluation, the thought that any idea being evaluated should be considered first from a Positive viewpoint, "What's good about this idea?" Next, "What is Interesting?" Finally, "What's wrong, or Negative?"

An initial theory of ours was that as the word got out about the innovation initiative, people would be beating down our doors with ideas. In retrospect, that proved to be idealistic! The Vice-Commander therefore created an Office of Innovation that was placed, organizationally speaking, above the Innovation Center. Its charter was to brief every one of the 13,000+ Electronic Security Command members on the initiative, set up a command-wide innovation network to share ideas, and to train interested people in the mechanics of idea generation and idea enhancement. We educated the Command, using the theme of the Vice-Commander, that ESC had to innovate or it would wither and die. We made up T-shirts showing first a skull, and later, a coiled snake with the phrase, "Innovate or Die!"

Our rewards for idea originators (people who submitted ideas) were psychic in nature; those who generated the best ideas received a "stargram," a hand-written note from the Vice-Commander. We also recognized that those who evaluated and implemented ideas were crucial to the program's success and started an Order of the Champions to recognize on a monthly basis the individual and the organization that most supported the program.

In addition to the ESC program, the Air Force Communications Command, the Air Training Command, the Air Force Space Command, the Air Force Office of the Surgeon General, units of the Air Force Systems Command, and the U.S. Army Health Services Command had programs with elements similar to those described for ESC. The recent Gulf War demonstrated how innovative the U.S. military could be in technology, such as the creation of the stealth fighter; in ad hoc structures, such as the formation of the coalition command structure; and in tactics, such as conducting the 100-hour ground war.

There are several lessons learned in our efforts that are applicable to any large organization. The first is that large organizations have many people that not only resist efforts aimed at change, they do their best to undermine them. The senior people have to be removed in order to further the program. People lower in the hierarchy must either be won over somehow or bypassed. We

Discovering Creativity   SUCCESS STORIES found that the involvement of senior leadership was essential; that while a bottom-up approach could have worked in the long run, the sort of change we were after required not only the acquiescence of the senior leadership but also their active participation. We decided that, in general, the greatest hindrance to innovative ideas was middle management in that they wanted to control their subordinates and protect their superiors. The effort required to effect change in a large organization was greater than any of us expected. We learned that telling people they were empowered to act didn't mean they would act; they often wanted permission or felt they should only work on things that directly related to their job. They also strongly avoided mistakes, wanting to be right at every stage and at all times. Innovation turned out to be a lot of work in order to make things happen. Without the support of the idea evaluators and implementers, nothing concrete would have ever happened. Champions and sponsors are key to the success of innovation programs too. Innovation has to be linked to all aspects of an organization: Excellence, productivity, leadership, teamwork, and quality all play a part in infusing innovation into a nurturing culture.

~~~

Dale W. Clauson, Director, The School for Innovators, 10682 Beinhorn Road, Houston, TX 77024. Tel: (713) 984-9611. Education: B.A. in mathematics; M.A. in business administration from San Diego State University.

CREATING AN INNOVATION COURSE IN A LARGE CORPORATION

Tony L. Jimenez

On February 15, 1990, the first two-day course called The Innovative Edge—An Introduction to Creativity and Innovation was offered. This course was designed for the Chevron Corporation. Over 1,500 employees have attended the course since its inception. This paper discusses the signposts, stepping stones, and speed bumps we encountered on the way to creating an innovation course in a large corporation. The thinking, what we add, what we leave out, and the intuitive choices are all parts of the process of creating a course. Interviews were held with Chevron leaders, managers, and employees in late 1988. Then, interviews were held with creativity experts across the United States and ideas tested on employees during 1989. This paper is a small glimpse into that process.

I encourage participants to look for signposts and stepping stones. Signposts are the assumptions course designers make, any discoveries about your potential participants, any experiences or biases you can use to assist your creating efforts. Stepping stones are the value-added connections participants make to their organization as a direct result of their participation in the course.

What Assumptions Would You Make If You Had to Create a Creativity Course?

The assumptions I made:

1. Creativity is for both your work life and your personal life.
2. The search for creativity and innovation is a lifelong process.
3. We must move beyond idea generation techniques; techniques are merely mental jumper cables.
4. You learn about creativity by creating.

Discoveries made during the early design work of the course:

1. Most Chevron employees had never taken a single course on creativity or innovation.
2. Biases for or against creativity were based upon extremely limited knowledge. Opinions about creativity and innovation were based upon limited experience.

The frequent question I would ask myself: "What biases, experiences, knowledge, values, or beliefs do I bring to the process of creating a creativity course?"

One bias comes from my experience. Whenever I created something in my life, it was *not* problem solving. As I examined the work of Edward DeBono, Robert Fritz, and Peter Drucker, they seemed to agree. Fritz believes that there is a profound difference between problem solving and creating. Problem solving is taking action to have something go away—the problem. Creating is taking action to have something come into being—the creation.

Another bias is the value of experiential learning for participants to discover creativity. This was a direct result of my discussions with managers who had a strong bias against creativity. When I triggered or stimulated their thinking to create ideas, it was hard for the managers to argue with their experience.

Another bias is using creativity to create the materials, exercises, and format of the course. Cartoons were first visualized and then drawn to match the image. A strong effort was made to stay away from exercises that have become clichés and therefore we created new ones.

Value-added factors of the Innovative Edge course for the Chevron Corporation are as follows:

1. Designed for Chevron managers, supervisors, and employees.
2. Supports corporation strategy of innovation, risk-taking, and an entrepreneurial approach.
3. Supports our performance management process—with regard to the dimension on Creativity and Innovation.
4. Parallels our quality effort by encouraging new ideas for exceeding customer needs, improving processes and breakthroughs.
5. Encourages synergy by cross-functional employees sharing ideas and approaches.
6. Supports the creative and innovative climate discussion held in the Chevron Managerial Leadership Forum.
7. Encourages an open discussion on the company's environmental stimulants and obstacles to creativity.

Another stepping stone is the design of a course that fits the company and its culture. The Innovative Edge course focuses on applied creativity. The working definition we use in the course is: Creativity is the generation of ideas and innovation is the application of ideas. The course could be subtitled: Learning to put your ideas into action. The course moves from classical to current thoughts on creativity and innovation. We use four questions to frame the lifelong search for creativity and innovation. The questions are:

1. How do we stimulate our creativity on and off the job?
2. What do we know about creativity?
3. What helps and hinders putting our ideas into action?
4. What are the do's and don'ts of selling ideas?

Finally, with regard to stepping stones, it should be noted that our two-day course offers clues to creativity and innovation and not answers.

Speed bumps are areas of caution or areas to slow down. Using faulty models or formulas instead of useful heuristics is a trap. The proper balance between validated instruments or material and creating what has not existed before is a potential trap. The work of the Center for Creative Leadership (Amabile & Gryskiewicz, 1987) on environmental stimulants and obstacles point to the many factors that modify, impede, or facilitate creativity in an organization. Attending to the speed bump encourages the appreciation of the complexity of trying to stimulate creativity in a large corporation. This complexity has given me great humility.

Imagine yourself at the edge of a beautiful blue ocean. You see water as far as the eye can see. The area of creativity and innovation is like a deep, huge ocean. You are about to do a little wading in the ocean of creativity and innovation. The storms of change and competition are strong in the business world. You can learn to navigate using your creativity and innovation.

The aim of the Innovative Edge course in Chevron is to encourage participants to use more of their creativity for innovation. Metaphorically, participants are encouraged to apply more of their creativity for themselves and their organization.

Reference

Amabile, T. M., & Gryskiewicz, S. S. (1987). *Creativity in the R&D lab.* (Technical Report No. 130). Greensboro, NC: Center for Creative Leadership.

Additional Sources

Amabile, T. M. (1989). *Growing up creative.* New York: Crown Publishers.
Burnside, R. M., Amabile, T. M., & Gryskiewicz, S. S. (1988). Assessing organizational climates for creativity and innovation. In Y. Ijiri & R. L. Kuhn (Eds.), *New directions in creative and innovative management* (pp. 169-185). Cambridge, MA: Ballinger.
DeBono, E. (1992). *Serious creativity.* New York: Harper Business.
Drucker, P. F. (1985). *Innovation and entrepreneurship.* New York: Harper & Row Publishers.
Fritz, R. (1991). *Creating.* New York: Ballantine Books.

Fritz, R. (1989). *The path of least resistance.* New York: Ballantine Books.
Isakson, S. G. (Ed.). (1987). *Frontiers of creativity research.* Buffalo, NY: Bearly Limited.
Kolb, D. A. (1984). *Experiential learning.* Englewood Cliffs, NJ: Prentice-Hall, Inc.

~~~

Tony L. Jimenez, Chevron Corporation, Room 1330, 575 Market Street, San Francisco, CA 94105-2856. Tel: (415) 894-9665.

PROMOTING TARGETED INNOVATION IN JAPAN THROUGH R&D DIVISION LIAISON BETWEEN DIFFERENT INDUSTRIES

Shigeru Kurebayashi

Since 1990, the JMA (Japan Management Association) Management Center, Inc., has cooperated with the Center for Creative Leadership to promote Targeted Innovation (TI) courses. As a means of encouraging innovation, public seminars were organized by each company, who established the following rules:

1. Participating companies are to be from different industries
2. Participating divisions are to be R&D divisions only
3. Participants are to range in age from late 20s to mid 30s

Targeted Innovation programs were held in accordance with the above conditions from the end of 1991 and were rated highly by individual participants and participating corporations. This report examines these programs according to:

1. Liaison between R&D divisions from different industries
2. Combinations of corporate participants
3. Participants' reactions to Targeted Innovation courses and liaison with different industries
4. Examples of problems identified and idea generation meetings
5. Ways to implement training
6. Creativity techniques

1. Liaison Between R&D Divisions From Different Industries

After confirming the merits of the Targeted Innovation program through internal and public implementation, we sought to improve TI's effectiveness through attention to the following points.
 • If the business of the participating companies is too different, the participants will not be able to understand each other's problems and will have little mutual interest.
 • Divisions within the same company may not be able to understand each other if their business is too different.
 • If there is poor understanding of each others' problems and little mutual interest, naturally, the quantity and quality of ideas will be low.

After investigation, we devised the following measures to compensate for these problems.
- Participants should be interested in other companies, divisions, and fields.
- The participating divisions should be R&D divisions. This would ensure interest and should enable the participants to basically understand problems even in different industries.
- R&D divisions were included because in all corporations the creative ability expected of R&D divisions is rising.

In November 1990, the first seminar promoting TI through liaison between R&D divisions in different industries was held in Tokyo. The next seminar, which used the same format, was held in Yokohama in August 1991. On average, the seminars, which have been successfully continued until the present time, have been held once every three months. In the initial stages, however, the following doubts, alongside findings, were raised:

1. Could corporations maintain their secrecy and security while discussing actual problems with other corporations?
   - Before the course, training managers make arrangements and seek to obtain the approval of their superiors.
   - Participants, who are from the middle ranks of R&D teams, are capable of discerning which issues are confidential.
2. While the participants are R&D personnel, could they properly understand problems in other fields and produce appropriate ideas?
   - There is no need to fully understand the details of the problem. As long as the basics of the problem are grasped adequate ideas can be deduced.

This is a description of Targeted Innovation through R&D division liaison between different industries.

2. Combinations of Corporate Participants

Currently, the seminars are held in Tokyo and Yokohama. Details are as follows.

1. Period—three days (accommodation in area)
2. Numbers of participating individuals—around 20
3. Numbers of participating corporations—4 to 6

The combination of corporations participating in TI is as follows.

*Tokyo
   a) Kirin Brewery Co., Ltd., Kao Corporation, Nippon Telegraph and Telephone Corporation (NTT), Mitsubishi Rayon Co., Ltd., IBM Japan Ltd.
   b) Kirin Brewery Co., Ltd., Sony Corporation, Nippon Telegraph and Telephone Corporation (NTT), Ricoh Co., Ltd.

*Yokohama
   a) IBM Japan Ltd., NKK Corporation, Ajinomoto Co., Inc., Nissan Motor Co., Ltd., Matsushita Communication Industrial Co., Ltd.
   b) Canon Co., Inc., Fuji Photo Film Co., Ltd., Tokyu Car Corporation, Showa Electric Wire and Cable Co., Ltd., Nissan Motor Co., Ltd., Lion Corporation, Mitsubishi Kasei Corporation, Amada Co., Ltd.

The combinations of participating corporations were respectively different in Tokyo and Yokohama. In the Tokyo seminars, the corporate participants were limited to six companies with four to six persons from each. In Yokohama, around ten corporations participated each time, with two to four persons representing each. The Tokyo and Yokohama seminars were of equal importance.

*Toyko seminars—characteristics and format
   1. The culture of each corporation was evident.
   2. To some extent, each corporation organized its own acitivities, with the corporations able to realize their ideas by forming a group.

*Yokohama seminars—characteristics and format
   1. Wide participation, presenting opportunities to develop business connections.
   2. There was a broad spectrum of ideas.

It is important to choose the form of the seminar in accordance with its purpose.
   The following table is a list of the corporations participating in TI and the divisions the team members represented.

Table 1
List of Corporations Participating in Targeted Innovation Through Liaison Between Different Industries (Tokyo Seminar)

Kirin Brewery Co., Ltd.
    Technology Development Division
    Pharmaceutical Development and Research Center
    Engineering Business Division
    Packaging Development Division

Kao Corporation
    Information Science Research Center
    Information Science Research Center
    Second Production Technology Development and Research Center
    First Production Technology Development and Research Center

Nippon Telegraph and Telephone Corporation (NTT)
    LSI Research Center
    LSI Research Center
    LSI Research Center

Mitsubishi Rayon Co., Ltd.
    Central Research Center
    Central Research Center
    Product Development Research Center
    Product Development Research Center
    Tokyo Research Center
    Tokyo Research Center

IBM Japan, Ltd.
    Yamato Research Center
    Yamato Research Center
    Yamato Research Center
    Yamato Research Center
    Yamato Research Center

Kirin Brewery Co., Ltd.
    Pharmaceutical Development and Research Center
    Engineering Business Division
    Application Development Center
    Basic Research and Development Center
    Kirin Technosystem
    Yeast Development Center

Sony Corporation
    R&D Strategic Group
    R&D Strategic Group
    R&D Strategic Group
    R&D Strategic Group

Nippon Telegraph and Telephone Corporation (NTT)
    Interdisciplinary Research Center
    Interdisciplinary Research Center
    Interdisciplinary Research Center
    Interdisciplinary Research Center
    Software Research Center
    Software Research Center

Ricoh Co., Ltd.
    RP Business Headquarters Image Technology Research Center
    RP Business Headquarters Image Technology Research Center
    RP Business Headquarters, PD Business Headquarters
    Communications Systems Business Division

Table 2
List of Corporations Participating in Targeted Innovation
Through Liaison Between Different Industries (Yokohama Seminar)

1	IBM Japan, Ltd.	Entry Systems
2	IBM Japan, Ltd.	Personal Systems
3	IBM Japan, Ltd.	Personal Systems
4	IBM Japan, Ltd.	Technology Promotion, Development Division
5	NKK Corporation	Central Research Center
6	NKK Corporation	Steel Research Center
7	NKK Corporation	Application Technology Research Center
8	Ajinomoto Co., Ltd.	Central Research Center
9	Ajinomoto Co., Ltd.	Foods Integrated Research Center
		Oils Development Research Center
10	Ajinomoto Co., Ltd.	Production Technology Research Center
11	Nissan Motor Co.	Electronics Technology Headquarters
		Electronics Design Division
12	Nissan Motor Co.	Body Design Division
13	Nissan Motor Co.	Chassis Design Division
14	Nissan Motor Co.	Mechanical Design Division
15	Matsushita Industrial Communication Co., Ltd.	Development and Research Center Transmission Systems Development Division
16	Matsushita Industrial Communication Co., Ltd.	Development and Research Center Transmission Systems Development Division
17	Matsushita Industrial Communication Co., Ltd.	Development and Research Center Mobile Communications Development Division
18	Matsushita Industrial Communication Co., Ltd.	Systems Technology Center Systems Development Division
19	Canon Inc.	B Third Development Division
20	Canon Inc.	Electronics Image Technology Development Division
21	Canon Inc.	Production Technology Research Center
22	Canon Inc.	Camera Fourth Development Division
23	Fuji Photo Film Co., Ltd., Odawara Plant	Chemicals Production Division
24	Tokyu Car Corporation	Technical Headquarters, Development Division
25	Showa Electric Wire and Cable	Technical Research Headquarters
26	Nissan Motor Co., Ltd., Industrial Equipment Plant	Industrial Equipment Design Section
27	Lion Corporation Research and Development HQ	Bioscience Research Center
28	Lion Corporation Research and Development HQ	Bioscience Research Center
29	Lion Corporation Research and Development HQ	Fourth Application Research Section
30	Lion Corporation Research and Development HQ	Fifth Application Research Section
31	Mitsubishi Kasei Corporation Integrated Research Center	Chemical Research Center Research Personnel
32	Mitsubishi Kasei Corporation Integrated Research Center	Business Division Personnel Group
33	Amada Co., Ltd.	Technical Research Center

SUCCESS STORIES   *Discovering Creativity*

3. Participants' Reactions to Targeted Innovation Courses and to Liaison With Different Industries (From Questionnaires)

After TI seminars, questionnaires were collected from participants, and the liaison seminar for R&D divisions of different industries examined. (Please refer to the table of questionnaire ratings.)

Question 1: "Did you understand the content of the seminar?" The overall rating was 4.5 indicating that the TI content was clearly understood.

Question 2: "Was the seminar profitable for you?" The overall rating was 4.0, indicating that it was indeed profitable.

Question 3: "How was the seminar compared with the ones organized at individual company-level?" The overall rating was 4.5, a high rating showing the success of combining different industries.

The questionnaire indicated that R&D divisions were highly interested in liaison with different industries.

Table 3
Results of the Questionnaire

Question 1: Did you understand the content of the seminar?

	Understood 5	4	3	2	Did not understand 1	Average
OVERALL	21	20				4.5
Third seminar	12	11				4.5
Fourth seminar	9	9				4.5
Kirin Brewery Overall	5	6				4.5
Third seminar	4	2				4.7
Fourth seminar	1	4				4.2
NTT Overall	9	4				4.7
Third seminar	4	3				4.6
Fourth seminar	5	1				4.8
Mitsubishi Rayon Overall	3	9				4.3
Third seminar		6				4.0
Fourth seminar	3	3				4.5
Ricoh Overall (Fourth seminar)	4	1				4.8

Question 2: Was the seminar profitable for you?

	Extremely profitable 5	Profitable 4	No interest 3	Not very profitable 2	Not profitable at all 1	Average
OVERALL	9	24	7			4.0
Fifth seminar	1	15	2			3.8
Sixth seminar	8	9	5			4.1
Kirin Brewery Overall	2	6	2			3.8
Fifth seminar		4	1			3.5
Sixth seminar	2	2	1			4.2
NTT Overall	4	5	2			4.2
Fifth seminar		4	1			3.8
Sixth seminar	4	1	1			4.5
Mitsubishi Rayon Overall		4	2			3.7
Sixth seminar						
Ricoh Overall	3	5	1			4.2
Fifth seminar	1	3				4.3
Sixth seminar	2	2	1			4.2
Sony Overall		4				4.0

Question 3: How was the seminar compared with ones organized at individual company-level?

	Extremely good 5	Profitable 4	No interest 3	Not very profitable 2	Not very good 1	Average
OVERALL	50	23	9			4.5
Third seminar	11	6	2			4.5
Fourth seminar	15	6	1			4.6
Fifth seminar	9	6	4			4.3
Sixth seminar	15	5	2			4.6
Kirin Brewery Overall	15	5	2			4.6
Third seminar	4	1	1			4.5
Fourth seminar	4	1				4.8
Fifth seminar	3	3				4.5
Sixth seminar	4		1			4.6
NTT Overall	15	6	3			4.5
Third seminar	4	2	1			4.2
Fourth seminar	4	2				4.7
Fifth seminar	2	1	2			4.0
Sixth seminar	5	1				4.8

Mitsubishi Rayon Overall	8	8	2	4.3
Third seminar	3	3		4.5
Fourth seminar	4	1	1	4.5
Fifth seminar	1	4	1	4.0
Ricoh Overall	10	4		4.7
Fourth seminar	3	2		4.6
Fifth seminar	2	2		4.5
Sixth seminar	5			5.0
Sony Overall (Fifth seminar)	2			4.0

4. Examples of Problems Identified and Idea Generation Meetings

At seminars, R&D divisions from different industries separate into groups and hold idea generation meetings concerning specific problems. Below are some examples of problems identified and raised.

We have left aside problems that require special knowledge, and selected just one idea for reference from among more than 100 deduced in each case. Below we examine six cases in terms of initial problem restatement, idea, and comments.

Example 1
i) Initial problem—How to scan whole interior of the cylinder with a laser beam.
ii) Problem statement—How to improve the method of revolving or scanning a laser beam around the cylinder's interior.
Comment: The problem is restated from the point of view of the revolving or scanning aspect.
iii) The idea—Changing from the premise of revolving the beam to one of scanning in a straight out and back loop.
Comment: The idea overturned the premise of revolving. A straight out and back loop can be more precisely controlled than a revolving motion.

Example 2
i) Initial problem—To remove jaggedness from facsimile images.
ii) Problem restatement—Transmit dots to avoid jaggedness.
Comment: The problem statement approaches the problem from the viewpoint of methods of sending the dots.
iii) Idea—Magnify and correct. The image is reduced at the receiving end.
Comment: If magnified, correction is simplified. Then when reduced again, the jaggedness is not noticeable.

Example 3
   i) Initial problem—To lengthen the preservation of plant matter inside a test-tube (sterilized), from one to three years.
   ii) Problem restatement—To lengthen the preservation period mainly through physical means.
   Comment: Although a chemical approach was possible, a physical approach was chosen.
   iii) Idea—Change the culture container from a hard material like glass to a soft material like vinyl chloride.
   Comment: Because the operation switches from the interior of the container to outside it, the task becomes easier.

Example 4
   i) Initial problem—Expand the uses of the optical fibers for communications.
   ii) Problem restatement—Utilize optical fibers in the housing industry.
   Comment: The problem restatement changes the focus to daily lifestyle, from which ideas will emerge more readily.
   iii) Idea—Fix a fish-eye lens to the door so that a person within the room can see outside beyond it.
   Comment: A practical idea that solves an inconvenience in daily life.

Example 5
   i) Initial problem—To prevent stacked cartons from tumbling over.
   ii) Problem restatement—Change the structure of the carton to prevent tumbling.
   Comment: A restatement of the problem from tumbling prevention to carton structure.
   iii) Idea—Change the carton structure to a diamond or rhomboid shape.
   Comment: An idea that challenges the shape of the carton, usually square.

Example 6
   i) Initial problem—Early detection of virus-infected plant material.
   ii) Problem restatement—To identify the virus-infected plant material at the seedling stage.
   iii) Idea—Accelerate the lifecycle of the virus to its end.
   Comment: It takes time to detect the disease under natural circumstances so the virus is activated to make appear sooner.

5. Ways to Implement Training

a. Course orientation—R&D division personnel are usually quiet persons. To promote mutual understanding and trust between R&D personnel from different industries, participants should wear paper nametags showing their business, specialty, nickname, etc.

b. Examining problems—It is difficult for R&D personnel from different industries to explain thier problems to each other in a short time. Therefore, if possible, practice explaining problems to members on three separate occasions, including once at the Problem Exploration Meeting. Choose a creative problem from among these.

c. Idea generation meeting—Four meetings per individual are generally held. For example, if there are 20 participants, five groups of four can each meet four times, constituting four meetings for each person. Alternatively, four groups of five can each meet five times. Over three days, however, this can be difficult because of time constraints.

d. Converging and evaluation—Each person produces around 100 ideas, which are jotted down at random on paper or worksheets. From these the individual selects about 30 ideas, writes them down on labels, and classifies them into groups of five to ten. This is a simple but extremely effective technique from which the most effective direction or approach becomes clear.

6. Creativity Techniques

The process of an idea being stimulated by words is very simple indeed. But it is often unclear what associations or impressions triggered the idea or from which fellow participants the idea came. To clarify the origin and process of the idea, on a single card, write down (1) hints (triggers), (2) the idea, and (3) the name of the person from whose idea yours was sparked. This will make the course of the idea's development very clear. Points entered on each label:

```
(1) HINT

(2) IDEA

(3) Name
```

Recording the process on paper also makes it easy to produce diagrams such as the one in Figure 2 (p. 236). This method is called the Perspectives Label Method.

Discovering Creativity *SUCCESS STORIES*

Time	1st Day	2nd Day	3rd Day
7:00 A.M.			
8:00			
9:00		Problem Exploration Meeting	Idea Generation Meeting (4)
10:00	Orientation		
11:00	Considering Creative Ability	Idea Generation Meeting (1)	Converging and Evaluation
12:00	Lunch & Break	Lunch & Break	Lunch & Break
1:00 P.M.			
2:00	Feedback from Diagnosing Creative Ability	Idea Generation Meeting (2)	Enjoying Creative Ability
3:00			
4:00			Conclusion
5:00	Examining Issues	Idea Generation Meeting (3)	
6:00	Dinner & Break	Dinner & Break	
7:00	Party		
8:00			
9:00			

Figure 1
Program Outline

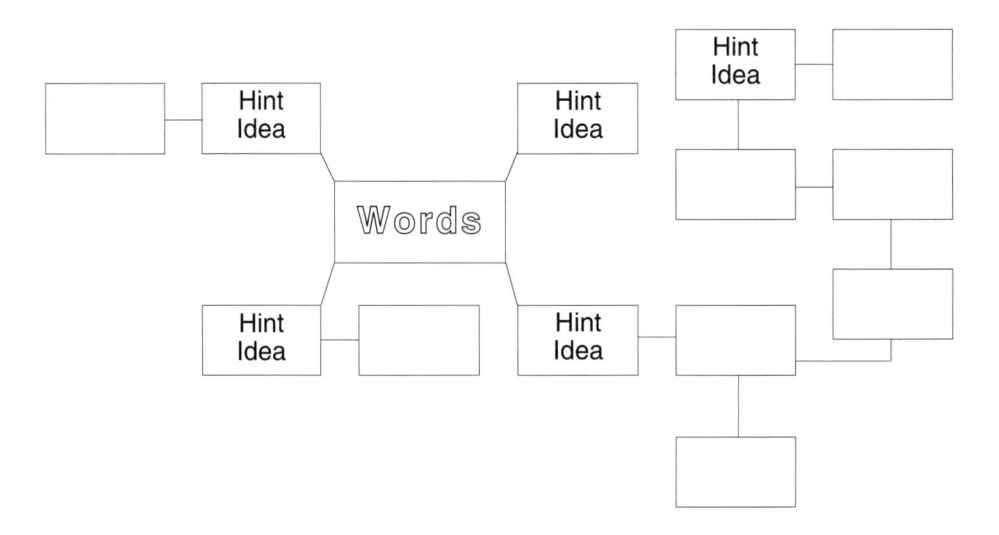

Figure 2
Perspectives Label Method

The Perspectives Label Method has the following characteristics:
    a. The link between hint and idea can be seen from each person's label, and this can be referred to.
    b. If other members are interested, they can develop their own ideas from the labels.

~~~

Shigeru Kurebayashi, JMA Management Center, Inc., 3-1-22 Shiba Koen, Minato-Ku, Tokyo 105, Japan. Tel: 03 3434 2777. Education: Graduated the Department of Science, Kyoto University, in 1970.

DEVELOPING CREATIVITY IN JAPANESE COMPANIES
The Situation Today and Current Issues

Yuji Nakazono

1. From Corporate Imitation to Innovation

In the past, Japanese corporations have largely copied the actions of domestic competitors, based on the introduction or adaptation of the latest technologies and management techniques from overseas. With the maturation of Japanese markets and the internationalization of Japanese corporations, however, Japanese corporations must now change to an approach based on originality and creativity. This awareness, spreading throughout industrial circles in Japan, is revolutionizing Japanese corporate behavior. Once again the issue of developing the creativity of the individual and the corporation is being examined seriously.

2. Problems in Developing Creativity in Japanese Corporations

In the past, there have been two main problems in developing creativity in Japanese corporations. First, there has been overemphasis on knowledge and techniques of acquiring it, accompanied by a neglect of management-side approaches. Second, the ability to identify problems and solve them creatively is under-developed, despite advanced analytical problem-solving ability based on *kaizen* activities.

3. The JMA Proposals—Three Approaches to Developing Creativity

To develop corporate creativity really effectively, the following three points must be comprehensively implemented throughout the whole corporation.
   (i) Build a creative corporate culture—principally the role of managers.
   (ii) Implement creative management—principally the role of administrators.
   (iii) Train and educate in creativity—targeting all personnel.

4. From *Kaizen* to Innovation

While *kaizen* activities, which encourage factory floor personnel to exercise their creativity, will remain important as a major strength of Japanese corporations, the most important issues now are the development of the innovation and creativity of technicians and planning staff and the training and education of administrators who can exercise creative management.

These measures will promote truly original and creative corporate activities.

The Asahi Beer Challenge

Asahi Beer is a leading Japanese beer manufacturer, which celebrated its 100th anniversary in 1989. The company's market share in Japan was low for many years, however, dipping below 10% in 1984. Consistently relegated to third place after Kirin and Sapporo, Asahi Beer's long history and traditions stood in the way of innovation, kept profits down, and hindered changes within the company.

In 1984, Asahi Beer decided to adopt a corporate strategy to improve its image. At the same time, Asahi Beer inaugurated total quality control (TQC) activities that involved all its personnel. By January 1986, the company had redesigned its labels, changed its logo, and committed to new management policy and orientation to revitalize business.

As well as overhauling its corporate identity, Asahi Beer critically examined its products. In July 1985, the Business Department conducted a survey of customer tastes and preferences to find out what kind of beer consumers preferred. The 5,000 respondents in the survey showed a preference for a full-bodied, clean-tasting, easy-to-drink beer.

The company began research and development to produce the beer respondents indicated they preferred, finally producing a new type of draft based on yeast No. 508. In 1986, while continuing the revamping of its corporate identity, the beer maker ran taste panels throughout Japan prior to successfully launching its new beer. Sales in 1986 rose to 10.4% of the market, up from 9.6% the previous year and exceeding the 10% mark for the first time in three years.

The collaboration of R&D personnel with the Business Department in the development of the new beer, instead of the R&D division having sole responsibility as in the past, was a new characteristic of the Asahi Beer challenge.

In March 1987, a revitalized Asahi Beer launched its *Super Dry* beer with an alcohol content 0.5% higher than ordinary beers. Sales soared and Asahi's market share climbed to 20.8% in 1988, displacing Sapporo as the second best seller. In 1989, market share reached 25%, a level not attained for 25 years.

Asahi Beer's success was the result of a change in thinking. As Mr. Kotaro Higuchi, the new president of the company said in 1986, "Asahi Beer switched from producing beer that our technicians rate highly to one that our customers want to drink."

Discovering Creativity SUCCESS STORIES

The Dry War

Other beer manufacturers immediately followed suit in the wake of Asahi Beer's success. From 1987 to 1989, all Japan's brewers without exception were producing dry beers, which in 1989 cornered 30% of Japan's beer market.

Previous to that, the beer industry had seen an advertising war, with brewers making huge investments in product promotion, and then a packaging war with companies vying to present their beer in a variety of containers. Now came the "dry war."

Kirin Brewery, which has more than half of the market share in Japan, also produced a dry beer, but the more it advertised its *Kirin Malt Dry* the more Asahi *Super Dry's* sales went up. Consumers stubbornly associated dry beer with the Asahi brand. From 1987 to 1988, Kirin lost 11% of its market share.

In 1990, Kirin decided against imitating its competitor's product and developed an entirely new beer of its own, *Ichiban Shibori*, and withdrew from the dry beer war. Like Asahi's *Super Dry, Ichiban Shibori* was a clear sales success.

From Imitative to Creative Management

Referring to the example of Asahi's *Super Dry,* let us take a brief look at the principles of Japanese corporate behavior in the past and ask ourselves what kind of management style is required for the future.

1. Imitation-based Management Produced Corporate Development

In the past, Japan's corporate management has introduced technologies and management methods from the United States and Europe, adapted them to all areas of business, and applied them skillfully. In addition, Japanese corporations' ability to carve out niches and survive side-by-side with competitors in the relatively small domestic market, management's propensity to invest earnings, and employees' dedication to the company combined with excessive competition have fueled Japan's corporate engines of growth.

Japan has 11 car makers, a huge number for one country. Camera makers, who export more than 80% of their products, have shaken down from a very large number to seven makers today. Of the 40 calculator companies registered in 1971, 10 have survived the fierce development and price competition.

This excessive competition has contributed to increased quality and productivity levels, improved and strengthened management, and produced the Japanese corporations of today. On the other hand, imitation of each other's products, a by-product of the competition, has led to an excess of similar products on the market, and has shortened product life cycles. Frequent design modifications and model changes complicate production processes and marketing, and hinder productivity.

Imitative management also results in copyright violations, technical wrangles, and trade frictions with other countries.

2. From Imitation-based to Creative Management

While Japan's markets are saturated, user needs are diversifying and original products are needed. With the maturing of markets, it is clear that corporations can no longer expect growth simply by imitating competitors, as illustrated by the case of Asahi Beer.

Tonoshi Hiraiwa, the chairman of the 54th general meeting of the Federation of Economic Organizations, at the heart of the financial world in Japan, made the following points in his address to that meeting:

> The changes that are reshaping the world today demand a revision of the behavior and systems that have supported Japan's economic development in the past. Rather than competing side-by-side with many competitors for market share, relying on governmental administration measures, and attitudes that place the corporation toward the center of society, Japanese corporations must satisfy consumers through their behavior, coexist with overseas companies, and seek free corporate activity and fair competition based on common rules.

To realize these goals, *a corporate management revolution based on creativity is needed.*

Problems in Developing Creativity in Japanese Corporations

1. Is Idea-development Training Sufficient?

One problem in developing creativity in Japanese industrial circles in the past has been providing idea-development training for researchers, technicians, and personnel in general.

In 1955, the SANNO Institute of Business Administration developed Japan's first Creative Thinking Course, aimed mainly at teaching those in corporations how to develop ideas. In 1958, Japan's first creativity research group, the Japan Creative Thinking Association, was established, marking Japan's first creativity research boom.

In 1965, Jiro Kawakita announced the KJ method, an idea development technique followed in 1970 by Masakazu Nakayama's M Method. Around this time, a considerable amount of material on idea-development techniques (thinking methods) appeared, and idea development, now popular with corporations, was used in their creativity training programs. This marked Japan's second creativity boom.

JMA (Japan Management Association), a training association active in industrial circles, vigorously implemented idea-development training, promoting it throughout industrial circles. While idea development was important, applied only to individuals it had little impact on corporate behavior. Japan's economy at that time was growing rapidly, largely through imitation, and idea development did not realize its true potential or really take hold in Japan.

2. Are Kaizen Activities Sufficient?

A study of corporate creativity development in Japan would be incomplete without a look at *kaizen* activities. Represented by TQC, *kaizen* activities are associated uniquely with Japan. Corporate staff from management to operations personnel participate in *kaizen* activities in an attempt to improve quality, reduce costs, and shorten delivery dates by solving problems and devising, proposing, and implementing work changes. Naturally, all personnel are expected to demonstrate their creativity.

In 1950, Dr. W. E. Deming's seminar in Japan on statistical quality control through the establishment of quality circles marked the beginning of the SQC movement that held sway in Japanese corporations until 1960. In 1954, Dr. J. M. Juran, who sought to adapt SQC to Japanese management styles, developed SQC still further in Japanese corporations through his seminars for top management. In this way, SQC developed into TQC and then company-wide quality control (CWQC).

Today, TQC has been widely adopted by manufacturing, service, construction and other industries, and is promoted in the workplace by QC circles (usually consisting of ten members). In 1981, there were 127,000 registered QC circles in Japan, with a total of 1.15 million participants. The actual figures, however, are estimated to be nearly ten times higher.

The following are problem-solving steps through TQC, which is representative of *kaizen:*

1) Seek the problem at the site.
2) Analyze the problem.
3) Investigate the cause of the problem.
4) Seek ideas to solve the problem and devise countermeasures.
5) Implement countermeasures.
6) Maintain the result and take steps to prevent recurrence of the problem.

Kaizen activities generally include a proposal system. Line and business staff at the site propose work-improving measures to management at company or division level. Groups at work-site level compete to produce the largest number of proposals. Winners, whether individuals or groups, are rewarded with bonuses. The most prolific proposal-raising individuals produced as many as 15,000 proposals a year, and almost every company has individuals that produce 2,000 to 3,000 proposals a year.

The creative awareness and motivation of those participating in TQC and these proposal systems improves the system. This has played an important part in the success of Japanese corporations.

Kaizen activities seek to make operations better, cheaper, faster, and more pleasant through an analytical problem-solving approach. Today's *kaizen* creative activities therefore lean toward innovation in work processes rather than innovation in new product development or in R&D. But with Japanese corporations needing original new products and technologies to prosper in the future, personnel of all kinds, including research, development, and planning, need more creative problem-solving ability.

JMA Proposals

In July 1988, when I was a director of the Creativity Development Center, I promoted the following three proposals through the Japan Management Association of which I was a member. Based on existing research, these proposals promoted throughout Japan, concern philosophy and methods of developing the creative ability of Japanese corporations in the future.

1. Creative Ability is More Important than Creativity

In the past, creativity development in Japan has mainly focused on idea development based on creativity that everyone possesses. In industry and business, however, creative ability—the ability to realize an idea and develop it so that it bears fruit—is far more important that just having an idea. We must therefore develop creative ability as well as creativity based on idea development.

2. Organizations Can Strengthen Creative Ability

While we usually associate creative ability with individuals, creative activities utilizing the power of an organization can be far more effective than activities that rely solely on individuals. Japan, where group activities and homogeneity are more characteristic than individuality or originality, could profitably use its organizations to strengthen its creative resources.

3. Developing Creative Ability in the Corporation

Developing the creative ability of corporations requires removing restrictions of corporate history and tradition, conservative culture, attitudes of administration and other elements that tend to hinder creative activity in the corporation, while encouraging the creative abilities of personnel. This kind of corporate cultural revolution necessitates making the thinking and behavior of managers, administrators, technicians, and other employees more creative.

Creative ability in organizations must be developed at a comprehensive, company-wide level rather than merely at the individual level as in the past. In this, the following three strategies should be implemented.

a) A creative cultural revolution. Managers should decide on originality management, make their policy decision clear to others, and remove from company values or behavior anything that hinders creative activity.

b) Creative management. All administrators should take a personal lead in their divisions in performing creative activities and should ensure that the activities of their staff are creative.

c) Creative education for all. Managers, administrators, technicians, and other employees should receive training in creative thinking and idea development, and should understand individual and organizational creative activity.

The Implementation of Creativity Training in Japanese Companies

In 1990 the SANNO Institute of Business Administration conducted a survey of creative development in 394 Japanese corporations. Questions and findings were as follows.

What methods do you currently use to implement creative development?
Proposal system	76.7%
Internal training	70.1%
Participation in exhibitions	59.4%
External training	56.3%

What level do you target for training?
Middle-level personnel	62.9%
Chief clerk, chief	56.3%
Team leader	54.8%
Manager, section chief	35.3%

What training technique do you use?
Brainstorming	87.1%
KJ method	63.7%
Checklist method	36.5%
Characteristics listing method	28.4%
NM method	23.6%

What problems have you experienced with your technique(s)?

Cannot implement or apply	41.4%
Does not yield effective ideas	39.8%
Takes too much time	34.3%
Effectiveness not clear	23.6%

From *Kaizen* to Innovation

We have seen that relatively few Japanese corporations have systematic, organized training systems to develop creative ability. Many merely offer idea development training and their own study circles based on *kaizen* activities. The effectiveness of creative ability development is also inhibited because it currently leans too far toward idea development and ignores actual implementation or application of ideas.

Various idea-development techniques are readily adopted, but few are applied. Although corporate training managers and participants show a great deal of interest in creativity training and new idea-development techniques we have developed, they have relatively little understanding of problems and creativity issues.

According to JMA's Survey on the Development of Technicians (1986, N=430), the skills researchers and technicians most often lack are, "creativity or innovation, the ability to identify R&D issues." As to what ability was the most necessary, many answered "the ability to originate rather than the ability to cooperate."

In the sense that *kaizen* activities have not led to a high level of creativity in Japanese corporations, they have been misapplied. *Kaizen* activities seek to improve on the current level of quality by solving problems *(kaizen)* analytically. Most people involved in *kaizen* activities learn analytic problem-solving techniques; brainstorming and the KJ method are the most popular and well-known. In Japanese corporations problem solving at the *kaizen* level is normal.

The problem is where to go from here. It is time to look at a higher level of innovative thinking and try to understand creative problem-solving techniques. In the words of a Toyota training manager, "We cannot afford to remain forever stuck at the *kaizen* level."

The most frequently used words in the lexicon of Japanese corporate management philosophy and behavior are "challenge," "innovation," and "creativity." But these words have remained little more than exhortations. Or, alternatively, employees were expected to implement innovation and creativity themselves in their *kaizen* activities. Recently, however, managers have begun to take these frequently used words seriously, seeking to implement them rather than using them just as slogans.

While *kaizen* improvements can cumulatively produce important innovations, people increasingly expect innovation by breakthrough. To produce these breakthroughs, it is important for administrators and R&D personnel in particular to develop their creative abilities, and creativity training for all personnel should be given priority.

The development of creative ability in Japanese corporations is becoming a major issue. JMA will keep developing effective training programs and courses to help ensure that this creative ability is achieved.

~~~

Yuji Nakazono, Management Education Institute, JMA Management Center, Inc., 3-1-22 Shiba Koen, Minato-Ku, Tokyo 105, Japan. Tel: 03-3434-2777. Education: Graduated the Department of Law, Hosei University, in 1960.

INNOVATIVE AND CREATIVE CHANGE

David Tanner

At Du Pont, we recognize that we are in a competitive race, and to outperform our competitors in the marketplace depends on our ability to generate novel, useful ideas (creativity), and then take these ideas quickly to market (innovation). A creativity-friendly workplace fits with our vision of "being a great global company through people," since creativity relates to people—and with our emphasis on continuous improvement in serving our customers, people, society, and stockholders—since it affects speed of delivery of new products, processes, and work practices.

Several years ago, we began a program to enhance creativity and innovation. We started by educating company leaders and people at all levels in creative-thinking techniques and in applications of these techniques to affect bottom-line results. Key factors were the stepping up of local champions and enthusiastic involvement of our people. This effort materialized into many examples of high payoff.

We then participated in a corporate thrust, led by two senior vice presidents, to accelerate innovation. This led to our Center for Creativity & Innovation. Our mission is to help all Du Pont people to accelerate progress toward our corporate vision through education in creative-thinking techniques, application problem solving—or opportunity searching in-house and with customers—and helping line managers foster an environment for creativity and innovation.

Innovation is a process that starts with a need, generates an idea or discovery, and triggers a series of events including demonstration scale-up and commercialization (bringing the idea to reality). It happens in one of three time frames: (1) *decade-to-decade,* commercializing new products of step-changing new processes like Conoco's tension leg platform for oceanic oil drilling; (2) *year-to-year*, involving major shifts in existing businesses such as Stainmaster carpets or introducing an advanced new pesticide; (3) *day-to-day*, involving contributions on a daily basis from people at all levels worldwide. All three types of innovation are critical to corporate health. Creative thinking plays an essential role, both in generating original ideas and in overcoming barriers to bringing those ideas promptly to reality.

Techniques and Applications

People can learn to use various techniques for creative thinking, even if they don't perceive themselves as creative.

Everyone has the capacity to think creatively. For some, it comes naturally. But everyone can learn techniques to stimulate creative thinking. Creative thinking does not replace information, training, logic, or hard work, but is another factor in getting the job done better. And it is an important ingredient in the continuous improvement framework that aims at both incremental continuous improvements and breakthrough advances.

We use five creative-thinking techniques:

Lateral thinking. Lateral thinking is a term coined by Edward de Bono, scholar and author of several books on creative thinking. He teaches techniques that jar our normal patterns used in problem solving and shifts them to entirely new starting points. These techniques lead to alternative approaches that otherwise may not have been conceived. For example, a business team was searching for new applications for Lycra spandex fiber. After listing existing applications, we generated a list of new applications such as stretch clothing for dolls, stretch warm-up suits for race horses, and others.

Metamorphic thinking. Metamorphic thinking involves generating new ideas by connecting the problem you are tackling to something that occurs in a totally unrelated system, often in nature.

For example, a need existed to develop a fire-resistant Nomex aramid fiber that could be dyed without requiring special procedures in our customers' mills. For years, our researchers failed to do this because of the tight Nomex fiber structure. Then a researcher asked himself, "What makes it possible for people to enter a coal mine?" His answer: props that keep the dug-out hole from collapsing. Applying this metaphor, he imbibed a large organic chemical molecule into Nomex during the manufacturing process. This propped open the structure and allowed the entrance of dyes under standard mill dying procedures. Today, a dyeable flame resistant Nomex is available that satisfies new FAA regulations for aircraft interiors in a variety of colors.

Positive thinking. This involves viewing a negative from different angles and turning it into a positive. For example, two companies each sent a representative to a developing country to help decide whether to build a shoe factory. The first rep wired back: "Nobody wears shoes here, don't build factory." The second rep wired back: "Nobody wears shoes here—opportunity unlimited! Build two factories!"

One of our major new products was a result of a research chemist turning a negative into a positive. The need was for a more rapidly dyeable nylon fiber. His approach was to chemically modify the nylon. In one experiment, the chemically modified fiber was totally unreceptive to dyes. Instead of viewing this as a negative result, he took a positive view—and this was the birth of our dye-resistant nylon carpet styling yarn which materialized into an important product in our carpet line.

Association trigger. At Du Pont, we have an Oz Creative Thinking Group. One aim of this group is "to function as a creativity network in a way that is fun rather than drudgery." This last phrase triggered the idea of using cartoons to express concepts in creativity and innovation. We launched a company-wide contest in *Du Pont World* magazine for employees to pair their ideas or experiences about creativity and innovation with 150 Frank & Ernest cartoons. This effort materialized into a copyrighted cartoon book, *Are We Creative Yet?* (1990, The Du Pont Company), containing 60 essays, making serious points about creativity with a light touch. In a foreword to the book, Du Pont Chairman Edgar S. Woolard, Jr., wrote: *"We intend to provide hero status to those who show us how to get products to the marketplace more promptly and more creatively."*

Capturing and interpreting dreams. Did you ever experience going to sleep with a problem and waking up the next morning with a clearer view of the problem and new ways of tackling it? This is because our mind continues to function while we sleep. In the subconscious state, our mind is less inhibited. A creative-thinking technique for harnessing the subconscious is to capture and interpret dreams. Ned Herrmann's Applied Creative Thinking workshop teaches you to keep a pad and pencil by your bedside, to write down your dreams, then interpret their meaning in relation to your problem. We applied this technique successfully in our Richmond plant to solve a problem with delamination and collapsing of vacuum hoses. A manufacturing person said this problem was "throbbing in his head, like a toothache." One night he dreamed of slinky toys. It then occurred to him that if he used a slinky-like spring in the vacuum hoses, it would stop them from collapsing. He rushed to work early to test the idea. It worked.

Most good ideas are obvious in hindsight. How often has someone suggested a good idea and you wonder, "Why didn't we think of that!" It's like climbing a mountain and not seeing the best path up until you have reached the top and are looking down. These ideas may seem obvious in hindsight, but they weren't to the people who were "climbing that mountain."

Education in creative-thinking techniques is not enough. As in tennis, taking lessons is important, but it doesn't make you a good player. It takes practice on the court and playing more than just weekends. Soon you begin hitting winners, deriving personal satisfaction from your efforts. This motivates more learning, more playing, and intensifies your competitiveness on the court.

Environment for Innovation

Providing quality time for people to learn the techniques of creative thinking is a first step in promoting an environment for creativity and innovation. It satisfies a key criterion for culture shift, giving "status" to the effort.

Rewarding individuals and teams who apply creative-thinking techniques to deliver bottom-line results reinforces status but, more importantly, also provides role models. When I visit our Industrial Fibers R&D units, we frequently reserve time for "creativity social hours" highlighted by recognizing role models who describe their creative "Aha" that led to a concrete business contribution.

Even units that are less participative in formal creativity programs think and act creatively because of the general environment. They recognize that the management is supportive of creative thinking, provides space and freedom, encourages risk taking, and does not punish people for mistakes but instead focuses on learning.

Here are some characteristics of creative thinkers that we believe are important.

They have absolute discontent with the status quo. They are not satisfied with the way things are. They want to change things. These people are sometimes viewed as "troublemakers," but they often come up with the most creative ideas and drive them to reality. However, people don't have to be troublemakers to be creative thinkers and movers.

They seek alternative solutions to problems or opportunities. They don't grab at the first idea, but take the time to search for alternatives. Many creative-thinking techniques, including lateral thinking and metaphoric thinking, help stir the imagination and generate alternatives.

They have a "prepared" mind. Creative thinkers are alert to things around them that may trigger ideas to meet important needs. Many important discoveries often attributed to circumstance or luck really occur because the inventor has a "prepared" mind.

They think positively. Sometimes negative results are blessings in disguise. Creative thinkers turn a negative into a positive by viewing it from different angles.

They work hard at it. A study at the University of California of known creative thinkers (famous writers, artists, composers, and inventors) showed that of the many characteristics that emerged only one was common to them all: They all have an intense interest in what they are doing and work hard at it.

These characteristics are not necessarily innate. To be a creative thinker, a person just has to learn the techniques and work hard at applying them.

Note: This article is reprinted with permission from *Executive Excellence*, June 1992. Copyright ©1992 by the Institute for Principle-Centered Leadership.

~~~

David Tanner, Tanner & Associates, Inc., 712 Hertford Road, Wilmington, DE 19803. Tel: (302) 478-5177. Education: Doctorate in chemistry.

OTHER PUBLICATIONS

SELECTED REPORTS:

Off the Track: Why and How Successful Executives Get Derailed
Morgan W. McCall, Jr., & Michael M. Lombardo (1983, Stock #121R) $10.00
High Hurdles: The Challenge of Executive Self-Development
Robert E. Kaplan, Wilfred H. Drath, & Joan R. Kofodimos (1985, Stock #125R) $15.00
Eighty-eight Assignments for Development in Place: Enhancing the Developmental Challenge of Existing Jobs
Michael M. Lombardo & Robert W. Eichinger (1989, Stock #136R) $12.00
Why Executives Lose Their Balance
Joan R. Kofodimos (1989, Stock #137R) $15.00
Preventing Derailment: What To Do Before It's Too Late
Michael M. Lombardo & Robert W. Eichinger (1989, Stock #138R) $20.00
Traps and Pitfalls in the Judgment of Executive Potential
Marian N. Ruderman & Patricia J. Ohlott (1990, Stock #141R) $15.00
Redefining What's Essential to Business Performance: Pathways to Productivity, Quality, and Service
Leonard R. Sayles (1990, Stock #142R) $20.00
Character Shifts: The Challenge of Improving Executive Performance Through Personal Growth
Robert E. Kaplan (1990, Stock #143R) $25.00
Twenty-two Ways to Develop Leadership in Staff Managers
Robert W. Eichinger & Michael M. Lombardo (1990, Stock #144R) $12.00
Gender Differences in the Development of Managers: How Women Managers Learn From Experience
Ellen Van Velsor & Martha W. Hughes (1990, Stock #145R) $30.00
Effective School Principals: Competencies for Meeting the Demands of Educational Reform
Cynthia D. McCauley (1990, Stock #146R) $15.00
The Expansive Executive (Second Edition)
Robert E. Kaplan (1991, Stock #147R) $20.00
Understanding Executive Performance: A Life-Story Perspective
Charles J. Palus, William Nasby, & Randolph D. Easton (1991, Stock #148R) $15.00
Feedback to Managers, Volume I: A Guide to Evaluating Multi-rater Feedback Instruments
Ellen Van Velsor & Jean Brittain Leslie (1991, Stock #149R) $15.00
Feedback to Managers, Volume II: A Review and Comparison of Sixteen Multi-rater Feedback Instruments
Ellen Van Velsor & Jean Brittain Leslie (1991, Stock #150R) $75.00
Feedback to Managers, Volumes I and II
Ellen Van Velsor & Jean Brittain Leslie (1991, Stock #151R) $80.00
Upward-communication Programs in American Industry
Allen I. Kraut & Frank H. Freeman (1992, Stock #152R) $25.00
Training for Action: A New Approach to Executive Development
Robert M. Burnside & Victoria A. Guthrie (1992, Stock #153R) $12.00
Readers' Choice: A Decade of *Issues & Observations*
Wilfred H. Drath, Editor (1990, Stock #314R) $20.00

Coping With an Intolerable Boss
Michael M. Lombardo & Morgan W. McCall, Jr. (1984, Stock #305R) $10.00
Learning How to Learn From Experience: Impact of Stress and Coping
Kerry A. Bunker & Amy D. Webb (1992, Stock #154R) $25.00
The Creative Opportunists: Conversations With the CEOs of Small Businesses
James S. Bruce (1992, Stock #316R) $12.00
Why Managers Have Trouble Empowering: A Theoretical Perspective Based on Concepts of Adult Development
Wilfred H. Drath (1993, Stock #155R) $12.00

SELECTED BOOKS:

If You Don't Know Where You're Going You'll Probably End Up Somewhere Else
David P. Campbell (1974, Stock #203R) $8.95
Take the Road to Creativity and Get Off Your Dead End
David P. Campbell (1977, Stock #204R) $8.95
If I'm In Charge Here, Why Is Everybody Laughing?
David P. Campbell (1980, Stock #205R) $8.95
Breaking the Glass Ceiling: Can Women Reach the Top of America's Largest Corporations? (Updated Edition)
Ann M. Morrison, Randall P. White, & Ellen Van Velsor (1992, Stock #236R) $19.95
The Lessons of Experience: How Successful Executives Develop on the Job
Morgan W. McCall, Jr., Michael M. Lombardo, & Ann M. Morrison (1988, Stock #211R) $19.95
Measures of Leadership
Kenneth E. Clark & Miriam B. Clark (Eds.) (1990, Stock #215R) $59.50
Beyond Ambition: How Driven Managers Can Lead Better and Live Better
Robert E. Kaplan, Wilfred H. Drath, & Joan R. Kofodimos (1991, Stock #227R) $27.95
Inklings: Collected Columns on Leadership and Creativity
David P. Campbell (1992, Stock #233R) $15.00
Readings in Innovation
Stanley S. Gryskiewicz & David A. Hills (Eds.) (1992, Stock #240R) $20.00
The New Leaders: Guidelines on Leadership Diversity in America
Ann M. Morrison (1992, Stock #238R) $25.95
Impact of Leadership
Kenneth E. Clark, Miriam B. Clark, & David P. Campbell (Eds.) (1992, Stock #235R) $59.50
Developing Diversity in Organizations: A Digest of Selected Literature
Ann M. Morrison & Kristen M. Crabtree (1992, Stock #317R) $20.00
Healing the Wounds: Overcoming the Trauma of Layoffs and Revitalizing Downsized Organizations
David M. Noer (1993, Stock #245R) $22.95
Executive Selection: A Look at What We Know and What We Need to Know
David L. DeVries (1993, Stock #321R) $15.00
Discovering Creativity: Proceedings of the International Creativity and Innovation Networking Conference
Stanley S. Gryskiewicz (Ed.) (1993, Stock #319R) $25.00

Discounts are available. Please write for a comprehensive Resource Guide (reports, books, videotapes, and audiotapes). Address your request to: Publication, Center for Creative Leadership, P.O. Box 26300, Greensboro, NC 27438-6300, 910-288-7210, ext. 2805. All prices subject to change.

ORDER FORM

Name _____ Title _____

Organization _____

Mailing Address _____

City/State/Zip _____

Telephone _____

Quantity	Stock No.	Title	Unit Cost	Amount

Subtotal ____

Shipping and Handling ____
(Add 5% of subtotal–must be at least $3.00)

All NC Residents add 6% sales tax ____

TOTAL ____

METHOD OF PAYMENT

❏ Check or money order enclosed (payable to Center for Creative Leadership).

❏ Purchase Order No. _____ (Must be accompanied by this form.)

❏ Charge my order, plus shipping, to my credit card: ❏ VISA ❏ MasterCard
   ❏ American Express ❏ Discover

ACCOUNT NUMBER: _____ EXPIRATION DATE: MO. ____ YR. ____

NAME OF ISSUING BANK: _____

SIGNATURE _____

❏ Please put me on your mailing list.
❏ Please send me the Center's quarterly publication, *Issues & Observations*.

**Publication • Center for Creative Leadership • P.O. Box 26300
Greensboro, NC 27438-6300
910-545-2805 • FAX 910-288-3999**

11/93

fold here

PLACE
STAMP
HERE

CENTER FOR CREATIVE LEADERSHIP
PUBLICATION
P. O. Box 26300
Greensboro, NC 27438-6300